Topical Readings
in American History

Edited by Gerald R. Baydo

TOPICAL READINGS
IN
AMERICAN
HISTORY

Edited by

GERALD BAYDO

Grossmont College

Prentice-Hall, Inc.   Englewood Cliffs, New Jersey

Library of Congress Cataloging in Publication Data

BAYDO, GERALD   comp.
  Topical readings in American history.

  SUMMARY: A collection of readings from many sources
relating to America's past, present, and future, on
topics such as ecology, native Americans, foreign
policy, labor, baseball, the Jesus movement, and life
in the future.
  Includes bibliographical references.
  1. United States—History—Sources.   2. United
States—History—Addresses, essays, lectures.
[1. United States—History—Sources]   I. Title.
E173.B3   917.3'03'08   73-20160
ISBN 0-13-925487-0

© 1974 by Prentice-Hall, Inc.
Englewood Cliffs, New Jersey

10   9   8   7   6   5   4   3   2   1

Printed in the United States of America

Prentice-Hall International, Inc.,   *London*
Prentice-Hall of Australia, Pty. Ltd.,   *Sydney*
Prentice-Hall of Canada, Ltd.,   *Toronto*
Prentice-Hall of India Private Limited,   *New Delhi*
Prentice-Hall of Japan, Inc.,   *Tokyo*

To Robbie and Brian—
my sons

CONTENTS

five
The American Indian: The Stereotype Revisited, 74

PREFACE

Teaching survey courses in American history is more challenging than ever before. It is increasingly difficult to enliven the basic names, dates, and facts or to present them in an engrossing manner. This book of readings follows a topical format designed to enliven the material and to provide maximum course flexibility. Each chapter contains both primary and secondary readings that show the continuity of the topic and of American history. In addition there is a brief narrative introduction to each chapter and each topic. Specific discussion questions highlight each reading and thought questions at the end of each chapter stimulate discussion. Because of its unique structure, this reader could be used with topical or chronological survey texts or even alone.

This is not just another American history reader. Besides taking a topical approach, it also presents sources on unusual topics, such as ecology, moon exploration, the Jesus movement, Native Americans, La Raza, Orientals, baseball, and even life in the future. Students can read about subjects they can easily relate to and apply these readings to history in all seventeen chapter topics. This selection of topical readings means to awaken students to the relationship of past, present, and future and to allow them to acquire a more meaningful knowledge of American history from those who made, wrote, and lived it.

one

MAN AND THE ENVIRONMENT
IN AMERICAN HISTORY

Mankind's interaction with the environment has been a constant theme in history. Man *is* essentially a product of the earth, even though recently writers have discussed the possibility of man as a product of some other planet. The interaction with earth's environment is an important factor in the development of American civilization. Initially Europeans in the American wilderness had to fight just to establish settlements that would endure. As American society became more technologically advanced, mountains, rivers, and plains ceased to be such formidable barriers.

With the beginning of the 20th century, Americans began to see nature less as something to be conquered and wasted, and more as a force to coexist with and conserve. Early Americans such as Henry David Thoreau and John Wesley Powell had also seen the real value of nature and had demanded a conservation policy, but few listened. Conservation as a viable policy began when President Theodore Roosevelt made it a national issue. Although some of the presidents after T. R. did not believe as staunchly in conservation, by the time Franklin Roosevelt took office conservation efforts were being expanded. But the original philosophy of conservation was too limited to handle all the environmental problems evident in America of the 1960s. Since saving the land and the soil and the rivers—conservation—was not sufficient to building environmental crises, the ecology movement began.

1

Ecology is today not only an environmental issue but also a political one. It is a popular—but very serious—issue. The environmental concern now is not just to conserve, but to save. Because mankind's ultimate survival depends upon our treatment of the environment, our future is our greatest burden.

The Appalachian Barrier*

In their first frontier in the West, Europeans initially found the American environment formidable. Virgin forests, uncharted rivers and coastline, and extremes of climates challenged their ability to survive. The terrain both limited and molded the founding of settlements. Early cities, for example, were seacoast towns based on trading and fishing. Because of the Appalachian Mountains the original thirteen English colonies clustered along the Atlantic coast. In this reading, historian Albert Brigham describes the tremendous influences of the Appalachian Highlands on the course and structure of American history.

Questions

1. What were the influences of the Appalachian region?
2. Who entered this region and why?
3. How would United States history have been different without a mountain barrier?

We have dwelt upon the physiographic aspects of the Appalachian region because they are usually left by historical writers to the reader's imagination. Those writers, unfortunately, do not all have Parkman's appreciation of geographic setting or the artistic skill with which he makes pictures of the land rise in perspective and color out of his pages.

This great rampart of the East does not seem difficult now, when the forests have been so largely cut away, when engineers have found reasonable grades for steam passage, and when electricity bids defiance to grades of every degree. But the greatest influence of the barrier goes back to the time when

---

*Source: Albert Perry Brigham, *Geographic Influences in American History* (New York: Ginn and Company, 1903), pp. 86–87.

the forest was everywhere, when the wilderness was nearly unknown, and when even a country highway belonged to the future. The explorer, finding a gap, might encounter another mountain in front of him, for the ridges often "break joints," like bricks in a wall. And if he hit on the Susquehanna or the Potomac, it would lead him to the mazy wilderness of the Allegheny plateau. In addition to the physical difficulties of entering the mountain belt from the Atlantic plains, the pioneer must be ready for the prowling savage and count on the hostility of the French garrisons as he neared the Ohio River. Only the adventurer, or the man with a serious public errand, would be likely to leave the fertile fields of Penn's country, or the tidal low-lands of the Chesapeake, for the hard trails and doubtful goals of the Appalachian wilderness. It has required more than two centuries to clear the forests, lay the roads, and open the regions fully to civilized man. Even down to 1880, there was a stretch of 350 miles, from the Roanoke southward, that had never been crossed by a railway.

If, without a mountain barrier, the Atlantic plains had merged into a land like the prairies, it would be hard to say how American history would have shaped itself. If the fierce aborigines of the Southwest and the Northwest had been in the same relative positions, the new colonies would have been for them a more easy prey. And the colonists would have scattered, seeking the best lands, tending to individual rather than community life. This, in a medley population drawn from all the nations of Northwestern Europe, would have kept civilization back, and deferred the building of coherent states. But the new Americans were pressed between the sea and the base of the mountains, forced to be neighborly, to assimilate each other's ideas, provide for common defense, and build up common institutions. Kept on the sea border, the centers of life were maritime, and there was, for those old days of slow-going ships, active interchange of ideas and products between the Old World and the New. The education of the mountains and forest came later. Now the people were held somewhat to their ancestral tutor—the wide sea.

2

Virginia's Starving Time*

Because European settlers were often not wary enough of the American environment, they suffered the consequences of it. In 1607 the first successful English settlement at Jamestown was located in a low, swampy area on the James River, near Chesapeake Bay. Not only was the climate unhealthy, but the settlement depended upon supplies from England which did not arrive frequently enough. Half the settlers died from disease and starvation, yet the situation continued to worsen. In 1609 the Starving Time nearly caused the abandonment of the Virginia colony. Captain John Smith, one of the leaders of the Virginia colony, here relates the effect of the settlers' environmental ignorance.

Questions

1. What did the settlers eat during the Starving Time?
2. To what limits can people go when faced with starvation?

. . . Now we all found the loss of Captain Smith [i.e., the author], yea, his greatest maligners could now curse his loss: as for corn provision and contribution from the savages, we had nothing but mortal wounds with clubs and arrows; as for our hogs, hens, goats, sheep, horse, or what lived, our commanders, officers, and savages daily consumed them, some small proportions sometimes we tasted till all was devoured; then swords, arms, pieces, or anything, we traded with the savages, whose cruel fingers were so oft imbrewed in our bloods that what by their cruelty, our Governor's indiscretion, and the loss of our ships, of five hundred [people] within six months after Captain Smith's departure, there remained not past sixty men, women, and

*Source: Edward Arber, ed., "Captain John Smith," in *The General History of Virginia* (Birmingham, Eng.: The English Scholar's Library, #16, 1884), p. 498.

children, most miserable and poor creatures; and those were preserved, for the most part, by roots, herbs, acorns, walnuts, berries, now and then a little fish. They that had starch in these extremities made no small use of it; yea, even the very skins of our horses.

Nay, so great was our famine that a savage we slew and buried the poorer sort took him up again and eat him; and so did divers one another boiled and stewed with roots and herbs. And one amongst the rest did kill his wife, powdered [salted] her, and had eaten part of her before it was known, for which he was executed, as he well deserved. Now whether she was better roasted, boiled or carbonadoed [broiled], I know not, but of such a dish as powdered wife I never heard of.

3

Conservation from Roosevelt to Roosevelt*

Conservation as a cause had its ups and downs during the first thirty years of this century. Theodore Roosevelt set aside forest reserves, established national parks and wildlife reserves, appointed an Inland Water Commission, and called numerous conservation conferences. Taft, on a similar path, continued but the removal of Pinchot and Taft's unpopularity hurt the cause. Woodrow Wilson was more concerned with foreign policy than nature, and the lack of interest in conservation continued through the 1920s. Franklin Roosevelt not only renewed the conservation campaign, he also expanded it. Here Stewart L. Udall, former secretary of the interior under President John F. Kennedy, reviews the conservation movement in the early twentieth century.

Questions

1. What was Theodore Roosevelt's concept of conservation?
2. Describe the period following Roosevelt.

*Source: From *The Quiet Crisis* by Stewart L. Udall. Copyright © 1963 by Stewart L. Udall. Reprinted by permission of Holt, Rinehart and Winston, Inc.

3. What was the conservation campaign of Franklin Roosevelt?
4. Where do Udall's sympathies lie?

In the years following the turn of the century, the nation needed new direction, and TR was at his best as a teacher and preacher-at-large. The country had to be aroused, and the idealistic young President was an arouser whose revivalist zeal carried the crowd with him.

Where conservation was concerned, TR was not bashful about brandishing his big stick. Nor did he speak softly. A group of foresters never forgot how he threw away a written speech and roared, "I hate a man who skins the land." His denunciations of soft living and "the get-rich-quick theory of life" had the force of an Old Testament sermon. The animating thrust of his personality still burned brightly in the mind of his friend, William Allen White, when, in his old age, he recalled the tingling impact of their first encounter:

> . . . It was out of the spirit of the man, the undefinable equation of his identity, body, mind, emotion, the soul of him, that grappled with me and, quite apart from reason brought me into his train. It was youth and the new order calling youth away from the old order. It was the inexorable coming of change into life, the passing of the old into the new.

TR's influence did not end when he left the White House in 1909. His concept of conservation finally became fixed as a part of the American creed during the course of the rousing political campaign of 1912. Once TR reentered politics, it was certain that his opponents would have to compete with him as champions of the conservation cause. This made the campaign one of the most provocative contests in our history, and many of the men who were destined to lead the nation in the troubled days of the 30's—men like Ickes, Norris, Rayburn, Stimson, and FDR himself—lit their political torches at the great bonfire of 1912. TR failed to regain the White House, but his Bull Moose effort provoked a debate that educated the American people as they had never been educated before. Thereafter, conservation and democracy were a single, inseparable creed.

Theodore Roosevelt dealt a decisive blow to the Myth of Superabundance, slowed the raiders to a walk, and gave us new attitudes toward the land and a new appreciation of the nature of democratic government. His approach, however, had shortcomings, the most serious of which was related to the inherent limitation of his presidential stewardship policy. Executive action worked well as far as it went, but was essentially a policy to save what was left of the Western lands. Large-scale legislative action would be necessary to renew the vast areas of our continent damaged by the Big Raids. Roosevelt's tendency to carry the ball himself encouraged the public to adopt a let-Teddy-do-it attitude toward conservation. Congressional lethargy was underscored by the fact that in the decade following 1909 only two far-reaching conservation measures—the Weeks Act authorizing a system of Eastern national forests, and the National Park Service bill of 1916—were enacted.

No one realized yet the full scope of the conservation challenge: the task of land rehabilitation would be a long, costly process, and it would take a full-time partnership between the executive and the Congress to do the job right. Further, it would take bitter years of depression and defeat to drive the point home.

During the interval between the two Roosevelts, conservation moved forward in some areas, but on the whole our land continued to lose its vitality. The Reclamation Service was hard at work bringing water to farms in the Western valleys, but there was no organized program to renew the soils of the farmed-over lands of the East. The "wheat rush" of World War I had encouraged the improvident plowing of vast grassland tracts on the Great Plains and the Forest Service was spreading the sustained-yield gospel, but little was being done to reforest and repair the vast cutover woodlands; and although the Park Service was busy enlarging our scenic estate, wildlife habitat continued to shrink. One of the few constructive steps in this period was the Norbeck-Andresen Act of 1929 which became the basis of our national system of waterfowl refuges.

Both waste prevention and projects of positive development lagged far behind national needs. Although the Reclamation Service had built a number of irrigation projects, we rejected the advice of Powell and Pinchot and TR to make comprehensive plans for river-basin development, and the Hoover Dam project, the only big river-control structure that had been approved by the Congress, ignored principles of sound regional planning. Ninety-five per cent of the hydro-power of our rivers was unharnessed, and nearly all of our farm and ranch families were denied the benefits of electric power. Soil erosion, the primal form of waste, was a problem in the West where the public-domain grasslands were overgrazed and unregulated; and in the East the soil-saving and fertility-restoring practices of our farmers were either unsystematic or nonexistent.

The economic bankruptcy that gnawed at our country's vitals after 1929 was closely related to a bankruptcy of land stewardship. The buzzards of the raiders had, at last, come home to roost, and for each bank failure there were land failures by the hundreds. In a sense, the Great Depression was a bill collector sent by nature, and the dark tidings were borne on every silt-laden stream and every dust cloud that darkened the horizon. Land failure meant the failure of people, and in the early 30's mortgage foreclosures and a daily deposit of dust on some window sills underlined this lesson for those who lived in the mid-continent.

In the period which led up to this debacle, nothing depicted our indecision better than the fight over Muscle Shoals, a choice hydroelectric site near rich phosphate deposits on the lower reaches of the Tennessee River. The Muscle Shoals debate began in 1903 when TR vetoed a special bill that would have licensed the site to a private utility company. It flared up over the years and came to a head twice, in 1928 and 1931, when federal-development bills shepherded through the Congress by the dogged Nebraskan, Senator George Norris, were vetoed by Calvin Coolidge and Herbert Hoover. The latter drew a sharp issue for the 1932 campaign when he said the Norris bill would "break down the initiative and enterprise of the American people . . . [and was] the negation of the ideal upon which our civilization has been based. . . ." Franklin Delano Roosevelt gave public development of Muscle Shoals a ringing endorsement in his campaign, and raised the old banner of his cousin, Theodore, with his assertion that we lacked a land policy worthy of the name.

It would, in fact, take a much larger national effort than either TR or Pinchot had envisioned to arrest the land devitalization dramatized in the early 30's by the damaging floods of our major rivers, the spreading blight of rural poverty, and, finally, the sickening spectacle of dust arising from the Great Plains.

We learned, but the learning process was slow, and in the main we waited for the shock of man-caused disasters to awaken us to the full failure of land stewardship. When, in 1933, the second wave of the conservation movement belatedly arrived, under the second Roosevelt, it elicited enthusiastic congressional participation, a dozen or more new agencies and services, massive appropriations, and a series of new resource programs.

Roosevelt was superbly prepared to lead the new conservation campaign. Standing on a platform built by his predecessors, he could see clearly the mistakes of the past, and he realized that one of the best ways to galvanize a demoralized people was to institute programs that would renew and rehabilitate the land.

Conservation was more than a political creed to FDR. He cared about the continent, and his mind was bubbling with ideas about land and water and wildlife. Nurtured on TR's concepts, he had started his public service in the New York Senate in 1910, and once described himself in *Who's Who* as "a tree grower." For years he had personally supervised the rebuilding of the topsoil on his erosion-scarred farm at Hyde Park and had planted as many as 50,000 trees on his estate in one year. The forests, he once said, are "the lungs of our land, purifying our air and giving fresh strength to our people."

4

From Conservation to Ecology*

The late 1960s saw the conservation movement become the ecology campaign. Preservation and improvement of the environment were becoming more and more a necessity. Clean water and air were added to the older issues of national parks and recreation areas. The media in general reflected the growing interest in environmental survival. Norman Cousins, former editor of Saturday Review, *introduced the new environmental section of the magazine in 1970 and described the philosophy of ecology.*

Questions

1. To Cousins, what *is* the ecology movement?
2. What are the goals of ecology?

Philosophy precedes ecology. What is most needed today are new realizations about man's place in the universe, a new sense of life, a new pride in the importance of being human, a new anticipation of the enlarged potentialities of mind, a new joyousness in the possibilities for essential human unity, and a new determination to keep this planet from becoming uninhabitable.

The largest library on Earth is not big enough to contain a catalogue listing everything that goes into the making of a single living cell. Man has been able to comprehend everything in the world except the uniqueness of his own being. Perhaps it is just as well. If ever he begins to contemplate his own composite wonder, he would lose himself in celebration and have neither time nor energy for anything else.

With all his gifts, man has been able to effect vast change, making his life different from that of those who have lived before. His capacity for invention and his sense of creative splendor have constructed great civilizations. But he

*Source: Norman Cousins, "A Philosophy for the Environment," *Saturday Review,* March 7, 1970, p. 47. Copyright 1970 by Saturday Review, Inc.

has never been in command of his own works. He has never been in balance. The result today is that, for all his brilliance, he has thrown himself all the way back to his primitive condition, in which his dominant problem on Earth was coping with his environment. The difference between his situation today and his tribal beginnings is that the environmental threats today are of his own making. He has been hammering at the chain of life at its weakest link, impairing the ability of the forests and the seas to make oxygen, putting poisons in the air beyond the ability of his lungs to eliminate them, fouling his own soil and water so that they cannot provide him with food.

Man's greatest failure is that he is unable to see his planet as a single abode. He has had little difficulty in making all of it accessible, but he has never made it manageable. But the price of his survival is the management of his planet. This calls for a philosophy of the whole, and for new education in the comprehension and control of his environment. For it will not be enough to fashion the world's largest mop in an attempt to clean up the human habitat. Humanity needs a world order. The fully sovereign nation is incapable of dealing with the poisoning of the environment. Worse than that, the national governments are an important part of the problem. They create anarchy on the very level where responsible centers and interrelationships are most needed. Whatever their functions inside their own borders, the nations in their external roles become irresponsible engines of spoilage and destruction.

The management of the planet, therefore, whether we are talking about the need to prevent war or the need to prevent ultimate damage to the conditions of life, requires a world government. This will be the test of man's vision and greatness. He can either exhaust himself in speculation over the difficulty of achieving such a government, or he can get on with the essential business of bringing it about. It will be a test not of his skill but of his philosophy. Everything begins—or ends—with a view of life.

If supreme value is given to life, it will not be impossible to create and maintain those institutions that are required to serve and sustain man.

Hickel's Philosophy on the Environment*

In the twentieth century the secretaries of the interior have often been responsible for leadership of government ecology and conservation campaigns. Walter J. Hickel served as President Nixon's secretary of the interior for twenty-two months, and before that he was governor of Alaska. During his years in Alaska, he acquired a concern for environmental protection which he was able to put into practice at the national level. Here Hickel looks optimistically at America's treatment of the environment.

Questions

1. What does Hickel mean by a collective world?
2. Is there room enough for everyone and everything?
3. Are the river banks green?
4. Does this article have an optimistic outlook?

I want America to be the conscience of the world again. I want Americans to lead the world in showing that the human being is the most important thing in existence, and perhaps we are just the people to do it. We are a mongrel people. One hundred years ago hardly anyone outside the United States believed that we would ever create a great Nation. We are not German; we are not British; we are not Asian; we are not white; and we are not black. We are all of these things, and more. It may take a mongrel kind of people like ours to create an environment of hope for all people.

It is time that we switched the emphasis in America and showed the world how to live life. As long as national rivalries exist, we shall never eliminate

*Source: From the book *Who Owns America?* by Walter J. Hickel. © 1971 by Walter J. Hickel. Published by Prentice-Hall, Inc., Englewood Cliffs, New Jersey.

altogether the need for national defense, or abandon the responsibility to defend our country. But our priorities are shifting, slowly but positively, to the problems of living a better life. If you went out and asked a fellow raking leaves on his lawn, "What are the problems today?" he would say, "We are spending too much of our money on war." And I would agree, because our challenge is to satisfy the yearnings of the inner man. We worry, and rightly so, about the problems of the inner city, but we will never solve those until we solve the problems of the inner man.

The only adequate response to that challenge lies in a totally new national approach to government in the United States, and a totally new involvement of the individual in determining his destiny.

1. A Collective World—But So Private

The belief that we have too much government has been accepted without question by what must be a majority of Americans of all political persuasions. I totally disagree. There may be too many people in government, or government may be misdirected, but I will argue until I die that there is not enough government in those areas where life is being choked from living: transportation, the cities and the general environment.

What we must now realize for the first time in America is that it is really a collective world, but one in which we live so privately. Without concern for the other person, for his desires and wants, activities for strictly private gain become destructive not only to others but eventually to oneself. No matter how great, how vast or how simple individual ownership might be, it must be looked upon as a passing thing. What good would it be if one owned it all and left an emptiness in passing? In reality, one has but a lease on ownership during one's lifetime. The success or failure of how something is used depends on how it is left.

How will we leave America? Will the heritage our generation leaves behind be an exhausted earth and a human who is degraded? Will the rugged individualism on which we have prided ourselves result in collective destruction? Not if we have a truly *national* approach to government.

We must have more men with the courage to accept responsibility for planning and implementing policies that will lift us as a nation into the next century, the century of the human. Government must be visionary in nature and be prepared to "return to us" those things that only national government can give back, such as clean rivers, unpolluted air and a free spirit in the inner man.

At stake is the living of life, and this is not a narrow or regional thing. It cannot be sustained by a government based on the principle that the blending of a conglomeration of special interests will produce a truly national policy. An individual or local government can take care of a problem in an individual or local way, but there are very few local splashes that do not make waves across the country. They are problems of the community called the United States. Decisions on where to put a freeway or how to dispose of municipal sewage have repercussions important throughout the land.

2. Enough Room for All?

Although there are limitations to the resources we have in our country, there is still a vast potential to be explored and wisely planned for. Our population is growing, and our urban centers especially give the impression that we are rapidly running out of space. In reality, there are still great regions of private and public land available for both the living of life and the restoration of man's spirit. Anyone who crosses the country can readily see that the immediate problem is one of distribution—not only of goods but of people.

If all the people in the world—not just the United States, but the world—were placed in the State of Texas, each person could be given 2,000 square feet of land, the equivalent of a good-sized home. Interesting though this example is, it would not be acceptable. There would be too damned many Texans! But it illustrates the reality of the situation: Our greatest lack has not been one of space but the lack of imagination to care and plan for all our property and all our people.

Is it right to give a cow 100 acres of public land on which to roam, while we pen up a ghetto family in 100 square feet? We can no longer address ourselves to our resources of the land without relating them to our people resources. And we cannot talk about wise use of our resources by the people without knowing what is there. That is why the time has come to look in detail at the entire country; to catalogue all those lands and assets the public owns, and decide how they will be used and conserved for the maximum benefit of everyone. We must have a national land inventory—a stimulating and exciting challenge, a task big enough to enlist thousands.

As in other areas of the environment, the development of a comprehensive land-use policy would mean jobs. And these jobs would demand the creative and imaginative talent of everyone involved, because it would be a pioneering venture. The aim would be to put a value—a value that cannot be measured in dollars and cents—on a mountain stream, a prairie, a forest or a wilderness. This would demand people who understand the balance between meeting the needs of our population for minerals, energy, and all kinds of resources on the one hand, and for esthetics and recreation on the other.

Perhaps by the middle of the next century our land surfaces will be used primarily for the living and enjoyment of life, while the ocean, the ocean floor and the polar regions will be a major source of minerals and food production. In the meantime, the challenge we are confronted with is to live off the great resources of our land without desecrating it.

3. Green River Banks

What a magnificent nation we would have if the great rivers of America ran clean and blue—the Potomac, the Mississippi, the James, the Shenandoah, the Cuyahoga and the Missouri! Is this possible? Yes. As part of a national approach to the living of life, we should establish a network of national rivers throughout our country. Each of the great rivers should have its banks preserved as green belts to filter and purify the runoff from rains and agricultural irrigation. These forested banks would provide great park spaces for all the people. The waters could be clean and available for private use—but not abuse.

What will it cost? It is within reach. We could pay for it over twenty years. After all, what does a war cost? We have marshaled men and materiel to destroy nations and wreak havoc on their environment; surely we can learn how to turn around that vast machinery to the construction and conservation of our nation.

When I was in Washington, I wanted to make the Potomac our first National River. With all the squabbling and bickering going on over cleaning up the sewage presently pumped into the Potomac system, I knew we were really fighting over only one part of the problem. If all the sewage were stopped completely today, the Potomac would still be dirty. The banks and shores at various places along the way have been bulldozed and developed, destroying the natural filtration system. Unless that basic problem is faced, the Potomac will never again be the great river it once was.

Some psychologists say that the drive in man that takes him to war is rooted in his need for stimulation. But they also say that stimulation need not be satisfied by violence, that it can be channeled into creative and positive action. We are stimulated by challenges, and the creation of a national land-use policy and a national rivers policy are two of the greatest challenges that I know.

Thought Questions

1. How do Brigham's article on the Appalachian Barrier and Captain John Smith's description of the starving time reveal the influence of the environment in American history?
2. Compare and contrast the ideas of Hickel and Cousins on the environment.
3. How did the two Roosevelts view conservation?
4. What common themes are evident in all the readings concerning the relationship of man and the environment?

two

EXPLORATION:
From Columbus to
Outer Space

Our search for adventure and excitement seems insatiable. The compulsion to climb the highest mountain, fathom the ocean depths, and explore the endless reaches of outer space appears to be a spirit that is difficult to satisfy. And frequently material gain was and is intertwined with the love of adventure. Gold, silver, riches of the East, the lure of the fur trade, material leadership in the Cold War—all could be attributed to romantic as well as material motives.

Exploration has been a constant theme in American history. In fact exploration actually began America. Initially Europeans were attempting to find a water route to India, and discovered America in the process. England, Spain, France and Holland consequently established empires in the New World. By the American Revolution much of the land had become known, but the search now turned to the land over the nearest mountains. Exploration of the Trans-Appalachian West led to the settlement of Kentucky and Tennessee. A series of military explorations in the 1800s traversed the terrain from the Atlantic to the Pacific, so that by the close of the frontier in 1890 there was little unknown land left. But the American curiosity and quest for challenge were not quenched. Now that the land was known, conquest of the air was next. By 1969 America had landed men on the moon. Though the Apollo program is now over, Americans still talk of distant planets and space labs, and even of living in the depths of the ocean.

I

The Norse Exploration*

While Columbus, probably the best-known of the early European explorers, is considered to have discovered America, he was not first to travel to America. In the mid-400s Hwui-Shan was supposed to have come from China and landed along the West Coast. While his voyage had no tangible consequences, he may well be the discoverer of America. In the tenth and eleventh centuries Norsemen explored and settled Greenland. While there are no clear accounts of their discoveries, the Norse sagas give us a great deal of insight into the early voyages. Here are two passages from the Saga of Thorfinn Karlsefni, the leader of the Norse settlement in Greenland.

Questions

1. What does the saga tell of the preparations for the settlement of Greenland?
2. Was the episode of the Uniped believable?
3. What problems were there in the Greenland settlement?
4. How can you separate the actual from the fantastic?

Thorfinn, called Karlsefni ["Stuff of a Man"] because of his capacity and vigor, was the great-grandson of Thórð the pioneer, who had settled at Hofda in Iceland. Thorfinn's father also was named Thórð; he dwelt at Reyniness in Skagafjord. Thorfinn's clan was wealthy; he himself was a successful trader and skillful mariner.

One summer Thorfinn Karlsefni decided to sail to Greenland. With him went Snorri Thorbrandsson from Alptafjord, and they had forty men with them. Bjarni Grímulfsson from Breidafjord and Thorhall Gamlason from

*From Edward Reman, The Norse Discoveries and Explorations in America (Berkeley, Ca.: University of California Press, 1949), pp. 30–31 and 37–38. Originally published by the University of California Press; reprinted by permission of the Regents of the University of California.

Austfirdir were planning a voyage to Greenland that same summer; on their ship too there were forty men. The two ships arrived at Eiríksfjord in Greenland in the fall.

Eirík rode to meet them and made them welcome; and soon they commenced to trade. The mariners proffered Eirík whatever goods he desired; and Eirík, in turn, invited them to stay the winter with him at Brattahlíð.

As Yuletide drew near, it seemed to Thorfinn that Eirík's manner had changed: whereas he had been gay and glad-hearted, he now appeared troubled and embarrassed. When an opportunity arose, Karlsefni asked: "What's wrong, Eirík? You have showered us all with hospitality, and yet you seem ill at ease. Tell me your trouble; perhaps I can take the burden from your mind. We are greatly indebted to you for your kindness to us all."

"You have all taken what little we have to offer like good and courteous guests," Eirík replied. "That is not what troubles me. My worry is this: I should hate to have it said that the poorest Yule you ever spent was at my house."

"Don't talk like that," said Karlsefni. "We have malt and meal and grain on our ships; and what is ours is yours. Take as much of it as you want, and make the Yule feast such as your own generous heart would have it."

Eirík the Red accepted Karlsefni's offer, and a great Yule feast was held. Afterward Thorfinn asked Eirík for the hand of Gudrid, Thorbjörn's daughter; for now that her husband, Thorstein Eiríksson, was dead, Eirík was her guardian. This Eirík granted; and so Thorfinn married Gudrid, and there was great feasting at Brattahlíð that winter.

During the winter there was much talk of Vinland; and the Icelanders resolved to voyage thither. So they began—Karlsefni and Snorri, Bjarni and Thorhall—to overhaul their ships in preparation for sailing in the spring. Thorvard, who had married Eirík's daughter Freydís, and also Thorvald Eiríksson, planned to set out for the western lands with Thorfinn Karlsefni.

There was also with them another Thorhall, who had been a hunter and fisherman in Eirík's service. He was a big man, dark, and of great stature. Now he was old, crabbed and taciturn, sly, and prone to get into trouble. He had not troubled to accept Christianity when it was introduced into Greenland. He was on the same ship with Thorvald, for he was familiar with wild regions. On this ship there were mostly Greenlanders; it was the same ship in which Thorbjörn Vífilsson had come to Greenland from Iceland several years before. On the three ships there were, all told, about one hundred sixty persons.

One morning [in the course of their stay by the river] Karlsefni and his men saw something glittering in a clearing above them, and they shouted at it. As it moved, they saw it was a Uniped [a mythical beast having only one leg]. It darted down toward them. Thorvald Eiríksson was at the helm. The Uniped then ran back northward, having shot an arrow into Thorvald's vitals. He drew out the arrow, saying: "There is fat about my entrails. We have found a good land, but we shall hardly be able to make use of it." A little later he died of his wound. The others ran after the Uniped, catching occasional glimpses of him, but at last he jumped into a pool and vanished. They returned and sailed back northward, thinking they had come to the land of the Unipeds and being unwilling to risk losing more men.

They concluded that the mountains (*fjöll*) which they had found, and those in Hóp, were all one, and that both regions were equidistant from Straumfjord [i.e., the three regions formed the points of an isosceles triangle, of which the distance from Straumfjord to each of the others formed one leg].

They returned to Straumfjord, and stayed there the third winter. The men quarreled much, and the single men coveted the married men's wives; whence there arose bitter strife. Here Karlsefni's son Snorri was born, in the first fall; he was three winters old when they [finally] departed for Greenland.

They set sail in a southerly wind [AM 544 adds "from Vinland"], and came to Markland. There they found five Skrælings, a man, two women, and two boys. The man was bearded. They captured the boys, but the others got away and sank into the earth. The Northmen took the boys with them, taught them their language, and baptized them. The boys said their mother's name was Vætilldi and their father was called Vægi. They said also that two kings ruled the Skrælings: one was named Avalldamon and the other Valldidida [or Avalldidida]. They asserted that the Skrælings had no houses, but slept in caves or in holes in the earth. They also said there was another land, lying opposite their land, and that its people wore white clothing and carried poles and flags. It is supposed that this land must have been *Hvítramannaland* [White Men's Land] or Ireland the Great.

Then the Northmen reached Greenland, and spent the winter with Eirík the Red.

John Charles Fremont on the Oregon Trail*

Lewis and Clark, the first official government explorers, not only added to the scientific knowledge of the Louisiana Purchase region, but also stimulated further interest in that area. Zebulon Pike's military expedition was exploring the Colorado country in 1806. Though the Pike expedition was responsible for the Great American Desert Myth that retarded settlement of the Southwest for many years, it also helped stimulate interest in trade with Santa Fe. While Pike's exploring proved much less fruitful than that of Lewis and Clark, it did add considerable information about the remote West. During the 1820s government explorers filled in knowledge of the Transappalachian area.

With the creation of the Army Corps of Topographical Engineers in 1838, major scientific military expeditions began to go to the Far West. John Charles Fremont led three such government expeditions. His published and widely circulated reports helped create a growing interest in settlement of the area. Here are two brief episodes from his 1842 trip west.

Note his description of Nebraska and Independence Rock—a landmark along the Oregon Trail.

Questions

1. What took place on June 28th? What was the significance of the events?
2. What was Fremont's impression of the Platte River?

*John Charles Fremont, "A Report on the Exploration of the Country Lying between the Missouri River and the Rocky Mountains, on the Line of the Kansas and Great Platte Rivers," Senate Report 243, 27th Cong., 3rd sess. (Washington, D.C.: Government Printing Office, 1842–43), pp. 14–17 and 68–72.

June 28 We halted to noon at an open reach of the river, which occupies rather more than a fourth of the valley, here only about four miles broad. The camp had been disposed with the usual precaution, the horses grazing at a little distance attended by the guard, and we were all sitting quietly at our dinner on the grass, when suddenly we heard the startling cry *"du monde!"* In an instant, every man's weapon was in his hand, the horses were driven in, hobbled and picketed, and horsemen were galloping at full speed in the direction of the new comers, screaming and yelling with the wildest excitement. "Get ready, my lads!" said the leader of the approaching party to his men, when our wild-looking horsemen were discovered bearing down upon them; *'nous allons attraper des coups de baguette.'* They proved to be a small party of fourteen, under the charge of a man named John Lee, and, with their baggage and provisions strapped to their backs, were making their way on foot to the frontier. A brief account of their fortunes will give some idea of navigation in the Nebraska. Sixty days since, they had left the mouth of Laramie's fork, some three hundred miles above, in barges laden with the furs of the American Fur Company. They started with the annual flood, and, drawing but nine inches water, hoped to make a speedy and prosperous voyage to St. Louis; but, after a lapse of forty days, found themselves only one hundred and thirty miles from their point of departure. They came down rapidly as far as Scott's bluffs, where their difficulties began. Sometimes they came upon places where the water was spread over a great extent, and here they toiled from morning until night, endeavoring to drag their boat through the sands, making only two or three miles in as many days. Sometimes they would enter an arm of the river, where there appeared a fine channel, and, after descending prosperously for eight or ten miles, would come suddenly upon dry sands, and be compelled to return, dragging their boat for days against the rapid current; and at others, they came upon places where the water lay in holes, and, getting out to float off their boat, would fall into water up to their necks, and the next moment tumble over against a sandbar. Discouraged at length, and finding the Platte growing every day more shallow, they discharged the principal part of their cargoes one hundred and thirty miles below Fort Laramie, which they secured as well as possible, and, leaving a few men to guard them, attempted to continue their voyage, laden with some light furs and their personal baggage. After fifteen or twenty days more struggling in the sands, during which they made but one hundred and forty miles, they sunk their barges, made a *cache* of their remaining furs and property, in trees on the bank, and, packing on his back what each man could carry, had commenced, the day before we encountered them, their journey on foot to St. Louis.

We laughed then at their forlorn and vagabond appearance, and in our turn, a month or two afterward, furnished the same occasion for merriment to others. Even their stock of tobacco, the *sine qua non* of a *voyageur,* without which the night fire is gloomy, was entirely exhausted. However, we shortened their homeward journey by a small supply from our own provision. They gave us the welcome intelligence that the buffalo were abundant some two days' march in advance, and made us a present of some choice pieces, which were a very acceptable change from our salt pork. In the interchange of news, and the renewal of old acquaintanceships, we found wherewithal to fill a busy hour; then we mounted our horses, and they shouldered their packs, and we shook hands and parted. Among them I had found an old companion on the northern prairie, a hardened and hardly served veteran of the mountains, who had been as much hacked and scarred as an old *moustache* of Napoleon's "old guard." He flourished in the sobriquet of La Tulipe, and his real name I never knew. Finding that he was going to the States only because his company was bound in that direction, and that he was rather more willing to return with me, I took him again into my service. We travelled this day but seventeen miles.

At our evening camp, about sunset, three figures were discovered approaching, which our glasses made out to be Indians. They proved to be Cheyennes—two men, and a boy of thirteen. About a month since, they had left their people on the south fork of the river, some three hundred miles to the westward, and a party of only four in number had been to the Pawnee villages on a horse stealing excursion, from which they were returning unsuccessful. They were miserably mounted on wild horses from the Arkansas plains, and had no other weapons than bows and long spears; and had they been discovered by the Pawnees, could not, by any possibility, have escaped. They were mortified by their ill success, and said the Pawnees were cowards who shut up their horses in their lodges at night. I invited them to supper with me, and Randolph and the young Cheyenne, who had been eyeing each other suspiciously and curiously, soon became intimate friends. After supper we sat down on the grass, and I placed a sheet of paper between us, on which they traced rudely, but with a certain degree of relative truth, the water-courses of the country which lay between us and their villages, and of which I desired to have some information. Their companions, they told us, had taken a nearer route over the hills; but they had mounted one of the summits to spy out the country, whence they had caught a glimpse of our party, and, confident of good treatment at the hands of the whites, hastened to join company. Latitude of the camp 40° 39' 51".

We made the next morning sixteen miles. I remarked that the ground was covered in many places with an efflorescence of salt, and the plants were not numerous. In the bottoms was frequently seen *tradescantia,* and on the dry lenches were *carduus, cactus,* and *amorpha.* A high wind during the morning had increased to a violent gale from the northwest, which made our afternoon ride cold and unpleasant. We had the welcome sight of two buffaloes on one of the large islands, and encamped at a clump of timber about seven miles from our noon halt, after a day's march of twenty-two miles.

The air was keen the next morning at sunrise, the thermometer standing at 44°, and it was sufficiently cold to make overcoats very comfortable. A few miles brought us into the midst of the buffalo, swarming in immense numbers over the plains, where they had left scarcely a blade of grass standing. Mr. Preuss, who was sketching at a little distance in the rear, had at first noted them as large groves of timber. In the sight of such a mass of life, the traveller feels a strange emotion of grandeur. We had heard from a distance a dull and confused murmuring, and, when we came in view of their dark masses, there was not one among us who did not feel his heart beat quicker. It was the early part of the day, when the herds are feeding; and everywhere they were in motion. Here and there a huge old bull was rolling in the grass, and clouds of dust rose in the air from various parts of the bands, each the scene of some obstinate fight. Indians and buffalo make the poetry and life of the prairie, and our camp was full of their exhilaration. In place of the quiet monotony of the march, relieved only by the cracking of the whip, and an *"avance donc! enfant de garce!"* shouts and songs resounded from every part of the line, and our evening camp was always the commencement of a feast, which terminated only with our departure on the following morning. At any time of the night might be seen pieces of the most delicate and choicest meat, roasting *en appolas,* on sticks around the fire, and the guard were never without company. With pleasant weather and no enemy to fear, an abundance of the most excellent meat, and no scarcity of bread or tobacco, they were enjoying the oasis of a voyageur's life. Three cows were killed to day. Kit Carson had shot one, and was continuing the chase in the midst of another herd, when his horse fell headlong, but sprang up and joined the flying band. Though considerably hurt, he had the good fortune to break no bones; and Maxwell, who was mounted on a fleet hunter, captured the runaway after a hard chase. He was on the point of shooting him, to avoid the loss of his bridle, (a handsomely mounted Spanish one,) when he found that his horse was able to come up with him. Animals are frequently lost in this way; and it is necessary to keep close watch over them, in the vicinity of the buffalo, in the midst of which they scour off to the plains, and are rarely retaken. . . .

July 23 The present year had been one of unparalleled drought, and throughout the country the water had been almost dried up. By availing themselves of the annual rise, the traders had invariably succeeded in carrying their furs to the Missouri; but this season, as has already been mentioned, on both forks of the Platte they had entirely failed. The greater number of the springs and many of the streams which made halting places for the *voyageurs,* had been dried up. Every where the soil looked parched and burnt, the scanty yellow grass crisped under the foot, and even the hardiest plants were destroyed by want of moisture. I think it necessary to mention this fact, because to the rapid evaporation in such an elevated region, nearly 5,000 feet above the sea, almost wholly unprotected by timber, should be attributed much of the sterile appearance of the country, in the destruction of vegetation, and the numerous saline efflorescences which covered the ground. Such I afterward found to be the case.

I was informed that the roving villages of Indians and travellers had never met with difficulty in finding an abundance of grass for their horses; and now it was after great search that we were able to find a scanty patch of grass, sufficient to keep them from sinking, and in the course of a day or two they began to suffer very much. We found none today at noon; and, in the course of our search on the Platte, came to a grove of cottonwood where some Indian village had recently encamped. Boughs of the cottonwood yet green covered the ground, which the Indians had cut down to feed their horses upon. It is only in the winter that recourse is had to this means of sustaining them; and their resort to it at this time was a striking evidence of the state of the country. We followed their example, and turned our horses into a grove of young poplars. This began to present itself as a very serious evil, for on our animals depended altogether the further prosecution of our journey.

Shortly after we had left this place, the scouts came galloping in with the alarm of Indians. We turned in immediately towards the river, which here had a steep high bank, where we formed with the carts a very close barricade, resting on the river, within which the animals were strongly hobbled and picketed. The guns were discharged and reloaded, and men thrown forward, under cover of the bank, in the direction by which the Indians were expected. Our interpreter, who, with the Indian, had gone to meet them, came in in about ten mintues, accompanied by two Sioux. They looked sulky, and we could obtain from them only some confused information. We learned that they belonged to the party which had been on the trail of the emigrants, whom they had overtaken at Rock Independence, on the Sweet Water. Here the party had disagreed, and came nigh fighting among themselves. One portion were desirous of attacking the whites, but the others were opposed to it; and finally they had broken up into small bands and dispersed over the country. The greater portion of them had gone over into the territory of the Crows, and intended to return by way of the Wind River valley, in the hope of being able to fall upon some small parties of Crow Indians. The remainder were returning down the Platte in scattered parties of ten and twenty, and those whom we had encountered belonged to those who had advocated an attack on the emigrants. Several of the men suggested shooting them on the spot; but I promptly discountenanced any such proceeding. They further informed me that buffalo were very scarce, and little or no grass to be found. There had been no rain, and innumerable quantities of grasshoppers had destroyed the grass. This insect had been so numerous since leaving Fort Laramie, that the ground seemed alive with them; and in walking, a little moving cloud preceded our footsteps. This was bad news. No grass, no buffalo—food for neither horse nor man. I gave them some plugs of tabacco and they went off, apparently well satisfied to be clear of us; for my men did not look upon them very lovingly, and they glanced suspiciously at our warlike preparations, and the little ring of rifles which surrounded them. They were evidently in a bad humor, and shot one of their horses when they had left us a short distance.

We made the next day twenty-two miles, and encamped on the right bank of the Platte, where a handsome meadow afforded tolerably good grass. There were the remains of an old fort here, thrown up in some sudden emergency, and on the opposite side was a picturesque bluff of ferruginous sandstone. There was a handsome grove a little above, and scattered groups of trees bordered the river. Buffalo made their appearance this afternoon, and the hunters came in shortly after we had encamped, with three fine cows. The night was fine, and observations gave for the latitude of the camp, 42° 47' 40".

July 25 We made but thirteen miles this day, and encamped about noon in a pleasant grove on the right bank. Low scaffolds were erected, upon which the meat was laid, cut up into thin strips, and small fires kindled below. Our object was to profit by the vicinity of the buffalo, to lay in a stock of provisions for ten or fifteen days. In the course of the afternoon, the hunters brought in five or six cows, and all hands were kept busily employed in preparing the meat, to the drying of which the guard attended during the night. Our people had recovered their gaiety, and the busy figures around the blazing fires gave a picturesque air to the camp. A very serious accident occurred this morning, in the breaking of one of the barometers. These had been the object of my constant solicitude, and, as I had intended them principally for mountain service, I had used them as seldom as possible; taking them always down at night, and on the occurrence of storms, in order to lessen the chances of being broken. I was reduced to one, a standard barometer, of Troughton's construction. This I determined to preserve, if possible. . . .

August 23 Yesterday evening we reached our encampment at Rock Independence, where I took some astronomical observations. Here, not unmindful of the custom of early travellers and explorers in our country, I engraved on this rock of the Far West a symbol of the Christian faith. Among the thickly inscribed names, I made on the hard granite the impression of a large cross, which I covered with a black preparation of India rubber, well calculated to resist the influence of wind and rain. It stands amidst the names of many who have long since found their way to the grave, and for whom the huge rock is a giant grave stone.

One George Weymouth was sent out to Maine by the Earl of Southampton, Lord Arundel, and others; and in the narrative of their discoveries, he says: "The next day, we ascended in our pinnace, that part of the river which lies more to the westward, carrying with us a cross—a thing never omitted by any Christian traveller—which we erected at the ultimate end of our route." This was in the year 1605, and in 1842, I obeyed the feeling of early travellers, and left the impression of the cross deeply engraved on the vast rock one thousand miles beyond the Mississippi, to which discoverers have given the national name of *Rock Independence.*

In obedience to my instructions to survey the river Platte, if possible, I had determined to make an attempt at this place. The India rubber boat was filled with air, placed in the water, and loaded with what was necessary for our operations; and I embarked with Mr. Preuss and a party of men. When we had dragged our boat for a mile or two over the sands, I abandoned the impossible undertaking, and waited for the arrival of the party, when we packed up our boat and equipage, and at 9 o'clock were again moving along on our land journey. We continued along the valley on the right bank of the Sweet Water, where the formation, as already described, consists of a grayish micaceous sandstone, and fine-grained conglomerate, and marl. We passed over a ridge which borders or constitutes the river hills of the Platte, consisting of huge blocks sixty or eighty feet cube of decomposing granite. The cement which united them was probably of easier decomposition, and has disappeared and left them isolate, and separated by small spaces. Numerous horns of the mountain goat were lying among the rocks, and in the ravines were cedars whose trunks were of extraordinary size. From this ridge we descended to a small open plain at the mouth of the Sweet Water, which rushed with a rapid current into the Platte, here flowing along in a broad, tranquil, and apparently deep stream, which seemed, from its turbid appearance to be considerably swollen. I obtained here some astronomical observations, and the afternoon was spent in getting our boat ready for navigation the next day. . . .

3

Man on the Moon[*]

By the twentieth century the continental United States was completely known, so America continued to explore in the air. The desire

[*]Source: *First on the Moon* by Neil Armstrong, Michael Collins, and Edwin E. Aldrin, Jr., written with Gene Farmer and Jane Hamblin, by permission of Little, Brown and Co. Copyright © 1970 by Little, Brown and Company, Inc., pp. 280–82.

to fly was not a new one, but the Wright Brothers made it a reality. Charles Lindbergh, who flew solo across the Atlantic in 1927, and Richard Byrd, who flew over the North Pole in 1926, led in adventuring in the air. Through the airplane Americans traveled to remote parts of the globe, but in time they began to look to the exploration of space. In this quest America was not alone. On October 4, 1957, Russia sent Sputnik I, an artificial satellite, into orbit around the earth.

Russia led the space race until the late 1950s when America slowly began to make gains. In 1960 Alan B. Shepherd traveled 300 miles into space and was soon followed by Captain Virgil Grissom. In 1962 John Glenn became the first American to orbit the earth. With the Gemini and Apollo projects, America made remarkable achievements, and on July 20, 1969, an American walked on the moon. Though the Apollo 17 flight ended the Apollo project and marked an official deemphasis on space exploration, exploration, for political, economic or personal reasons, will continue. The depths of the sea and the reaches of outer space are still tempting. In this article Neil Armstrong and Edwin Aldrin verbalize their thoughts prior to their historic moon walks.

Questions

1. What were Armstrong's impressions?
2. How do the thoughts of Aldrin compare with those of Armstrong?
3. How do these reflections compare with the other earlier explorers?

It has a stark beauty all its own. It's like much of the high desert of the United States.

NEIL ARMSTRONG

I don't believe any pair of people had been more removed physically from the rest of the world than we were.

EDWIN E. ALDRIN JR.

It was time for Neil Armstrong to walk on the moon, and as Armstrong waited for Aldrin to follow him out in nineteen minutes his first reaction to the environment was a favorable one. He was able immediately to discard the theory, once widely held, that the windless surface of the moon was overlaid with a dangerously deep coating of dust in which men and manmade machines would founder. The lunar module's footpads had made only a shallow penetration, and Neil's boots sank only a fraction of an inch: "Maybe an eighth of an inch, but I can see the footprints of my boots and the treads in the fine sandy particles." And he could move around: "There seems to be no difficulty. . . . It's even perhaps easier than the simulations at one-sixth G. . . . It's actually no trouble to walk around. The descent engine did not leave a crater of any size. There's about one foot clearance on the ground. We're essentially on a very level place here. I can see some evidence of rays emanating from the descent engine, but very insignificant amounts. . . . Okay, Buzz, we're ready to bring down the camera."

"I'm all ready," Aldrin answered. . . . "Okay, you'll have to pay out all the LEC [lunar equipment conveyor]. It looks like it's coming out nice and evenly."

"Okay, it's quite dark here in the shadow and a little hard for me to see if I have good footing. I'll work my way over into sunlight here without looking directly into the sun."

"Okay, it's taut now," Aldrin said. "Don't hold it quite so tight."

Armstrong looked up at the LM and messaged: "I'm standing directly in the shadow now, looking up at Buzz in the window. And I can see everything clearly. The light is sufficiently bright, backlighted into the front of the LM, that everything is very clearly visible."

"Okay, I'm going to be changing this film magazine," Aldrin said.

"Okay," Armstrong said. "Camera installed on the RCU bracket [remote control unit]. I'm storing the LEC on the secondary strut. . . . I'll step out and take some of my first pictures here."

Houston (McCandless): Roger, Neil, we're reading you loud and clear. We see you getting some pictures and the contingency sample.

"This is very interesting," Armstrong said. "It's a very soft surface, but here and there where I plug with the contingency sample collector, I run into a very hard surface. . . . I'll try to get a rock in here. Here's a couple."

"That looks beautiful from here, Neil," Aldrin said from Eagle's cabin.

"It has a stark beauty all its own. It's like much of the high desert of the United States. It's different, but it's very pretty out here."

In El Lago Jan Armstrong was ticking off the minutes, but not out of any particular safety concern; her concern was still the one she had expressed much earlier: would they be able to do all they had been assigned to do on this first lunar landing mission? But there was tension in the small talk. Jan volunteered, "Buzz will not come down until Neil gets the contingency sample—which will fall out of his pocket." There was some discussion about how to tell who was saying what; Armstrong and Aldrin had voices of similar timbre, and even people who knew them well had had difficulty with voice identifications throughout the flight. Ricky Armstrong suggested, "You can recognize Daddy—he always says 'Uhhh.' " In Nassau Bay Pat Collins commented: "Look at Neil move. He looks like he's dancing—that's the kangaroo hop." Waiting for Buzz to come out, Joan Aldrin reacted to Armstrong's physical descriptions of the lunar surface with amazement: "He *likes* it!" Later Neil Armstrong said. . . .

The most dramatic recollections I had were the sights themselves. Of all the spectacular views we had, the most impressive to me was on the way to the moon, when we flew through its shadow. We were still thousands of miles away, but close enough so that the moon almost filled our circular window. It was eclipsing the sun, from our position, and the corona of the sun was visible around the limb of the moon as a gigantic lens-shaped or saucer-shaped light, stretching out to several lunar diameters. It was magnificent, but the moon was even more so. We were in its shadow, so there was no part of it illuminated by the sun. It was illuminated only by earthshine. It made the moon appear blue-gray, and the entire scene looked decidedly three-dimensional.

I was really aware, visually aware, that the moon was in fact a sphere, not a disc. It seemed almost as if it were showing us its roundness, its similarity in shape to our earth, in a sort of welcome. I was sure that it would be a hospitable host. It had been awaiting its first visitors for a long time.

"You can really throw things a long way up here," Armstrong said. "That pocket open, Buzz?"

"Yes, it is, but it's not up against your suit though. Hit it back once more. More toward the inside. Okay, that's good."

"That in the pocket?"

"Yes, push down," Aldrin said. "Got it? No, it's not all the way in. Push it. There you go."

"Contingency sample is in the pocket," Armstrong confirmed. ". . . Are you getting a TV picture now, Houston?"

Houston (McCandless): Neil, yes we are getting a TV picture. . . . You're not in it at the present time. We can see the bag on the LEC being moved by Buzz, though. Here you come into our field of view.

Aldrin: "Okay. Are you ready for me to come out?" *Armstrong:* "Yes. Just stand by a second. I'll move this over the handrail. Okay?" *Aldrin:* "All right. That's got it. Are you ready?" *Armstrong:* "All set. Okay, you saw what difficulties I was having. I'll try to watch your PLSS from underneath here. . . . Okay. Your PLSS is—looks like it is clearing okay. The shoes are about to come over the sill. Okay, now drop your PLSS down. There you go. . . . About an inch clearance on top of your PLSS. . . . Okay, you're right at the edge of the porch. . . . Looks good." *Aldrin:* "Now I want to back up and partially close the hatch, making sure not to lock it on my way out." *Armstrong:* "A particularly good thought." *Aldrin:* "That's our home for the next couple of hours and I want to take good care of it."

Watching television in Nassau Bay, Rusty Schweickart encouraged: "Don't close it all the way, Buzz. What do you mean? You forgot the key?" As Buzz started down the ladder Jan Armstrong wondered aloud, "Wouldn't that be something if they locked themselves out?" In the Aldrin home the astronaut Fred Haise, watching Armstrong move across the screen, laughed and said, "That's the fastest I've ever seen Neil move!" He warned Joan Aldrin, "Buzz is about to come out now, Joan." She said, "It's like making an entrance on stage." But as seconds passed with no sight of Buzz, she said, "You see, he's doing it just like on Gemini 12. He's going to explain every single thing he does." Then Buzz's legs did appear. Joan screamed and kicked her own legs up in the air. As he came slowly down the ladder she said, "He's going to analyze every step at a time."

Thought Questions

1. Analyze the different styles of recording experience of the Norsemen and Neil Armstrong.
2. How did John Fremont and Edwin Aldrin describe the terrain about them?
3. What different hardships did the explorers from the Norsemen to the astronauts suffer?

three

RELIGION:

From the Missionaries to
the Jesus People

Worship and religion are hardly indigenous to America, but they are persistent themes. Critics have talked recently of the end of organized religion and the birth of an era of disbelief. Religious enthusiasts, on the other hand, say that church attendance is at an all-time high and that the present Jesus movement is symptomatic of a growing revival of religion. Such paradox is not new. Critics and supporters and periods of religious revivalism have come and gone.

The colonial period reflected European religion in America. The Anglicans represented the English break with the Catholic Church, while the Puritans attempted to purify the Anglican Church, and the Catholics carried their traditional beliefs to the New World. Many other minor sects that grew out of the proliferation of beliefs in Europe also came to America. Religion affected everyday colonial life, particularly in Puritan New England. But by the early 1740s religious groups, noticing a lack in zeal, underwent a Great Awakening. It was during this awakening that American evangelism was born.

With the American Revolution churches shared in the spirit of independence and became much more Americanized. The early 1800s saw a continued growth in revivalism, with a Second Great Awakening, rising popularity of Baptist and Methodist sects, and religious experimentation. The Civil War split many denominations and led into the industrial, urban age. During the late 1900s American churches faced mass immigration, the evolutionist ideas of Charles Darwin, and the challenge of burgeoning cities. While they tried to adjust to the times, many of them split into liberal and conservative camps over ideas of evolution.

The twentieth century did little to help organized religion. Many of the problems of the 1800s remained unsolved. Evolution continued to plague biblical scholars, while war, birth control, abortion, and a general loosening of morals raised questions within the churches. Again they tried to change with the times and many new religious experiences were born. But in the late 1960s a new Great Awakening—the Jesus Movement—began a new phase of religion, evidently outside the confines of established religions. And the religious theme in American history continues.

Cotton Mather on Education*

In 1630 the English Puritans came to the Massachusetts area to create a "New Jersualem in America" and to "live" the Bible. They felt that the Anglican Church had not been completely purged of the influences of the Roman Catholic Church, and that God had destined them to come to America and establish a community of the elect. To them the church and state were inseparable, and their lives were such that civic and religious matters were often one and the same. Here Cotton Mather, one of the most influential Puritan clergymen, gives advice on the care and training of Puritan children.

Questions

1. What general guidelines does Mather establish for the guidance of children?
2. How "realistic" are his ideas?
3. How does this essay reflect his religious beliefs?
4. Would his plans for the care and training of children work today?

I. I pour out continual prayers and cries to the God of all grace for them, that He will be a Father to my children, and bestow His Christ and His Grace upon them, and guide them with His councils, and bring them to His glory. And in this action I mention them distinctly, every one by name, unto the Lord.

II. I begin betimes to entertain them with delightful stories, especially scriptural ones, and still conclude with some lesson of piety, bidding them to learn that lesson from the story. And thus every day at the table I have used myself to tell a story before I rise, and make the story useful to the olive plants about the table.

*Source: Worthington C. Ford, ed., *The Diary of Cotton Mather* in *Massachusetts Historical Society Collections* (1911), 7th Series, Vol. VII, pp. 534–37.

III. When the children at any time accidentally come in my way, it is my custom to let fall some sentence or other that may be monitory and profitable to them. This matter proves to me a matter of some study and labor and contrivance. But who can tell what may be the effect of a continual dropping?

IV. I essay betimes to engage the children in exercises of piety, and especially secret prayer, for which I give them very plain and brief directions, and suggest unto them the petitions which I would have them to make before the Lord and which I therefore explain to their apprehension and capacity. And I often call upon them, "Child, don't you forget every day to go alone and pray as I have directed you!"

V. Betimes I try to form in the children a temper of benignity. I put them upon doing of services and kindnesses for one another and for other children. I applaud them when I see them delight in it. I upbraid all aversion to it. I caution them exquisitely against all revenges of injuries. I instruct them to return good offices for evil ones. I show them how they will by this goodness become like to the good God and His glorious Christ. I let them discern that I am not satisfied except when they have a sweetness of temper shining in them.

VI. As soon as 'tis possible, I make the children learn to write. And when they can write, I employ them in writing out the most agreeable and profitable things that I can invent for them. In this way I propose to freight their minds with excellent things, and have a deep impression made upon their minds by such things.

VII. I mightily endeavor it that the children may betimes be acted by principles of reason and honor. I first beget in them an high opinion of their father's love to them, and of his being best able to judge what shall be good for them. Then I make them sensible, 'tis a folly for them to pretend unto any wit and will of their own; they must resign all to me, who will be sure to do what is best; my word must be their law. I cause them to understand that it is an hurtful and a shameful thing to do amiss. I aggravate this on all occasions, and let them see how amiable they will render themselves by well doing.

The first chastisement which I inflict for an ordinary fault is to let the child see and hear me in an astonishment, and hardly able to believe that the child could do so base a thing, but believing that they will never do it again. I would never come to give a child a blow, except in case of obstinacy or some gross enormity. To be chased for a while out of my presence I would make to be looked upon as the sorest punishment in the family.

I would by all possible insinuations gain this point upon them, that for them to learn all the brave things in the world is the bravest thing in the world. I am not fond of proposing play to them, as a reward of any diligent application to learn what is good, lest they should think diversion to be a better and a nobler thing than diligence. I would have them come to propound and expect at this rate: "I have done well, and now I will go to my father; he will teach me some curious thing for it." I must have them count it a privilege to be taught; and I sometimes manage the matter so that my refusing to teach them something is their punishment. The slavish way of education, carried on with raving and kicking and scourging (in schools as well as families), 'tis abominable, and a dreadful judgement of God upon the world.

VIII. Though I find it a marvellous advantage to have the children strongly biassed by principles of reason and honor (which, I find, children will feel sooner than is commonly thought for), yet I would neglect no endeavors to have higher principles infused into them. I therefore betimes awe them with the eye of God upon them. I show them how they must live Jesus Christ, and show it by doing what their parents require of them. I often tell them of the good angels who love them and help them and guard them, and who take notice of them, and therefore must not be disobliged. Heaven and Hell I set before them as the consequences of their behavior here.

IX. When the children are capable of it, I take them alone, one by one; and after my charges unto them to fear God and serve Christ and shun sin, I pray with them in my study and make them the witnesses of the agonies, with which I address the throne of grace on their behalf.

2

Joseph Smith and Mormonism[*]

By the 1700s the early enthusiasm of American religion was waning. The Puritan experiment had failed and other faiths suffered a noticeable drop in church attendance. A similar religious apathy was also reported in Europe. Everything changed with the Great Awakening, an international religious revival. In America revivals began locally in the early 1700s and by 1740 had spread to all

*Source: Joseph Smith, *The Pearl of Great Price: Being a Choice Selection from the Revelations, Translations, and Narrations of Joseph Smith, First Prophet, Seer, and Revelator to the Church of Latter-Day Saints* (Liverpool, 1851), pp. 37ff.

*thirteen colonies. One of the most effective preachers of the revival
was Jonathan Edwards. During the 1730s his preaching in the
Connecticut River village of Northampton aroused such a spectacular and contagious revival spirit that he became a center of the Great
Awakening.*

*Variety characterized the religious experiences of the first half of
the nineteenth century. Established religions vied with utopian
communities and many other new religious groups, such as the
Shakers. Experimentation sometimes led to discoveries of greater
authority and control. This was true of the Church of Jesus Christ
of Latter-Day Saints, best known as Mormons, and its founder
Joseph Smith. As a very young man, Smith began to distrust all
existing denominations and wanted a new answer. In 1822 he
found his answer in a "revelation" from God through a set of golden
plates containing the* Book of Mormon, *an ancient scripture. In
1830 he organized the Church of Jesus Christ of Latter-Day Saints.
Although Smith was eventually killed, the church continued under
Brigham Young. Today its members number more than two million.
In this reading Smith describes the anguish that preceded his "visions," the first visions themselves, and his discovery of the golden
plates.*

Questions

1. Why was Smith confused by the state of religion in his time?
2. How did he describe the "visions" and his discovery of the golden plates?
3. From this reading what impressions do you have of Joseph Smith and his religion?

My mind at different times was greatly excited, the cry and tumult was so
great and incessant. The Presbyterians were most decided against the Baptists
and Methodists, and used all their powers of either reason or sophistry to
prove their errors, or, at least, to make the people think they were in error.
On the other hand the Baptists and Methodists, in their turn, were equally
zealous to establish their own tenets, and disprove all others.

In the midst of this war of words and tumult of opinions, I often said to
myself, what is to be done? Who of all these parties are right? or, are they
all wrong together? If any one of them be right, which is it, and how shall
I know it?

While I was labouring under the extreme difficulties, caused by the contests
of these parties of religionists, I was one day reading the Epistle of James, first
chapter and fifth verse, which reads, "If any of you lack wisdom, let him ask

of God, that giveth unto all men liberally and upbraideth not, and it shall be given him." Never did any passage of scripture come with more power to the heart of man than this did at this time to mine. It seemed to enter with great force into every feeling of my heart. I reflected on it again and again, knowing that if any person needed wisdom from God, I did; for how to act I did not know, and unless I could get more wisdom than I then had, would never know; for the teachers of religion of the different sects understood the same passage so differently as to destroy all confidence in settling the question by an appeal to the Bible. At length I came to the conclusion that I must either remain in darkness and confusion, or else I must do as James directs, that is, ask of God. I at length came to the determination to "ask of God," concluding that if he gave wisdom to them that lacked wisdom, and would give liberally and not upbraid, I might venture. So, in accordance with this my determination to ask of God, I retired to the woods to make the attempt. It was on the morning of a beautiful clear day, early in the spring of eighteen hundred and twenty. It was the first time in my life that I had made such an attempt, for amidst all my anxieties I had never as yet made the attempt to pray vocally.

After I had retired into the place where I had previously designed to go, having looked around me and finding myself alone, I kneeled down and began to offer up the desires of my heart to God. I had scarcely done so, when immediately I was seized upon by some power which entirely overcame me, and had such astonishing influence over me as to bind my tongue so that I could not speak. Thick darkness gathered around me, and it seemed to me for a time as if I were doomed to sudden destruction. But exerting all my powers to call upon God to deliver me out of the power of this enemy which had seized upon me, and at the very moment when I was ready to sink into despair and abandon myself to destruction, not to an imaginary ruin, but to the power of some actual being from the unseen world, who had such a marvelous power as I had never before felt in any being. Just at this moment of great alarm, I saw a pillar of light exactly over my head, above the brightness of the Sun, which descended gradually until it fell upon me. It no sooner appeared than I found myself delivered from the enemy which held me bound. When the light rested upon me, I saw two personages, whose brightness and glory defy all description, standing above me in the air. One of them spake unto me, calling me by name, and said (pointing to the other) "THIS IS MY BELOVED SON, HEAR HIM."

My object in going to enquire of the Lord was to know which of all the sects was right, that I might know which to join. No sooner therefore did I get possession of myself, so as to be able to speak, than I asked the personages who stood above me in the light, which of all the sects was right (for at this time it had never entered into my heart that all were wrong), and which I should join. I was answered that I must join none of them, for they were all wrong, and the personage who addressed me said "that all their creeds were an abomination in his sight; that those professors were all corrupt, they draw near to me with their lips, but their hearts are far from me; they teach for doctrine the commandments of men, having a form of godliness, but they deny the power thereof."

He again forbade me to join with any of them; and many other things did he say unto me which I cannot write at this time. When I came to myself again, I found myself lying on my back, looking up into heaven. . . .

I often felt condemned for my weakness and imperfections; when on the evening of the above mentioned twenty-first of September, after I had retired to my bed for the night, I betook myself to prayer and supplication to Almighty God, for forgiveness of all my sins and follies, and also for a manifestation to me, that I might know of my state and standing before him; for I had full confidence in obtaining a divine manifestation, as I had previously had one.

While I was thus in the act of calling upon God, I discovered a light appearing in the room, which continued to increase until the room was lighter than at noonday, when immediately a personage appeared at my bedside, standing in the air, for his feet did not touch the floor. He had on a loose robe of most exquisite whiteness. It was a whiteness beyond anything earthly I had ever seen; nor do I believe that any earthly thing could be made to appear so exceedingly white and brilliant; his hands were naked, and his arms also, a little above the wrist; so, also, were his feet naked, as were his legs, a little above the ankles. His head and neck were also bare. I could discover that he had no other clothing on but this robe, as it was open, so that I could see into his bosom.

Not only was his robe exceedingly white, but his whole person was glorious beyond description, and his countenance truly like lightning. The room was exceedingly light, but not so very bright as immediately around his person. When I first looked upon him I was afraid, but the fear soon left me. He called me by name and said unto me, that he was a messenger sent from the presence of God to me, and that his name was Nephi.[1] That God had a work for me to do, and that my name should be had for good and evil among all nations, kindreds, and tongues; or that it should be both good and evil spoken of among all people. He said there was a book deposited, written upon gold plates, giving an account of the former inhabitants of this continent, and the source from whence they sprang. He also said that, the fulness of the everlasting gospel was contained in it, as delivered by the Saviour to the ancient inhabitants. Also, that there were two stones in silver bows (and these stones, fastened to a breastplate, constituted what is called the Urim and Thummim) deposited with the plates, and the possession and use of these stones was what constituted Seers in ancient or former times, and that God had prepared them for the purpose of translating the book. . . .

I . . . went to the place where the messenger had told me the plates were

---

[1]Later editions read "Moroni."

deposited, and owing to the distinctness of the vision which I had had concerning it, I knew the place the instant that I arrived there. Convenient to the village of Manchester, Ontario county, New York, stands a hill of considerable size, and the most elevated of any in the neighbourhood. On the west side of this hill, not far from the top, under a stone of considerable size, lay the plates deposited in a stone box; this stone was thick and rounding in the middle on the upper side, and thinner towards the edges, so that the middle part of it was visible above the ground, but the edge all round was covered with earth. Having removed the earth and obtained a lever which I got fixed under the edge of the stone, and with a little exertion raised it up; I looked in, and there indeed did I behold the plates, the Urim and Thummim, and the breast-plate, as stated by the messenger. The box in which they lay was formed by laying stones together in some kind of cement. In the bottom of the box were laid two stones crossways of the box, and on these stones lay the plates and the other things with them. I made an attempt to take them out, but was forbidden by the messenger, and was again informed that the time for bringing them forth had not yet arrived, neither would until four years from that time. . . .

At length the time arrived for obtaining the Plates, the Urim and Thummim, and the Breast-plate. On the 22nd day of September, 1827, having gone, as usual, at the end of another year, to the place where they were deposited; the same heavenly messenger delivered them up to me with this charge, that I should be responsible for them; that if I should let them go carelessly or through any neglect of mine, I should be cut off; but that if I would use all my endeavours to preserve them, until he, the messenger, should call for them, they should be protected.

I soon found out the reason why I had received such strict charges to keep them safe, and why it was that the messenger had said, that when I had done what was required at my hand, he would call for them; for no sooner was it known that I had them, than the most strenuous exertions were used to get them from me; every stratagem that could be invented was resorted to for that purpose; the persecution became more bitter and severe than before, and multitudes were on the alert continually to get them from me if possible, but by the wisdom of God they remained safe in my hands, until I had accomplished by them what was required at my hand; when, according to arrangements, the messenger called for them, I delivered them up to him, and he has them in his charge until this day, being the 2nd day of May, 1838.

The Scopes Trial*

The split between religious liberals and conservatives, formerly initiated by the ideas of Charles Darwin, reemerged as an issue in the 1920s. The liberals were trying to reconcile religion with the rapid changes in American society, while the conservatives reflected older, more traditional views. The bitter controversy between the two forces reached its climax in 1925 with the trial of John Scopes. Scopes was a Tennessee high school biology teacher who had taught evolution in his class in defiance of a state law. Clarence Darrow defended Scopes, while the political figure of William Jennings Bryan led the prosecution. Though the liberals lost the trial, Bryan's views appeared unacceptable to most Americans. This selection from the trial record relates the struggle between Darrow and Bryan over the interpretation of the Bible.

Questions

1. What was Bryan's interpretation of the Bible?
2. How did Darrow challenge Bryan's views?
3. In your estimation who had the stronger arguments and why?

[*Examination of W. J. Bryan by Clarence Darrow, counsel for the Defense:*]

Q—You have given considerable study to the Bible, haven't you, Mr. Bryan?

A—Yes, sir, I have tried to.

Q—Well, we all know you have; we are not going to dispute that at all. But you have written and published articles almost weekly, and sometimes have made interpretations of various things.

*Source: State of Tennessee v. John Thomas Scopes, Nos. 5231, 5232, pp. 733–38.

A—I would not say interpretations, Mr. Darrow, but comments on the lesson.

Q—If you comment to any extent these comments have been interpretations?

A—I presume that any discussion might be to some extent interpretations, but they have not been primarily intended as interpretations. . . .

Q—Then you have made a general study of it?

A—Yes, I have; I have studied the Bible for about fifty years, or some time more than that, but, of course, I have studied it more as I have become older than when I was but a boy.

Q—Do you claim that everything in the Bible should be literally interpreted?

A—I believe everything in the Bible should be accepted as it is given there; some of the Bible is given illustratively. For instance: "Ye are the salt of the earth." I would not insist that man was actually salt, or that he had flesh of salt, but it is used in the sense of salt as saving God's people.

Q—But when you read that Jonah swallowed the whale—or that the whale swallowed Jonah—excuse me please—how do you literally interpret that?

A—When I read that a big fish swallowed Jonah—it does not say whale.

Q—Doesn't it? Are you sure?

A—That is my recollection of it. A big fish, and I believe it; and I believe in a God who can make a whale and can make a man and make both do what He pleases.

Q—Mr. Bryan, doesn't the New Testament say whale? [*Matthew 12:40.*]

A—I am not sure. My impression is that it says fish; but it does not make so much difference; I merely called your attention to where it says fish—it does not say whale.

Q—But in the New Testament it says whale, doesn't it?

A—That may be true; I cannot remember in my own mind what I read about it.

Q—Now, you say, the big fish swallowed Jonah, and he there remained how long? three days? and then he spewed him upon the land. You believe that the big fish was made to swallow Jonah?

A—I am not prepared to say that; the Bible merely says it was done.

Q—You don't know whether it was the ordinary run of fish, or made for that purpose?

A—You may guess; you evolutionists guess.

Q—But when we do guess, we have a sense to guess right.

A—But do not do it often.

Q—You are not prepared to say whether that fish was made especially to swallow a man or not?

A—The Bible doesn't say, so I am not prepared to say.

Q—You don't know whether that was fixed up specially for the purpose?

A—No, the Bible doesn't say.

Q—But you do believe He made them—that He made such a fish and that it was big enough to swallow Jonah?

A—Yes, sir. Let me add: one miracle is just as easy to believe as another.

Q—It is for me.

A—It is for me.

Q—Just as hard?

A—It is hard to believe for you, but easy for me. A miracle is a thing performed beyond what man can perform. When you get beyond what man can do, you get within the realm of miracles; and it is just as easy to believe the miracle of Jonah as any other miracle in the Bible.

Q—Perfectly easy to believe that Jonah swallowed the whale?

A—If the Bible said so; the Bible doesn't make as extreme statements as evolutionists do.

Mr. Darrow—That may be a question, Mr. Bryan, about some of those you have known.

A—The only thing is, you have a definition of fact that includes imagination.

Q—And you have a definition that excludes everything but imagination.

Gen. Stewart—I object to that as argumentative.

The Witness—You—

Mr. Darrow—The witness must not argue with me, either.

Q—Do you consider the story of Jonah and the whale a miracle?

A—I think it is.

Q—Do you believe Joshua made the sun stand still?

A—I believe what the Bible says. I suppose you mean that the earth stood still?

Q—I don't know. I am talking about the Bible now.

A—I accept the Bible absolutely.

Q—The Bible says Joshua commanded the sun to stand still for the purpose of lengthening the day, doesn't it? and you believe it?

A—I do.

Q—Do you believe at that time the entire sun went around the earth?

A—No, I believe that the earth goes around the sun.

Q—Do you believe that men who wrote it thought that the day could be lengthened or that the sun could be stopped?

A—I don't know what they thought.

Q—You don't know?

A—I think they wrote the fact without expressing their own thoughts.

Q—Have you an opinion as to whether or not the men who wrote that thought—

Gen. Stewart—I want to object, your Honor; it has gone beyond the pale of any issue that could possibly be injected into this lawsuit, except by imagination. I do not think the defendant has a right to conduct the examination any further and I ask your Honor to exclude it.

The Court—I will hear Mr. Bryan.

The Witness—It seems to me it would be too exacting to confine the Defense to the facts; if they are not allowed to get away from the facts, what have they to deal with?

The Court—Mr. Bryan is willing to be examined. Go ahead.

Mr. Darrow—Have you an opinion as to whether—whoever wrote the book, I believe it is, Joshua, the Book of Joshua, thought the sun went around the earth or not?

A—I believe that he was inspired.

Mr. Darrow—Can you answer my question?

A—When you let me finish the statement.

Q—It is a simple question, but finish it.

The Witness—You cannot measure the length of my answer by the length of your question.

[*Laughter in the courtyard.*]

Mr. Darrow—No, except that the answer be longer.

[*Laughter in the courtyard.*]

A—I believe that the Bible is inspired, an inspired author, whether one who wrote as he was directed to write understood the things he was writing about, I don't know.

Q—Whoever inspired it? Do you think whoever inspired it believed that the sun went around the earth?

A—I believe it was inspired by the Almighty, and He may have used language that could be understood at that time.

Q—Was—

The Witness—Instead of using language that could not be understood until Mr. Darrow was born.

The Jesus Movement*

Modern religion, as difficult to define as the direction of modern American society, has seen its most noticeable change in the forming of the Jesus Movement. This youth-oriented movement in the tradition of evangelism is Jesus-centered as is evident from the movement's preaching and writing. Whether it is merely students reacting to the twentieth century American materialism or a reaffirmation of the evangelical spirit is not yet clear. Here is a description of a typical day in a Jesus community in Ellenville, New York.

Questions

1. What is "normal" living like here?
2. Where does religion fit into the community?
3. What does the purpose of the colony appear to be?

This sleepy town on the edge of the Catskills has a population of 5,000, a collection of peeling Victorian mansions and—since last June—a colony of more than 100 transients who call themselves the "Children of God."

They are part of a sect within the "Jesus movement" which claims anywhere from 2,000 to 3,000 members in small colonies in the U.S., and some in Europe.

The "Children" live by sharing, adopt Biblical names and follow a strict schedule daily of study, work, prayer and singing in their cluster of houses.

Most of the "Children" in the Ellenville colony are in their early 20s but there have been some as old as 55.

*Reprinted from *U.S. News and World Report,* "A Day in the Life of the 'Children of God,' " March 20, 1972, p. 65. Copyright 1972 U.S. News and World Report, Inc.

"We Shall Try."

Nominally in charge is David Cook—known in the colony as "Jared" —who is a licensed minister. He says:

"In the book of Acts, it is written that the early Christians sold what they had and shared with each other. That is what we try to do."

Apparently this arrangement works. A recent convert says:

"Lots of kids come here with quite a bit of money. Some still get money from home. We don't have money problems. We don't need much money."

Most "Children" admit to having had bad experiences with drugs, sex or family. Now they have abandoned worldly goods and have turned to what one calls "the ultimate trip"—namely, Jesus.

Robert Miller, who calls himself "Barnabas" and is an assistant to Mr. Cook, explained his own experience:

"Life had lost its meaning. I was involved in psychedelic drugs.

"At Woodstock, I tried to kill myself, built a fire and stood in it. This guy pulled me out and beat out the flames. Then I heard the Children of God singing on a hillside. It was beautiful. I was drawn to it and accepted Jesus Christ. It was heavy, man. I haven't used drugs since. Now I just want to help other people."

Such people stir mixed feelings, here and elsewhere in the nation.

Many parents of the Children are up in arms about the colonists' life style, and have formed a national organization in opposition—"Parents' Committee to Free Our Children From the Children of God," or FREECOG.

These parents say their children in the colonies have been mesmerized, brainwashed or forcibly detained by their leaders. Lawsuits are threatened in some places to force youngsters to return home.

Here in Ellenville, there are complaints about "goings on" at the settlement, about rock music the "Children" play, and "the money up there."

Yet most in Ellenville accept the sincerity of the "Children." Chief of Police William Trapnell said:

"We have very good relations with the group. There has never been any trouble. I have made several visits up there and the atmosphere is good. It's always 'God bless you, brother.' It beats being called 'pig.' "

A Roman Catholic priest, the Rev. John Budwick, also is persuaded of the group's sincerity. "They may be in a transitional phase," he said, "but what they are doing is not so different from what I am doing."

"Called Me Brother."

A filling-station attendant talked about the colony's nightly "Jesus-jamming" at which the "Children" sing original hymns pegged to the Scriptures and set to music played by musicians with electric guitars and banjos.

"I'm not much on religion, but I went up there one night," he said. "I was accepted. Everybody called me 'brother.' This rock stuff was never my bag but when they started singing their own hymns, man, I got goose bumps."

Organizationally, each unit within the colony is described as self-governing, and self-sufficient.

All members are called disciples. The new member, called a "babe," must give his full name, his drug history, his chosen Biblical name, and allow his mail to be censored.

After intensive Bible instruction, which is vigorous enough to make many leave after a few days, the persevering become "younger brothers." With full acceptance comes the title of "elder brother."

At this stage, the disciple must learn a trade. The popular ones are photography, auto mechanics, printing, leather and art crafts.

Plan of the Day.

The daily schedule is spartan. It begins at 7 A.M. with cleanup. Then come tribe meetings, morning prayers and classes on eternal salvation. Breakfast, one of the day's two meals, is at 11 A.M., accompanied by songs, Scripture reading and recitation.

Afternoons are devoted to work, more classes and leadership training. Dinner is at 6. Most of the "Children" watch evening news on television. Evenings are devoted to celebrating Christ with rock bands, the reading of letters from other colonies and quiet conversation. All lights go out at midnight.

There are separate quarters for men and women, except for a few married couples. Once in the colony, a man or woman may not marry for six months.

All possessions are shared. The "Children" often give away clothing to the poor in the town. In return, Ellenville merchants give their visitors supplies of day-old bread, dented cans of food and sometimes bulk supplies of rice and flour.

Godly Revolution.

These are not hippies. Only a few have long hair. But an application form for membership says a good revolutionary is "rebellious against society because society is anti-God." It adds that the "Children" rebel against "self-destructing capitalism with its hellish wars and fiendish weapons."

The "Children" see their colony as a springboard for foreign evangelism. Already the "Children" have colonies in established centers of Europe's hippie culture—in Amsterdam, London, Bonn, Essen, Stockholm and Brussels.

Meantime, evangelism consists of boarding one of the colony's ancient buses and heading into New York City's Greenwich Village on week-ends to recruit colonists.

The bus has a built-in stove, food, blankets and medical supplies. The "Children" talk to Village hippies about God and the peaceful life in the Catskills.

There is no coercion. But each trip produces a few more converts for this sect that is stirring controversy and wonderment in so much of the nation today.

Thought Questions

1. Compare and contrast Cotton Mather's and Joseph Smith's views on religion and the religious experience.
2. How does the Scopes Trial indicate the liberal-conservative split in modern religion?
3. What direction is modern religion taking and how does the Jesus Movement fit into it?
4. What were the differences and similarities in the expression of religion in this chapter?

four

WAR:
From the French and Indian War
to Vietnam

In American history war has played a persistent and troubling role. Looking at our history it sometimes seems that periods of peace have only occasionally disturbed the continuous eras of war. From the beginning, Americans have had to become used to war and its horrors—throughout the many wars and our different enemies and varied rationales.

The French and Indian War was a struggle between England and France for control of North America. Colonists frequently fought on the English side, but found the results and processes of the war bitter. After England changed her colonial policy, the American Revolution followed. But the Revolution did not solve all Anglo-American problems, and in 1812 America and England again clashed. In 1846 the Mexican War, an imperialistic struggle which left the United States in command in the Southwest, began moving America to the Civil War. The War between the States, of all our wars, is most unique in that it has been the only internecine clash in our history. After this divisive struggle, the nation found temporary unity in another imperialist war with Spain in 1898 some thirty years later. America first felt its imperial power in 1898. The conclusion of the Spanish-American War found America a possessor of extracontinental territories.

World Wars I and II were much different from earlier ones; they were fought throughout the world and were very crucial to American survival. The

Korean and Vietnamese conflicts followed closely after World War II. These limited wars exemplified American willingness to fight in foreign lands, as "policeman of the globe," against an enemy that offered no immediate danger.

The Coming of the American Revolution*

War usually occurs for a complex of reasons; and the American Revolution is no exception. Taxation, a new imperial policy, general restlessness, radical leadership—all contributed. The following two readings help explain the coming of the American Revolution: in the first a revolutionary veteran views that war as a blow for self-government; in the second historian George Bancroft sees the Revolution as a rebellion of liberty-loving Americans against a tyrannical and oppressive British government.

Questions

CHAMBERLAIN

1. How did Preston explain the war?
2. Are his arguments too simple?

BANCROFT

1. How does Bancroft explain the American Revolution?
2. Which of the two readings seems the more reasonable explanation?

Chamberlain

When the action at Lexington, on the morning of the 19th [of April], was known at Danvers, the minute men there, under the lead of Captain

*Sources: Mellen Chamberlain, *John Adams: The Statesman of the American Revolution* (1898), pp. 248–49; and George Bancroft, *History of the United States of America from the Discovery of the Continent* (Boston, Mass.: Little, Brown and Company, 1876), Vol. 3, pp. 9–13.

Gideon Foster, made that memorable march—or run, rather—of sixteen miles in four hours, and struck Percy's flying column at West Cambridge. Brave but incautious in flanking the Redcoats, they were flanked themselves and badly pinched, leaving seven dead, two wounded, and one missing. Among those who escaped was Levi Preston, afterwards known as Captain Levi Preston.

When I was about twenty-one and Captain Preston about ninety-one, I "interviewed" him as to what he did and thought sixty-seven years before, on April 19, 1775. And now, fifty-two years later, I make my report—a little belated perhaps, but not too late, I trust, for the morning papers!

At that time, of course, I knew all about the American Revolution—far more than I do now! And if I now know anything truly, it is chiefly owing to what I have since forgotten of the histories of that event then popular.

With an assurance passing even that of the modern interviewer—if that were possible—I began: "Captain Preston, why did you go to the Concord fight, the 19th of April, 1775?"

The old man, bowed beneath the weight of years, raised himself upright, and turning to me said: "Why did I go?"

"Yes," I replied; "my histories tell me that you men of the Revolution took up arms against 'intolerable oppressions.' What were they?"

"Oppressions? I didn't feel them."

"What, were you not oppressed by the Stamp Act?"

"I never saw one of those stamps, and always understood that Governor Bernard [of Massachusetts] put them all in Castle William [Boston]. I am certain I never paid a penny for one of them."

"Well, what then about the tea-tax?"

"Tea-tax! I never drank a drop of the stuff; the boys threw it all overboard."

"Then I suppose you had been reading Harrington or Sidney and Locke about the eternal principles of liberty."

"Never heard of 'em. We read only the Bible, the Catechism, Watts' Psalms and Hymns, and the Almanack."

"Well, then, what was the matter? and what did you mean in going to the fight?"

"Young man, what we meant in going for those Redcoats was this: we always had governed ourselves, and we always meant to. They didn't mean we should."

Bancroft

The American Revolution, of which I write the history, essaying to unfold the principles which organized its events, and bound to keep faith with the ashes of its heroes, was most radical in its character, yet achieved with such benign tranquility that even conservatism hesitated to censure. A civil war armed men of the same ancestry against each other, yet for the advancement of the principles of everlasting peace and universal brotherhood. A new plebeian democracy took its place by the side of the proudest empires. Religion was disenthralled from civil institutions; thought obtained for itself free utterance by speech and by the press; industry was commissioned to follow the bent of its own genius; the system of commercial restrictions between states was reprobated and shattered; and the oceans were enfranchised for every peaceful keel. International law was humanized and softened; and a new, milder, and more just maritime code was concerted and enforced. The trade in slaves was branded and restrained. . . . The equality of all men was declared; personal freedom secured in its complete individuality; and common consent recognised as the only just origin of fundamental laws: so that in thirteen separate states, with ample territory for creating more, the inhabitants of each formed their own political institutions. By the side of the principle of the freedom of the individual and the freedom of the separate states, the noblest work of human intellect was consummated in a federative union; and that union put away every motive to its destruction, by insuring to each successive generation the right to better its constitution, according to the increasing intelligence of the living people. . . .

Yet the thirteen colonies, in whom was involved the futurity of our race, were feeble settlements in the wilderness, scattered along the coast of a continent, little connected with each other, little heeded by their metropolis, almost unknown to the world; they were bound together only as British America, that part of the western hemisphere which the English mind had appropriated. England was the mother of its language, the home of its traditions, the source of its laws, and the land on which its affections centered. And yet it was an offset from England, rather than an integral part of it; an empire of itself, free from nobility and prelacy; not only Protestant, but by a vast majority dissenting from the church of England; attracting the commoners and plebeian sects of the parent country, and rendered cosmopolitan by recruits from the nations of the European continent. By the benignity of the law, the natives of other lands were received as citizens; and political liberty, as a birthright, was the talisman that harmoniously blended all differences, and inspired a new public life, dearer than their native tongue, their memories, and their kindred. Dutch, French, Swede, and German renounced their nationality, to claim the rights of Englishmen.

The extent of those rights, as held by the colonists, had never been precisely ascertained. Of all the forms of civil government of which they had ever heard or read, no one appeared to them so well calculated to preserve liberty, and to secure all the most valuable advantages of civil society, as the English; and of this happy constitution of the mother country, which it was usual to represent, and almost to adore, as designed to approach perfection, they held their own to be a copy, or rather an improvement, with additional privileges not enjoyed by the common people there. The elective franchise was more equally diffused; there were no decayed boroughs, or unrepresented towns; representation, which was universal, conformed more nearly to population; for more than half the inhabitants, their legislative assemblies were chosen annually and by ballot, and the time for convening their legislatures was fixed by a fundamental law; the civil list in every colony but one was voted annually, and annually subjected to scrutiny; appropriations of money often, for greater security against corruption and waste, included the nomination and appointment of the agents who were to direct the expenditures; municipal liberties were more independent and more extensive; in none of the colonies was there an ecclesiastical court, and in most of them there was no established church or religious test of capacity for office; the cultivator of the soil was, for the most part, a freeholder; in all the continent the people possessed arms, and the able-bodied men were enrolled and trained to their use: so that in America there was more of personal independence, and far more of popular power, than in England.

2

Lincoln and Davis on the Civil War*

After the War of 1812 tension began to build between North and South, and by 1861 they were at war. There has never been complete agreement what its causes were or whether war was unavoidable. Slavery has been considered the major cause of the war, but it is not the only one. Their distinctly sectional, almost totally different lifestyles, made them very imcompatible. One particularly sore point between the two regions was each's opinion of the nature of the federal government. In these two readings, Lincoln and then Davis argue the nationalist and states' rights arguments, respectively.

*James D. Richardson, ed., *A Compilation of the Messages and Papers of the Presidents* (Washington, D.C.: Government Printing Office, 1897), Vol. 7, pp. 5–12; and Frank Moore, ed., *The Rebellion Record* (1861), Vol. 1, pp. 166ff.

Questions

LINCOLN

1. What was Lincoln's opinion of the Union?
2. What did Lincoln feel was the basic cause of the war?

DAVIS

1. How did Davis give an historic basis for states' rights?
2. How was the states' rights position violated?

Lincoln

Apprehension seems to exist among the people of the Southern States that by the accession of a Republican Administration their property and their peace and personal security are to be endangered. There has never been any reasonable cause for such apprehension. Indeed, the most ample evidence to the contrary has all the while existed, and been open to their inspection. It is found in nearly all the published speeches of him who now addresses you. . . .

I now reiterate these sentiments, and in doing so I only press upon the public attention the most conclusive evidence of which the case is susceptible that the property, peace, and security of no section are to be in any wise endangered by the now incoming Administration. I add, too, that all the protection which, consistently with the Constitution and the laws, can be given will be cheerfully given to all the States when lawfully demanded, for whatever cause—as cheerfully to one section as to another. . . .

It is seventy-two years since the first inauguration of a President under our National Constitution. During that period fifteen different and greatly distinguished citizens have in succession administered the executive branch of the Government. They have conducted it through many perils, and generally with great success. Yet, with all this scope of precedent, I now enter upon the same task for the brief constitutional term of four years under great and peculiar difficulty. A disruption of the Federal Union, heretofore only menaced, is now formidably attempted.

I hold that in contemplation of universal law and of the Constitution the Union of these States is perpetual. Perpetuity is implied, if not expressed, in the fundamental law of all national governments. It is safe to assert that no government proper ever had a provision in its organic law for its own termination. Continue to execute all the express provisions of our National Constitution, and the Union will endure forever, it being impossible to destroy it except by some action not provided for in the instrument itself.

Again: If the United States be not a government proper, but an association of States in the nature of contract merely, can it, as a contract, be peaceably unmade by less than all the parties who made it? One party to a contract may violate it—break it, so to speak—but does it not require all to lawfully rescind it?

Descending from these general principles, we find the proposition that in legal contemplation the Union is perpetual confirmed by the history of the Union itself. The Union is much older than the Constitution. It was formed, in fact, by the Articles of Association in 1774. It was matured and continued by the Declaration of Independence in 1776. It was further matured, and the faith of all the then thirteen States expressly plighted and engaged that it should be perpetual, by the Articles of Confederation in 1778. And finally, in 1787, one of the declared objects for ordaining and establishing the Constitution was *"to form a more perfect Union."*

But if destruction of the Union by one or by a part only of the States be lawfully possible, the Union is *less* perfect than before the Constitution, having lost the vital element of perpetuity.

It follows from these views that no State upon its own mere motion can lawfully get out of the Union; that *resolves* and *ordinances* to that effect are legally void, and that acts of violence within any State or States against the authority of the United States are insurrectionary or revolutionary, according to circumstances.

I therefore consider that in view of the Constitution and the laws the Union is unbroken, and to the extent of my ability I shall take care, as the Constitution itself expressly enjoins upon me, that the laws of the Union be faithfully executed in all the States. Doing this I deem to be only a simple duty on my part, and I shall perform it so far as practicable unless my rightful masters, the American people, shall withhold the requisite means or in some authoritative manner direct the contrary. I trust this will not be regarded as a menace, but only as the declared purpose of the Union that it *will* constitutionally defend and maintain itself. . . .

Plainly the central idea of secession is the essence of anarchy. A majority held in restraint by constitutional checks and limitations, and always changing easily with deliberate changes of popular opinions and sentiments, is the only true sovereign of a free people. Whoever rejects it does of necessity fly to anarchy or to despotism. Unanimity is impossible. The rule of a minority, as a permanent arrangement, is wholly inadmissible; so that, rejecting the majority principle, anarchy or despotism in some form is all that is left. . . .

The Chief Magistrate derives all his authority from the people, and they have conferred none upon him to fix terms for the separation of the States. The people themselves can do this . . . if they choose, but the Executive as such has nothing to do with it. His duty is to administer the present Government as it came to his hands and to transmit it unimpaired by him to his successor. . . .

In *your* hands, my dissatisfied fellow-countrymen, and now in *mine,* is the momentous issue of civil war. The Government will not assail *you.* You can have no conflict without being yourselves the aggressors. *You* have an oath registered in heaven to destroy the Government, while *I* shall have the most solemn one to "preserve, protect, and defend it."

I am loath to close. We are not enemies, but friends. We must not be enemies. Though passion may have strained, it must not break our bonds of affection. The mystic chords of memory, stretching from every battlefield and patriot grave to every living heart and hearthstone all over this broad land, will yet swell the chorus of the Union, when again touched, as surely they will be, by the better angels of our nature. . . .

Davis

The declaration of war made against this Confederacy, by Abraham Lincoln, President of the United States, in his proclamation, issued on the 15th day of the present month, renders it necessary, in my judgment, that you should convene at the earliest practicable moment to devise the measures necessary for the defence of the country.

The occasion is, indeed, an extraordinary one. It justifies me in giving a brief review of the relations heretofore existing between us and the States which now unite in warfare against us, and a succinct statement of the events which have resulted to the end, that mankind may pass intelligent and impartial judgment on our motives and objects.

During the war waged against Great Britain by her colonies on this continent, a common danger impelled them to a close alliance, and to the formation of a Confederation by the terms of which the colonies, styling themselves States, entered severally into a firm league of friendship with each other for their common defense, the security of their liberties, and their mutual and general welfare, binding themselves to assist each other against all force offered to, or attacks made upon them, or any of them, on account of religion, sovereignty, trade, or any other pretence whatever.

In order to guard against any misconstruction of their compact, the several States made an explicit declaration in a distinct article—that each State retain its sovereignty, freedom and independence, and every power of jurisdiction and right which is not by this said confederation expressly delegated to the United States in Congress assembled under this contract of alliance.

The war of the Revolution was successfully waged, and resulted in the treaty of peace with Great Britain in 1783, by the terms of which the several States were each by name recognized to be independent.

The articles of confederation contained a clause whereby all alterations were prohibited, unless confirmed by the Legislatures of every State after being agreed to by the Congress; and in obedience to this provision, under the resolution of Congress of the 21st of February, 1787, the several States appointed delegates for the purpose of revising the articles of confederation, and reporting to Congress and the several Legislatures such alterations and provisions therein as shall, when agreed to in Congress, and confirmed by the States, render the Federal Constitution adequate to the exigencies of the Government, and the preservation of the Union.

It was by the delegates chosen by the several States under the resolution just quoted, that the Constitution of the United States was formed in 1787, and submitted to the several States for ratification, as shown by the seventh article, which is in these words: "The ratification of the conventions of nine States shall be sufficient for the establishment of this Constitution between the States so ratifying the same."

I have italicized certain words in the resolutions just made for the purpose of attracting attention to the singular and marked caution with which the States endeavored in every possible form to exclude the idea that the separate and independent sovereignty of each State was merged into one common government or nation; and the earnest desire they evinced to impress on the Constitution its true character—that of a compact between independent States—the Constitution of 1787, however, admitting the clause already recited from the articles of confederation, which provided in explicit terms that each State reclaimed its sovereignty and independence.

Some alarm was felt in the States, when invited to ratify the Constitution, lest this omission should be construed into an abandonment of their cherished principles, and they refused to be satisfied until amendments were added to the Constitution, placing beyond any pretence of doubt the reservation by the States of their sovereign rights and powers not expressly delegated to the United States by the Constitution.

Strange, indeed, must it appear to the impartial observer, that it is none the less true that all these carefully worded clauses proved unavailing to prevent the rise and growth in the Northern States of a political school which has persistently claimed that the Government set above and over the States, an organization created by the States, to secure the blessings of liberty and independence against foreign aggression, has been gradually perverted into a machine for their control in their domestic affairs.

The creature has been exalted above its Creator—the principals have been made subordinate to the agent appointed by themselves.

The people of the Southern States, whose almost exclusive occupation was agriculture, early perceived a tendency in the Northern States to render a common government subservient to their own purposes by imposing burthens on commerce as protection to their manufacturing and shipping interests.

Long and angry controversies grew out of these attempts, often successful, to benefit one section of the country at the expense of the other, and the danger of disruption arising from this cause was enhanced by the fact that the Northern population was increasing, by emigration and other causes, more than the population of the South.

By degrees, as the Northern States gained preponderance in the National Congress, self-interest taught their people to yield ready assent to any plausible advocacy of their right as majority to govern the minority. Without control, they learn to listen with impatience to the suggestion of any constitutional impediment to the exercise of their will, and so utterly have the principles of the Constitution been corrupted in the Northern mind that, in the inaugural address delivered by President Lincoln in March last, he asserts a maxim which he plainly deems to be undeniable, that the theory of the Constitution requires, in all cases, that the majority shall govern. And in another memorial instance the same Chief Magistrate did not hesitate to liken the relations between States and the United States to those which exist between the county and the State in which it is situated, and by which it was created.

This is the lamentable and fundamental error in which rests the policy that has culminated in his declaration of war against these Confederate States.

In addition to the long-continued and deep-seated resentment felt by the Southern States at the persistent abuse of the powers they had delegated to the Congress for the purpose of enriching the manufacturing and shipping classes of the North at the expense of the South, there has existed for nearly half a century another subject of discord, involving interests of such transcendent magnitude as at all times to create the apprehension in the minds of many devoted lovers of the Union that its permanence was impossible.

3

The Rough Riders*

After the Civil War the nation turned to industrial and urban expansion. Isolation generally characterized foreign policy; business and government were closely allied. Agrarian America was becoming industrial America, and by 1890 the frontier was officially closed. While we had been growing in power, it was not until the Spanish-American War of 1898 that America became a world power.

In 1895 Cuba revolted against Spanish rule. In response the Spanish sent General "Butcher" Weyler to put down all insurrection. The United States press seized upon the concentration camps and Weyler's other atrocities, depicting them sensationally and arousing Americans against Spain. Although Weyler was removed, the sinking of the battleship Maine and the DeLome letter incident further angered Americans. McKinley declared war. Here Rough Rider Teddy Roosevelt tells of the hardships and valor of his men.

Questions

1. What were some of the "heroics" of the Rough Riders?
2. Why were they so successful?
3. How can this reading by Roosevelt be included in the tradition of an adventure story?

When the shrapnel burst among us on the hillside we made up our minds that we had better settle down to solid siege work. All of the men who were not in the trenches I took off to the right, back of the Gatling guns, where there was a valley, and dispersed them by troops in sheltered parts. It took

*Source: Theodore Roosevelt, *The Rough Riders* (Boston, 1899), pp. 110ff.

us an hour or two's experimenting to find out exactly what spots were free from danger, because some of the Spanish sharpshooters were in trees in our front, where we could not possibly place them from the trenches; and these were able to reach little hollows and depressions where the men were entirely safe from the Spanish artillery and from their trench fire. Moreover, in one hollow, which we thought safe, the Spaniards succeeded in dropping a shell, a fragment of which went through the head of one of my men, who, astonishing to say, lived, although unconscious, for two hours afterward. Finally, I got all eight troops settled and the men promptly proceeded to make themselves as much at home as possible. For the next twenty-four hours, however, the amount of comfort was small, as in the way of protection and covering we only had what blankets, raincoats, and hammocks we took from the dead Spaniards. Ammunition, which was, of course, the most vital need, was brought up in abundance; but very little food reached us. That afternoon we had just enough to allow each man for his supper two hardtacks, and one hardtack extra for every four men.

During the first night we had dug trenches sufficient in length and depth to shelter our men and insure safety against attack, but we had not put in any traverses or approaches, nor had we arranged the trenches at all points in the best places for offensive work; for we were working at night on ground which we had but partially explored. Later on an engineer officer stated that he did not think our work had been scientific; and I assured him that I did not doubt that he was right, for I had never before seen a trench, excepting those we captured from the Spaniards, or heard of a traverse, save as I vaguely remembered reading about them in books. For such work as we were engaged in, however, the problem of intrenchment was comparatively simple, and the work we did proved entirely adequate. No man in my regiment was ever hit in the trenches or going in or out of them.

But on the first day there was plenty of excitement connected with relieving the firing line. Under the intense heat, crowded down in cramped attitudes in the rank, newly dug, poisonous soil of the trenches, the men needed to be relieved every six hours or so. Accordingly, in the late morning, and again in the afternoon, I arranged for their release. On each occasion I waited until there was a lull in the firing and then started a sudden rush by the relieving party, who tumbled into the trenches every which way. The movement resulted on each occasion in a terrific outburst of fire from the Spanish lines, which proved quite harmless; and as it gradually died away the men who had been relieved got out as best they could. Fortunately, by the next day I was able to abandon this primitive, though thrilling and wholly novel, military method of relief.

When the hardtack came up that afternoon I felt much sympathy for the hungry unfortunates in the trenches and hated to condemn them to six hours more without food; but I did not know how to get food in to them. Little McGinty, the bronco buster, volunteered to make the attempt, and I gave him permission. He simply took a case of hardtack in his arms and darted toward the trenches. The distance was but short, and though there was an outburst of fire, he was actually missed. One bullet, however, passed through the case of hardtack just before he disappeared with it into the trench. A trooper named Shanafelt repeated the feat, later, with a pail of coffee. Another trooper, George King, spent a leisure hour in the rear making soup out of some rice and other stuff he found in a Spanish house; he brought some of it to General Wood, Jack Greenway, and myself, and nothing could have tasted more delicious.

At this time our army in the trenches numbered about 11,000 men; and the Spaniards in Santiago about 9,000, their reinforcements having just arrived. Nobody on the firing line, whatever was the case in the rear, felt the slightest uneasiness as to the Spaniards being able to break out; but there were plenty who doubted the advisability of trying to rush the heavy earthworks and wire defenses in our front.

All day long the firing continued—musketry and cannon. Our artillery gave up the attempt to fight on the firing line, and was withdrawn well to the rear out of range of the Spanish rifles; so far as we could see, it accomplished very little. The dynamite gun was brought up to the right of the regimental line. It was more effective than the regular artillery because it was fired with smokeless powder, and as it was used like a mortar from behind the hill, it did not betray its presence, and those firing it suffered no loss. Every few shots it got out of order, and the Rough Rider machinists and those furnished by Lieutenant Parker—whom we by this time began to consider as an exceedingly valuable member of our own regiment—would spend an hour or two in setting it right. Sergeant Borrowe had charge of it and handled it well. With him was Sergeant Guitilias, a gallant old fellow, a veteran of the Civil War, whose duties were properly those of standard-bearer, he having charge of the yellow cavalry standard of the regiment; but in the Cuban campaign he was given the more active work of helping run the dynamite gun. The shots from the dynamite gun made a terrific explosion, but they did not seem to go accurately. Once one of them struck a Spanish trench and wrecked part of it. On another occasion one struck a big building, from which there promptly swarmed both Spanish cavalry and infantry, on whom the Colt automatic guns played with good effect, during the minute that elapsed before they could get other cover.

These Colt automatic guns were not, on the whole, very successful. The gun detail was under the charge of Sergeant (afterward Lieutenant) Tiffany, assisted by some of our best men, like Stephens, Crowninshield, Bradley, Smith, and Herrig. The guns were mounted on tripods. They were too heavy for men to carry any distance and we could not always get mules. They would have been more effective if mounted on wheels, as the Gatlings were. Moreover, they proved more delicate than the Gatlings, and very readily got out of order. A further and serious disadvantage was that they did not use the

Krag ammunition, as the Gatlings did, but the Mauser ammunition. The Spanish cartridges which we captured came in quite handily for this reason. Parker took the same fatherly interest in these two Colts that he did in the dynamite gun, and finally I put all three and their men under his immediate care, so that he had a battery of seven guns.

In fact, I think Parker deserved rather more credit than any other one man in the entire campaign. I do not allude especially to his courage and energy, great though they were, for there were hundreds of his fellow officers of the cavalry and infantry who possessed as much of the former quality, and scores who possessed as much of the latter; but he had the rare good judgment and foresight to see the possibilities of the machine guns, and, thanks to the aid of General Shafter, he was able to organize his battery. He then, by his own exertions, got it to the front and proved that it could do invaluable work on the field of battle, as much in attack as in defense. Parker's Gatlings were our inseparable companions throughout the siege. After our trenches were put in final shape, he took off the wheels of a couple and placed them with our own two Colts in the trenches. His gunners slept beside the Rough Riders in the bombproofs, and the men shared with one another when either side got a supply of beans or of coffee and sugar; for Parker was as wide awake and energetic in getting food for his men as we prided ourselves upon being in getting food for ours. Besides, he got oil, and let our men have plenty for their rifles. At no hour of the day or night was Parker anywhere but where we wished him to be in the event of an attack. If I was ordered to send a troop of Rough Riders to guard some road or some break in the lines, we usually got Parker to send a Gatling along, and whether the change was made by day or by night, the Gatling went, over any ground and in any weather. He never exposed the Gatlings needlessly or unless there was some object to be gained, but if serious fighting broke out, he always took a hand. Sometimes this fighting would be the result of an effort on our part to quell the fire from the Spanish trenches; sometimes the Spaniards took the initiative; but at whatever hour of the twenty-four serious fighting began, the drumming of the Gatlings was soon heard through the cracking of our own carbines.

4

World War II*

With the acquisition of Guam and the Philippines and the protector-ate over Cuba, the United States emerged as an imperial power. President Theodore Roosevelt, first elected in 1901, was well suited to imperialism. The building of the Panama Canal, the Roosevelt Corollary, and the Great White Fleet all characterized his approach to foreign policy. Dollar diplomacy—the practice of capital invest-ment in underdeveloped countries—expanded under William How-ard Taft. Though Woodrow Wilson attempted to bring morality to American imperialism, he was challenged by European turmoil. The assassination of Archduke Ferdinand in 1914 began a world war that threatened American neutrality. The United States was eventually drawn into armed conflict.

The Versailles Treaty that ended World War I did not solve the basic problems of European nationalism. The United States did not join the League of Nations, choosing instead isolation from world affairs. While Hitler and Mussolini were rising gradually to power, the United States generally ignored the rest of the world, especially in the 1920s. The national depression held the attention of the nation in the 1930s, but as the decade closed, news from Asia and Europe was ominous. Japan and Germany were on the move. Presi-dent Franklin Roosevelt feared that the neutrality laws would have to be modified, and by 1939 had suggested a modified cash-and-carry system for munitions.

In the first reading Secretary of State Cordell Hull argues for a revision of the neutrality laws; in the next selection historian Robert A. Divine describes the Pearl Harbor attack and subsequent Ameri-can entrance into World War II.

*Sources: From the *Congressional Record,* 76th Cong., 1st sess., LXXXI (Washington, D.C.: Government Printing Office, July 14, 1939), pp. 9127–28; and from *The Reluctant Belligerent: American Entry into World War II,* by Robert A. Divine. Copyright © 1965 by John Wiley & Sons, Inc. Reprinted by permission.

Questions

HULL

1. What were the major arguments Hull used for revision of neutrality laws?
2. What specific changes did he want?

DIVINE

1. What is Divine saying about the coming of World War II?
2. What is the importance of Pearl Harbor in American involvement in World War II?

Hull

The Congress has pending before it at the present time certain proposals providing for the amendment of the existing so-called neutrality legislation. Some of these proposed changes I regard as necessary to promote the peace and security of the United States.

There is an astonishing amount of confusion and misunderstanding as regards the legislation under consideration, and particularly with regard to the operation of the existing arms embargo. . . .

The proponents, including the executive branch of the government, at the time when the arms embargo was originally adopted called attention to the fact that its enactment constituted a hazardous departure from the principle of international law which recognizes the rights of neutrals to trade with belligerents and of belligerents to trade with neutrals.

They believe that neutrality means impartiality, and, in their view, an arms embargo is directly opposed to the idea of neutrality. It is not humanly possible, by enacting an arms embargo, or by refraining from such enactments, to hold the scales exactly even between two belligerents. In either case and due to shifting circumstances one belligerent may find itself in a position of relative advantage or disadvantage. . . .

There is no theory or practice to be found in international law pertaining to neutrality to the effect that the advantages that any particular belligerent might procure through its geographic location, its superiority on land or at sea, or through other circumstances, should be offset by the establishment by neutral nations of embargoes.

The opposition to the present substitute proposal joins issue on this point and stands for existing rigid embargo as a permanent part of our neutrality policy.

And yet by insisting on an arms embargo in time of war they are, to that extent, for the reasons I have stated, urging not neutrality but what might well result in actual unneutrality, the serious consequences of which no one can predict.

Those who urge the retention of the present embargo continue to advance the view that it will keep this country out of war—thereby misleading the American people to rely upon a false and illogical delusion as a means of keeping out of war.

I say it is illogical, because, while the trade in "arms, ammunition and implements of war" is at present banned, the trade in equally essential war materials, as well as all the essential materials out of which the finished articles are made, can continue.

For example, in time of war, we can sell cotton for the manufacture of explosives, but not the explosives; we can sell the steel and copper for cannon and for shells, but not the cannon nor the shells; we can continue to sell to belligerents the high-powered fuel necessary for the operation of airplanes, but we are not able to sell the airplanes.

I say it is a false delusion because a continuation of the trade in arms is a clearly recognized and traditional right of the nationals of a neutral country in time of war, subject only to effective blockade and to the right of belligerents to treat any such commodities as contraband.

The assertion frequently made that this country has ever engaged or may become engaged in serious controversy solely over the fact that its nationals have sold arms to belligerents is misleading and unsupportable.

All available evidence is directly to the contrary. Every informed person knows that arms, as absolute contraband, are subject to seizure by a belligerent and that neither the neutral shipper nor his government has the slightest ground for complaint.

There is, therefore, no reason to suppose that the sale of arms may lead to serious controversy between a neutral and a belligerent. Furthermore, under the proposals that have been made American nationals would be divested of all right, title and interest in these and other commodities before they leave our shores and American citizens and ships would be kept out of the danger zones.

As regards possible complications which might arise as a result of the extension of credits to belligerents or of extraordinary profits accruing to any group of producers in this country, it is wholly within the power of Congress at all times to safeguard the national interest in this respect.

Controversies which would involve the United States are far more likely to arise from the entrance of American ships or American citizens in the danger zones or through the sinking on the high seas of American vessels carrying commodities other than those covered by the arms embargo.

In the recommendations formulated by the Executive as a substitute for the present legislation it was especially urged that provisions be adopted which would exclude American nationals and American ships from zones where real danger to their safety might exist and which would divest goods of American ownership, thereby minimizing to the fullest extent the danger of American involvement.

Those of us who support the recommendations formulated for the elimination of the embargo are convinced that the arms embargo plays into the hands of those nations which have taken the lead in building up their fighting power.

It works directly against the interests of the peace-loving nations, especially those which do not possess their own munitions plants.

It means that if any country is disposed toward conquest and devotes its energy and resources to establish itself as a superior fighting power, that country may be more tempted to try the fortunes of war if it knows that its less well prepared opponents would be shut off from those supplies which, under every rule of international law, they should be able to buy in all neutral countries, including the United States.

It means also that some of those countries, which have only limited facilities for the production of arms, ammunition and implements of war, are put in a position of increased dependence. During peacetime they would feel the compulsion of shaping their political as well as their economic policy to suit the military strength of others, and during wartime their powers of defense would be limited.

For these reasons those who are supporting the recommendations for the amendment of existing legislation recognize definitely that the present embargo encourages a general state of war both in Europe and Asia. Since the present embargo has this effect its results are directly prejudicial to the highest interests and to the peace and to the security of the United States. . . .

I must also refer to the impression sedulously created to the effect that the sale of arms, munitions and implements of war by this country is immoral and that on this ground it should be suppressed in time of war.

As a matter of fact, almost all sales of arms and ammunition made in recent years by our nationals have been made to governments whose policies have been dedicated to the maintenance of peace, but who have felt the necessity of creating or of augmenting their means of national self-defense, thereby protecting otherwise helpless men, women and children in the event that other powers resort to war.

In the face of the present universal danger, all countries, including our own, feel the necessity of increasing armament, and small countries in particular are dependent upon countries like the United States, which have the capacity to produce armaments.

Our refusal to make it possible for them to obtain such means of necessary self-defense in a time of grave emergency would contribute solely towards making more helpless the law-abiding and peace-devoted peoples of the world.

If such action is moral, and if, on the contrary, sales of the means of self-defense for the protection of peaceful and law-abiding peoples are immoral, then a new definition of morality and immorality must be written. This task might be left to the proponents of the arms embargo. . . .

The legislative proposals which were recommended to the Congress through the communications which I transmitted to Senator Pittman and to Congressman Bloom on May 27 providing for the safe-guarding of our nation to the fullest possible extent from incurring the risks of involvement in war contemplate the elimination of the existing arms embargo and are as follows:

1. To prohibit American ships from entering combat areas;
2. To restrict travel by American citizens in combat areas;
3. To require that goods exported from the United States to belligerent countries shall be preceded by the transfer of title to the foreign purchasers;
4. To continue the existing legislation respecting loans and credits to belligerent nations;
5. To regulate the solicitation and collection in this country of funds for belligerents; and
6. To continue the national munitions control board and the licensing system with respect to the importation and exportation of arms, ammunition, and implements of war. . . .

There has thus been offered as a substitute for the present act a far broader and more effective set of provisions, which in no conceivable sense could breed trouble, but which to a far greater extent than the present act would both aid in making less likely a general war, and, while keeping strictly within the limits of neutrality, would reduce as far as possible the risk of this nation of being drawn into war if war comes. . . .

Divine

The State Department dispatched this urgent message at 9 P.M., December 6, instructing Ambassador Grew to deliver it as soon as possible. At the same time, the long-awaited Japanese reply to the ten-part American note of November 26 was coming in over the cables. The first thirteen parts of a fourteen-part message were deciphered almost simultaneously in the Japanese Embassy and in the offices of U.S. Naval Intelligence. The message consisted of a tedious review of Japanese-American relations and a verbose analysis of the American note of November 26. More ominous was the instruction to Nomura and Kurusu not to present the message to the State Department until the fourteenth part arrived the next day, December 7. Copies of the Japanese message were handed to State Department officials and the President during the evening. According to the naval officer who delivered the message to the White House, the President read through the dispatch and then turned to Harry Hopkins and said, "This means war."[1] Nevertheless, no further action was taken that evening. The next morning the fourteenth part of the Japanese note arrived. Charging that the United States was conspiring with Britain to block the New Order in Asia, the message concluded, "The Japanese Government regrets to have to notify hereby the American Government that in view of the attitude of the American Government it cannot but consider that it is impossible to reach an agreement through further negotiations."[2]

The intercepted Japanese message indicated clearly that Japan was severing diplomatic relations and planning on war. But the precise place where the first blow would fall remained unknown. In the Pentagon General Marshall belatedly prepared an additional warning message to American commanders in the Pacific. At the State Department Hull learned that Nomura and Kurusu had asked for an audience at 1 P.M. to deliver the fourteen-point message. At the White House Roosevelt met with Hu Shih, the Chinese ambassador, and read him the text of his personal appeal to the Emperor. "This is my last effort at peace," Roosevelt told Hu Shih. "I am afraid it may fail." Then the President voiced his fear that Japan would try "foul play," saying that something "nasty" might take place within the next 48 hours in Thailand, Malaya, the East Indies, or "possibly" the Philippines.[3]

At the very time that Roosevelt was speaking, a Japanese task force had launched its planes for a devastating raid on the American Pacific Fleet at Pearl Harbor. The Japanese ships had left the Kurile Islands on November 25 and had passed unnoticed through the icy waters of the North Pacific. Japan could have recalled this striking force if the United States had made a sudden diplomatic surrender; instead, it was ordered to fulfill its mission. By knocking out the American fleet, Japan could safely carry out her major thrust into Southeast Asia and the Philippines.

When Nomura and Kurusu arrived an hour late at the State Department to deliver the last note, Hull already knew of the attack on Pearl Harbor. He pretended to read the message that the two envoys handed him; he already knew its contents and significance. Then, unable to repress his fury any longer, the Secretary denounced the Japanese Government in scathing language and dismissed the envoys.

Throughout the afternoon reports came in to the President and his advisers. The Pacific fleet at Pearl Harbor was crippled; 2400 Americans had lost their lives. For years afterward investigating committees would sift through the voluminous evidence in the search for scapegoats for this national tragedy. At the time, however, there was a sense of release, if not relief. When Roosevelt summoned his advisers to a late afternoon conference, Harry Hopkins

---

[1] *Pearl Harbor Attack*, Part 10, p. 4662.
[2] *Foreign Relations: Japan, 1931–1941*, II, 792.
[3] Feis, *Road to Pearl Harbor*, p. 340.

recorded the mood they shared. "The conference met in not too tense an atmosphere because I think that all of us believed that in the last analysis the enemy was Hitler and that he could never be defeated without force of arms; that sooner or later we were bound to be in the war and that Japan had given us an opportunity."[4]

One critical question still remained unanswered—did war with Japan mean war with Germany as well? When Roosevelt read a draft of a message to Congress calling for war with Japan, Secretary Stimson objected. "I pointed out," Stimson recorded in his diary, "that we knew . . . that Germany had pushed Japan into this and that we should ask for a declaration of war against Germany also."[5] No one supported this suggestion. The next day President Roosevelt delivered a brief message to Congress. Declaring that December 7 was "a date which will live in infamy," Roosevelt presented a simple resumé of the Japanese attacks in Hawaii, the Philippines and Southeast Asia, and asked Congress to recognize that a state of war existed between the United States and Japan.[6] With only one dissenting vote, Congress complied.

Hitler resolved the dilemma over war in the Atlantic. Although uninformed by the Japanese in advance, Hitler was pleased with the strike at Pearl Harbor. On December 11 the German Foreign Office handed a note to the American Chargé d'Affaires in Berlin severing diplomatic relations and declaring war. There was no mention of Japan. Instead, Germany stated that "the Government of the United States from initial violations of neutrality, had finally proceeded to open acts of war against Germany."[7] In short, Germany was masquerading as the defender of international law self-righteously fighting against American encroachments. Later the same day Roosevelt willingly faced the Nazi challenge· "The forces endeavoring to enslave the entire world are moving towards this hemisphere," he proclaimed to Congress.[8] Virtually without debate Congress unanimously passed a Joint Resolution affirming a state of war with Germany.

Thus to the very end, the pattern of American reaction to events abroad held true. From the first signs of aggression in the 1930's to the attack on Pearl Harbor, the United States refused to act until there was no other choice. The American people believed in the 1930's that they could escape the contagion of war. When the fall of France destroyed this illusion, they embraced the comforting notion that through material aid they could defeat Hitler without entering the conflict. When Japan threatened all Asia, Americans naively believed that economic pressure would compel her to retreat. Even when Japan responded with the attack on Pearl Harbor, the United States ignored

[4]Robert Sherwood, *Roosevelt and Hopkins* (New York, 1948), p. 431.
[5]Langer and Gleason, *Undeclared War*, p. 938.
[6]State Department, *Peace and War*, p. 839.
[7]Langer and Gleason, *Undeclared War*, p. 940.
[8]State Department, *Peace and War*, p. 849.

the Axis alliance and waited for Hitler to force America into the European war.

American foreign policy was sterile and bankrupt in a period of grave international crisis. Although it was the single most powerful nation on the globe, the United States abdicated its responsibilities and became a creature of history rather than its molder. By surrendering the initiative to Germany and Japan, the nation imperiled its security and very nearly permitted the Axis powers to win the war. In the last analysis the United States was saved only by the Japanese miscalculation in attacking Pearl Harbor. Japan's tactical victory quickly led to strategic defeat as the United States finally accepted the challenge of aggression.

5

The Vietnam War*

Korea was not the only limited war of the twentieth century; it was followed closely by our involvement in Vietnam. Although the Vietnam War is over, its scars and divisiveness are still deeply felt. No one person or group can be blamed for Vietnam. Presidents Dwight Eisenhower and John Kennedy initially sent aid to South Vietnam. President Johnson ordered American troops over there, directed bombing of North Vietnam, and received congressional approval of the Gulf of Tonkin Resolution. President Richard Nixon attempted to disengage America and followed his Vietnamization policy. In early 1973 a truce was signed, the American prisoners of war were returned, and an uneasy peace came to Vietnam. These two readings feature a letter from President Kennedy in support of Ngo Dinh Diem, and the Gulf of Tonkin Resolution.

*Sources: *Department of State Bulletin,* XXXVII (Washington, D.C.: Government Printing Office, January 1, 1962), pp. 13–14; *Department of State Bulletin,* VI, 268 (Washington, D.C.: Government Printing Office, August, 1964).

Questions

KENNEDY

1. What were Kennedy's reasons for support?
2. Is Kennedy still in the spirit of the Cold War?

TONKIN RESOLUTION

1. What did the resolution state?
2. Did the resolution give Johnson a blank check?

President Kennedy to President Diem

December 14, 1961

Dear Mr. President:

I have received your recent letter in which you described so cogently the dangerous condition caused by North Vietnam's efforts to take over your country. The situation in your embattled country is well known to me and to the American people. We have been deeply disturbed by the assault on your country. Our indignation has mounted as the deliberate savagery of the Communist program of assassination, kidnapping, and wanton violence became clear.

Your letter underlines what our own information has convincingly shown —that the campaign of force and terror now being waged against your people and your Government is supported and directed from the outside by the authorities at Hanoi. They have thus violated the provisions of the Geneva Accords designed to ensure peace in Vietnam and to which they bound themselves in 1954.

At that time, the United States, although not a party to the Accords, declared that it "would view any renewal of the aggression in violation of the Agreements with grave concern and as seriously threatening international peace and security." We continue to maintain that view.

In accordance with that declaration, and in response to your request, we are prepared to help the Republic of Vietnam to protect its people and to preserve its independence. We shall promptly increase our assistance to your defense effort as well as help relieve the destruction of the floods which you describe. I have already given the orders to get these programs underway.

The United States, like the Republic of Vietnam, remains devoted to the cause of peace and our primary purpose is to help your people maintain their independence. If the Communist authorities in North Vietnam will stop their campaign to destroy the Republic of Vietnam, the measures we are taking to assist your defense efforts will no longer be necessary. We shall seek to persuade the Communists to give up their attempts of force and subversion. In any case, we are confident that the Vietnamese people will preserve their independence and gain the peace and prosperity for which they have sought so hard and so long.

Gulf of Tonkin Resolution

TO PROMOTE THE MAINTENANCE OF INTERNATIONAL PEACE AND SECURITY IN SOUTHEAST ASIA

Whereas naval units of the Communist regime in Vietnam, in violation of the principles of the Charter of the United Nations and of international law, have deliberately and repeatedly attacked United States naval vessels lawfully present in international waters, and have thereby created a serious threat to international peace; and

Whereas these attacks are part of a deliberate and systematic campaign of aggression that the Communist regime in North Vietnam has been waging against its neighbors and the nations joined with them in the collective defense of their freedom; and

Whereas the United States is assisting the peoples of southeast Asia to protect their freedom and has no territorial, military or political ambitions in that area, but desires only that these people should be left in peace to work out their own destinies in their own way: Now, therefore, be it

Resolved by the Senate and House of Representatives of the United States of America in Congress assembled,

That the Congress approves and supports the determination of the President, as Commander in Chief, to take all necessary measures to repel any armed attack against the forces of the United States and to prevent further aggression.

Sec. 2. The United States regards as vital to its national interest and to world peace the maintenance of international peace and security in southeast Asia. Consonant with the Constitution of the United States and the Charter of the United Nations and in accordance with its obligations under the Southeast Asia Collective Defense Treaty, the United States is, therefore, prepared, as the President determines, to take all necessary steps, including the use of armed force, to assist any member or protocol state of the Southeast Asia Collective Defense Treaty requesting assistance in defense of its freedom.

Sec. 3 This resolution shall expire when the President shall determine that the peace and security of the area is reasonably assured by international conditions created by action of the United Nations or otherwise, except that it may be terminated earlier by concurrent resolution of the Congress.

Thought Questions

1. Compare and contrast historian George Bancroft's reasons for the American Revolution with Robert Divine's reasons for World War II.
2. Compare and contrast the coming of the American Revolution and Civil War.
3. Is there any similarity between World War II and the Vietnam War?
4. Were any of the causes of the wars similar at all?

five

THE AMERICAN INDIAN:
The Stereotype Revisited

In March, 1973, members of the American Indian Movement occupied Wounded Knee, South Dakota, site of an 1890 Sioux massacre. In November, 1972, members of the same organization had seized, occupied, and ransacked the Bureau of Indian Affairs building in Washington. That same month, in protest of a Massachusetts Thanksgiving celebration, a group of Indians had driven the tourists from the *Mayflower* and seized Plymouth Rock. What is happening? What point is being made? The Red Power movement is becoming more active, involves more Indians, and works harder at making white America aware of its existence. But while the Red Power Movement is new, Indians in America are not.

There were, according to current data, no human beings in North America until about 50,000 years ago. Until the arrival of Columbus, Mongoloid peoples who had migrated from Asia occupied North and South America. The Spanish, French, and English all encountered native Americans, and Europeans acted in a generally very bad way towards them. While it may be true that cultural understanding was lacking on both sides, the Indian suffered most—and still does today. During the English colonial period treatment of Indians differed from colony to colony, but in the push westward an extermination policy became evident. By the American Revolution the United States assumed full control of Indian affairs.

Early United States policy used the treaty or sovereign agreement method of legally acquiring Indian land. Of course the United States army frequently implemented the treaty, and wars usually followed. From the Pequot War in 1636 to Wounded Knee in 1890, Indian wars marred relations with whites. President Andrew Jackson used the treaty to remove tribes west of the Mississippi. After 1850 treaty negotiations placed tribes on permanent reservations. Indian leaders such as King Philip, Pontiac, Logan, Joseph Brant, Tecumseh, John Ross, Red Cloud, Sitting Bull, Chief Joseph, and many others challenged the white man, but failed.

In the twentieth century the Indian wars have continued in a different way. The Dawes Act of 1887 gave way to the Indian Reorganization Act of 1934, which emphasized Indian self-government, yet gave the Bureau of Indian Affairs ultimate veto power. In the 1950s Congress attempted to terminate relations with specific tribes by cutting their aid from the federal government, but this policy was disastrous. Relocation of reservation Indians in urban centers supplanted termination. By the 1960s the Indians began to fight back. Protests, demonstrations, songs, books are all part of the Red Power movement and have frequently evoked much white sympathy. President Richard Nixon emphasized Indian self-determination as a national policy and reorganized the Department of the Interior, Bureau of Indian Affairs. Still many Indians feel that more positive action is needed before a permanent peace can exist between whites and Indians.

The Stereotype*

The persistent stereotypes of the American Indian as savage warrior or drunken brute or cowering squaw have often prevented understanding of the real people. Literature and the media have been most responsible for creating the false impressions. James Fenimore Cooper, to name one author, in the early 1800s wrote of noble savages and savages. The dime novels of the late 1800s continued to picture the same savage Indian stereotype. Hollywood movies did little to change those images. Some recent television programs and movies have attempted to picture Indians as individuals, but many viewers, used to familiar patterns, wonder what happened to the "real" Indians that they have come to know and love. In this reading Stephen Powers of the Department of the Interior illustrates the problem of challenging stereotypes. In this excerpt from his report in 1877, he attempts to clarify some stereotypes but actually perpetuates others.

Questions

1. What stereotypes does Powers deal with?
2. What were his general feelings about California Indians?
3. What stereotypes did Powers perpetuate?
4. Do any of these stereotypes still exist today?

Physically considered the California Indians are superior to the Chinese, at least to those brought over to America. There is no better proof of this than the wages they receive for labor, for in a free and open market like ours a thing will always eventually fetch what it is worth. Chinamen on the railroad

*Source: Stephen Powers, *Tribes of California* (Washington, D.C.: Government Printing Office, 1877), pp. 401–2, 418.

receive $1 a day and board themselves; Indians working in gangs on public roads receive seventy-five cents a day, sometimes $1, and their board, the whole equal to $1.25 or $1.50. But on the northern ranches the Indian has $1.50 to $2 a day and his board, or $1 a day when employed by the year. Farmers trust Indians with valuable teams and complicated agricultural machinery far more than they do the Chinese. And the Indian endures the hot and heavy work of the ranch better than even the Canton Chinaman, who comes from a hot climate but wants an umbrella over his head. The valley Indians are more willing to labor and more moral now than the mountain Indians, because the latter have better opportunities to hunt game and can pick up small change and old clothes about the mining towns.

There is a common belief among the prejudiced and ignorant that the Indian is such an enormous eater as to overbalance his superior value as a laborer over the Chinaman. This is untrue. It is the almost universal testimony of men who have employed them and observed their habits to any purpose, that when they first come in from the rancheria with their stomachs distended from eating the innutritious aboriginal diet, for a day or two they eat voraciously until they become sated on our richer food; and after that they consume no more than an American performing the same labor.

I am inclined to attribute something of the mental weakness of the California aborigines to the excessive amount of fish which they consumed in their native state; also, perhaps, to the quantity of bitter acorns they ate. It is generally accounted that fish is rich in brain-food, but it is an indisputable fact that the grossest superstitions and lowest intellects in the race are found along the sea-coast.

Another erroneous impression generally prevails among Americans as to their physique, because they have seen only the wretched remnants of the race, the inferior lowlanders, whereas the nobler and more valorous mountaineers were early cut off. On the Round Valley Reservation the Pit River men wear shoes averaging five and six in size, the women two and three. The Potter Valley men are, however, a little larger in the feet; their shoes run from seven to ten, averaging eight and nine; the women of the same tribe range from four to seven, averaging five and six. The men's hands are as small and handsome as their feet, and so are the women's when young, but the hard and unremitting toil of after-life makes their hands grow large, coarse, and ugly. . . .

But, after all, let no romantic reader be deceived, and long to escape from the hollow mockeries and the vain pomps and ambitions of civilization, and mingle in the free, wild, and untrammeled life of the savage. It is one of the greatest delusions that ever existed. Of all droning and dreary lives that ever the mind of man conceived this is the chief. To pass long hours in silence, so saturated with sleep that one can sleep no more, sitting and brushing off the flies! Savages are not more sociable than civilized men and women, but less; they talk very fast when some matter excites them, but for the most part they are vacuous, inane, and silent. Kindly Nature, what beneficence thou hast displayed in endowing the savage with the illimitable power of doing nothing, and of being happy in doing it! I lived nearly two years in sufficient proximity to them, and I give it as the result of my extended observations that they sleep, day and night together, from fourteen to sixteen hours out of the twenty-four. They lie down at night-fall, for they have no lights; and they seldom rise before the sun, in summer generally an hour or two after. During the day they are constantly drowsing. When on a march they frequently chatter a good deal, but when a halt is called they all drop on the ground, as if overcome by the heat, and sink into a torpid silence. They will lie in the shade for hours in the middle of the day, then slowly rouse up, commence chattering, and march until night-fall.

2

Chief Joseph and the Last of the Wars of the West*

In the wars between Indians and whites both sides were to blame. Because of the predominance of conflict in United States relations with Indians, the army played a major role in implementing trea- ties, enforcing removal, and safeguarding reservation policy. Al- though many older American history texts reveal little of the Indian's viewpoint during the wars—or generally—voices of protest were loud and clear. Many leaders such as King Philip, Pontiac, Tecumseh, and Sitting Bull saw great value in unity, but were unable to realize their ideas. Today Indian leaders such as Russell Means of the American Indian Movement talk of Indian unity too.

In this reading Chief Joseph of the Nez Percé expresses his views of the white man and his wars with Indians. (In 1877 Chief Joseph fled with his people from the United States Army, but was eventu- ally forced to surrender in one of the last Indian wars.)

*Source: Chief Joseph, "Chief Joseph's Own Story," *North American Review,* CXXVII (April 1879), pp. 415ff.

Questions

1. What was Chief Joseph's opinion of the white man?
2. How did he view treaties?
3. What Indian outlook does he express here?
4. What does Chief Joseph want?

My friends, I have been asked to show you my heart. I am glad to have a chance to do so. I want the white people to understand my people. Some of you think an Indian is like a wild animal. This is a great mistake. I will tell you about our people, and then you can judge whether an Indian is a man or not. I believe much trouble and blood would be saved if we opened our hearts more. I will tell you in my way how the Indian sees things. The white man has more words to tell you how they look to him, but it does not require many words to speak the truth. What I have to say will come from my heart, and I will speak with a straight tongue. Ah-cum-kin-i-ma-me-hut (the Great Spirit) is looking at me, and will hear me.

My name is In-mut-too-yah-lat-lat (Thunder-traveling-over-the-mountains). I am chief of the Wal-lam-wat-kin band of Chute-pa-lu, or Nez Percés (nose-pierced Indians). I was born in eastern Oregon, thirty-eight winters ago. My father was chief before me. When a young man he was called Joseph by Mr. Spalding, a missionary. He died a few years ago. There was no stain on his hands of the blood of a white man. He left a good name on the earth. He advised me well for my people.

Our fathers gave us many laws, which they had learned from their fathers. These laws were good. They told us to treat all men as they treated us; that we should never be the first to break a bargain; that it was a disgrace to tell a lie; that we should speak only the truth; that it was a shame for one man to take from another his wife, or his property, without paying for it. We were taught to believe that the Great Spirit sees and hears everything, and that He never forgets; that hereafter He will give every man a spirit-home according to his deserts; if he has been a good man, he will have a good home; if he has been a bad man, he will have a bad home. This I believe, and all my people believe the same.

The first white men of your people who came to our country were named Lewis and Clark. They also brought many things that our people had never seen. They talked straight, and our people gave them a great feast, as a proof that their hearts were friendly. These men were very kind. They made presents to our chiefs and our people made presents to them. We had a great many horses of which we gave them what they needed, and they gave us guns and tobacco in return. All the Nez Percés made friends with Lewis and Clark, and agreed to let them pass through their country, and never to make war on white men. This promise the Nez Percé have never broken. . . .

Next there came a white officer (Governor Stevens) who invited all the Nez Percé to a treaty council. After the council was opened he made known his heart. He said there were a great many white people in the country, and many more would come; that he wanted the land marked out so that the Indians and white men could be separated. If they were to live in peace it was necessary, he said, that the Indians should have a country set apart for them, and in that country they must stay. My father, who represented his band, refused to have anything to do with the council, because he wished to be a free man. He claimed that no man owned any part of the earth, and a man could not sell what was not his own.

Mr. Spalding took hold of my father's arm and said: "Come and sign the treaty." My father pushed him away and said: "Why do you ask me to sign away my country? It is your business to talk to us about spirit matters, and not to talk to us about parting with our land." Governor Stevens urged my father to sign his treaty, but he refused. "I will not sign your paper," he said, "you go where you please, so do I; you are not a child, I am no child; I think for myself. No man can think for me. I have no other home than this. I will not give it up to any man. My people would have no home. Take away your paper. I will not touch it with my hand." . . .

The United States Government again asked for a treaty council. My father had become blind and feeble. He could no longer speak for his people. It was then I took my father's place as chief. In this council I made my first speech to white men. I said to the agent who held the council:

"I did not want to come to this council, but I came hoping that we could save blood. The white man has no right to come here and take our country. We have never accepted presents from the Government. Neither Lawyer nor any other chief had authority to sell this land. It has always belonged to my people. It came unclouded to them from our fathers, and we will defend this land as long as a drop of Indian blood warms the heart of our men."

The agent said he had orders, from the Great White Chief at Washington, for us to go upon the Lapwei reservation, and that if we obeyed he would help us in many ways. "You must move to the agency," he said. I answered him: "I will not. I do not need your help; we have plenty, and we are contented and happy if the white man will let us alone. The reservation is too small for so many people with all their stock. You can keep your presents; we can go to your towns and pay for all we need; we have plenty of horses and cattle to sell, and we won't have any help from you; we are free now; we can go where we please. Our fathers were born here. Here they lived, here they died, here are their graves. We will never leave them." The agent went away, and we had peace for awhile. . . .

For a short time we lived quietly. But this could not last. White men had found gold in the mountains around the land of the winding water. They stole a great many horses from us, and we could not get them back because we were Indians. . . . We could have avenged our wrongs many times, but we did not.

Whenever the Government has asked us to help them against other Indians we have never refused. When the white men were few and we were strong we could have killed them off, but the Nez Percés wished to live at peace. . . .

In the treaty councils the commissioners have claimed that our country had been sold to the Government. Suppose a white man should come to me and say, "Joseph, I like your horses, and I want to buy them." I say to him, "No, my horses suit me, I will not sell them." Then he goes to my neighbor, and says to him: "Joseph has some horses. I want to buy them, but he refuses to sell." My neighbor answers, "Pay me the money, and I will sell you Joseph's horses." The white man returns to me and says, "Joseph, I have bought your horses, and you must let me have them." If we sold our lands to the Government, this is the way they were bought. . . .

Year after year we have been threatened, but no war was made upon my people until General Howard came to our country two years ago and told us that he was the white war-chief of all that country. He said: "I have a great many soldiers at my back. I am going to bring them up here, and then I will talk to you again. I will not let white men laugh at me the next time I come. The country belongs to the Government, and I intend to make you go upon the reservation."

3

Indian Voices through Poetry*

Although the Dawes Severalty Act of 1887 attempted to legislate a uniform Indian policy, it was a failure. With its emphasis on allotment and private property, the act undermined basic Indian philosophy, and in the process many Indians lost a great deal of their land. With the appointment of John Collier as Commissioner of

---

*Sources: Edwin T. Denig, *Indian Tribes of the Upper Missouri,* 46th Annual Report of the Bureau of American Ethnology (Washington, D.C.: Government Printing Office, 1930), pp. 483–84; and Alice Fletcher and Francis LaFleche, *The Omaha Tribe,* 27th Report of the Bureau of American Ethnology (Washington, D.C.: Government Printing Office, 1911), p. 13.

Indian Affairs under Franklin Roosevelt came one of the most progressive eras in Indian history. Under the Indian New Deal the recognition of the basic strength of the tribal structure was made official government policy. The passage of the Indian Reorganization Act of 1934 allowed tribes self-government for the first time since they had settled on reservations and no longer attempted to break up tribal and communal aspects of Indian life. Under the act Indian land holdings were slowly built up and tribal governments were encouraged. Although the Bureau of Indian Affairs had ultimate veto power and the Indians that voted against forming a government could not enforce their decision, it was a step in the right direction.

Since World War II Americans have become more aware of the existence of Indians and their problems. The termination policy of the 1950s was disastrous to the tribes involved, and Presidents Kennedy, Johnson, and Nixon have not completely reversed that trend to an emphasis on self-determination. The changes that have slowly occurred in government policy have been accompanied by new Indian organizations, pro-Indian movies and songs, and a growing Indian literature. Here are two Indian poems: the first is an Assiniboine prayer of a warrior; the second is a lyric treatment of an Osage myth of creation.

Questions

PRAYER OF A WARRIOR

1. What is the purpose of the prayer?
2. How does it express the feelings of the warrior?

MYTH OF CREATION

1. What is the Osage story of creation?
2. Is there any similarity between this story and the Christian story of creation?

Prayer of a Warrior (Assiniboine)

> O Wakonda, you see me a poor man.
> Have pity on me.
> I go to war to revenge the death of my brother.
> Have pity upon me.

I smoke this tobacco taken from my medicine sack,
where it has been enveloped with the remains of my
dead brother [a lock of his hair]. I smoke it to my
tutelary, to you; aid me in revenge.
On my path preserve me from mad wolves.
Let no enemies surprise me.
I have sacrificed, I have smoked, my heart is low,
have pity upon me. Give me the bows and arrows of
my enemies. Give me their guns. Give me their horses.
Give me their bodies. Let me have my face blackened
on my return. Let good weather come that I can see.
Good dreams give that I can judge where they are. I
have suffered. I wish to live. I wish to be revenged. I
am poor. I want horses. I will sacrifice. I will smoke.
I will remember. Have pity on me.

Myth of Creation (Osage)

Way beyond, a part of the Osage lived in the sky. They desired to know their origin, the source from which they came into existence. They went to the sun. He told them that they were his children. Then they wandered still farther and came to the moon. She told them that she gave birth to them, and that the sun was their father. She told them that they must leave their present abode and go down to the earth and dwell there. They came to the earth, but found it covered with water. They could not return to the place they had left, so they wept, but no answer came to them from anywhere. They floated about in the air, seeking in every direction for help from some god; but they found none. The animals were with them, and of all these the elk was the finest and most stately, and inspired all the creatures with confidence; so they appealed to the elk for help. He dropped into the water and began to sink. Then he called to the winds, and the winds came from all quarters and blew until the waters went upward as in a mist.

At first rocks only were exposed, and the people traveled on the rocky places that produced no plants, and there was nothing to eat. Then the waters began to go down until the soft earth was exposed. When this happened, the elk in his joy rolled over and over on the soft earth, and all his loose hairs clung to the soil. The hairs grew, and from them sprang beans, corns, potatoes, and wild turnips, and then all the grasses and trees.

Alcatraz*

The Red Power movement began in 1964 when the Indians of Washington state staged a fish-in in protest of the loss of their fishing rights. Soon after that the Makah Indians of the same state closed their seashore to the public. In 1968 a group of Indians representing all tribes seized Alcatraz Island and planned to make it an Indian cultural center. Members of the American Indian Movement seized and occupied the Bureau of Indian Affairs Office in Washington, D.C. in 1972. Then in 1973, the American Indian Movement seized the town of Wounded Knee on the Pine Ridge Sioux Reservation of South Dakota. Indians are clearly taking action. This selection features two brief editorials from one of the best Indian newspapers, Akesasne Notes, dealing with the removal of the Alcatraz Indians.

Questions

1. What was the symbol of Alcatraz?
2. What were the Indian plans for Alcatraz?
3. Evaluate the proposal to the citizens of the United States.
4. What are the Indians saying in the proposals?
5. Are these two editorials "reasonable"?

Alcatraz Is Not An Island

We came to Alcatraz with an idea. We would unite our people and show the world that the Indian spirit would live forever. There was little hate or anger in our hearts, for the very thought of a lasting unity kept us whole and in harmony with life. From this island would grow a movement which

*Source: From "Alcatraz Is Not an Island," and "Indians of All Tribes Proposal to the Citizens of the United States," Akesasne Notes, Mohawk Nation, via Rooseveltown, New York, 13683. Late Summer, 1971, p. 7. Reprinted with permission.

must surely encompass the world. All men of this earth must hunger for peace and fellowship.

The idea was born and spread across this land, not as a fire of anger, but as a warming glow.

Alcatraz was born a mountain, surrounded by the waters of a great salt sea. By hands of hate was this island transformed into a symbol of fear and oppression. For too short a time this same island was held in trust by Indians of all tribes, who sang its praise as a part of mother earth, and who cleansed the evil with the sacred tobacco.

Alcatraz is again the hateful symbol of oppression. Our Indian people have been removed from sacred ground, our children have felt guns at their heads. Steel fences are again being put up. All approaches to the island are being guarded and patrolled. Armed with weapons of war and the sterile theories of law, they try desperately to keep out the Indian spirit. We send out our voices to that desolate rock, and are gifted with echoes which resound our strength.

Alcatraz, the idea, lives. We can only pray the Great Spirit that all brothers and sisters who can understand our song join us. Speak now your love of the Indian people. Dance with us the great unity. Chant with us the earth renewal. Let all men and women be proud. Let our children bathe in truth and never know the broken promises of the past.

Let Indians of all tribes be the pathway to People of one earth.

Indians of All Tribes Proposal to the Citizens of the United States

After having held the island of Alcatraz for a period of 19 months, November 20, 1969 to June 11, 1971, Indians of All Tribes were forcibly removed from the Island by federal marshals. Despite all the injustices we American Indian people have suffered in the past and even today, we hold a hope that the citizens of this great country will at last hear our words.

The ideas born and nourished on Alcatraz were never based upon hate. The occupation of this island has seen the beginnings of a unity between Indian tribes as foretold in many of our ancient prophesies. As we worked to develop these ideas we knew the necessity of co-operating with all other brothers and sisters in this land to assure a lasting success.

Our plans for a cultural and study center are now being acted upon at Davis, Toyon, and other appropriate locations across this land. Spiritual centers are being planned in many areas which will include the study and preservation of the local ecology. More and more, our Indian people are concerned with the loss of natural resources and with the ever-increasing dangers of pollution. Many species of plants and animals are extinct, and many others are threatened with extinction by current practices of conservation which lack so much. We realize, fully, the necessary duty of modern technology to begin working closer with nature, rather than against. We also feel that many of our ancient practices of conservation and coexistence with all of nature can contribute much enlightenment in this new direction.

But what of Alcatraz? The government's proposal that a park be created, with monuments of noted Indians, and Indian park rangers, is, of course, not what Indians of All Tribes has in mind. Should hundreds of tourists be visiting Alcatraz daily, it would become just another park, trampled and noisy. As for monuments, that is a thing very few of us can imagine. Each of our tribes identifies with mountains, rivers, valleys, deserts, and other natural landmarks. These are the only monuments we need or want. Alcatraz is a very important symbol of unity for all Indians. It is with this in mind, and with the fact that so many people are beginning to realize the importance of protecting our environment, that we submit this proposal.

1. That the deed to the island of Alcatraz be given to the Indians of All Tribes, with the stipulation that the Indians of All Tribes act as guardians of this island, in the name of the Great Spirit, and for the benefit of all men and women who respect our earth mother.

2. That work begin immediately to level all manmade structures (excepting the lighthouse and necessary generators) so that nature can once more return to this island.

3. That the stone and concrete be made into blocks for a seawall as a protective barrier for the return of fish, sea otters, sea lions, and other creatures of the sea and air who would take shelter here.

4. That the steel bars and plates be given to children's playgrounds and parks across this land, to be made into forms and structures which the children can climb upon and enjoy.

5. That because we lost a young sister here, and because this island has been cleansed and declared sacred ground by many of our traditional leaders, that it be allowed to remain as such forever.

6. That one small roundhouse be erected, to be used once yearly, each time by representatives of a different tribe, in a ceremony of earth renewal and purification to re-dedicate it to all who love and respect our earth.

Let this proposal be acted upon immediately! Let this be a first step toward sane policies and practices regarding nature and our environment. Let us set an example that all nations of this earth can approve and accept. We must restore all that has been destroyed by greed and ignorance.

In 1976, on the 200th Anniversary of the United States of America, let us truly celebrate. Let us know that the future unborn generations will remember us with love.

This proposal, then, we offer to the citizens of this country, hoping that by its acceptance, a new era of understanding and cooperation between a people of varied cultural backgrounds can at least begin.

Indian Humor*

Who today is the spokesman for the Indian? Some feel that the Bureau of Indian Affairs or the president speaks for Indians. Militants such as Russell Means and Dennis Banks say that they represent the tribes. One spokesperson is Vine Deloria, Jr., an early leader in the National Indian Youth Council who has written many articles and books on Indians past and present. This reading from Deloria's book, Custer Died for Your Sins, *explains Indian humor.*

Questions

1. What are Indian jokes?
2. How does Indian humor differ from white humor?
3. What does Indian humor accomplish?

One of the best ways to understand a people is to know what makes them laugh. Laughter encompasses the limits of the soul. In humor life is redefined and accepted. Irony and satire provide much keener insights into a group's collective psyche and values than do years of research.

It has always been a great disappointment to Indian people that the humorous side of Indian life has not been mentioned by professed experts on Indian Affairs. Rather the image of the granite-faced grunting redskin has been perpetuated by American mythology.

People have little sympathy with stolid groups. Dick Gregory did much more than is believed when he introduced humor into the Civil Rights struggle. He enabled non-blacks to enter into the thought world of the black community and experience the hurt it suffered. When all people shared the

---

*Source: Reprinted with permission of The Macmillan Company from *Custer Died for Your Sins* by Vine Deloria, Jr. Copyright © 1969 by Vine Deloria, Jr.

humorous but ironic situation of the black, the urgency and morality of Civil Rights was communicated.

The Indian people are exactly opposite of the popular stereotype. I sometimes wonder how anything is accomplished by Indians because of the apparent overemphasis on humor within the Indian world. Indians have found a humorous side of nearly every problem and the experiences of life have generally been so well defined through jokes and stories that they have become a thing in themselves.

For centuries before the white invasion, teasing was a method of control of social situations by Indian people. Rather than embarrass members of the tribe publicly, people used to tease individuals they considered out of step with the concensus of tribal opinion. In this way egos were preserved and disputes within the tribe of a personal nature were held to a minimum.

Gradually people learned to anticipate teasing and began to tease themselves as a means of showing humility and at the same time advocating a course of action they deeply believed in. Men would depreciate their feats to show they were not trying to run roughshod over tribal desires. This method of behavior served to highlight their true virtues and gain them a place of influence in tribal policy-making circles.

Humor has come to occupy such a prominent place in national Indian affairs that any kind of movement is impossible without it. Tribes are being brought together by sharing humor of the past. Columbus jokes gain great sympathy among all tribes, yet there are no tribes extant who had anything to do with Columbus. But the fact of white invasion from which all tribes have suffered has created a common bond in relation to Columbus jokes that gives a solid feeling of unity and purpose to the tribes.

The more desperate the problem, the more humor is directed to describe it. Satirical remarks often circumscribe problems so that possible solutions are drawn from the circumstances that would not make sense if presented in other than a humorous form.

Often people are awakened and brought to a militant edge through funny remarks. I often counseled people to run for the Bureau of Indian Affairs in case of an earthquake because nothing could shake the BIA. And I would watch as younger Indians set their jaws, determined that they, if nobody else, would shake it. We also had a saying that in case of fire call the BIA and they would handle it because they put a wet blanket on everything. This also got a warm reception from people.

Columbus and Custer jokes are the best for penetration into the heart of the matter, however. Rumor has it that Columbus began his journey with four ships. But one went over the edge so he arrived in the new world with only three. Another version states that Columbus didn't know where he was going, didn't know where he had been, and did it all on someone else's money. And the white man has been following Columbus ever since.

It is said when Columbus landed, one Indian turned to another and said, "Well, there goes the neighborhood." Another version has two Indians watching Columbus land and one saying to the other, "Maybe if we leave them alone they will go away." A favorite cartoon in Indian country a few years back showed a flying saucer landing while an Indian watched. The caption was "Oh, no, not again."

The most popular and enduring subject of Indian humor is, of course, General Custer. There are probably more jokes about Custer and the Indians than there were participants in the battle. All tribes, even those thousands of miles from Montana, feel a sense of accomplishment when thinking of Custer. Custer binds together implacable foes because he represented the Ugly American of the last century and he got what was coming to him.

Some years ago we put out a bumper sticker which read "Custer Died for Your Sins." It was originally meant as a dig at the National Council of Churches. But as it spread around the nation it took on additional meaning until everyone claimed to understand it and each interpretation was different.

Originally, the Custer bumper sticker referred to the Sioux Treaty of 1868 signed at Fort Laramie in which the United States pledged to give free and undisturbed use of the lands claimed by Red Cloud in return for peace. Under the covenants of the Old Testament, breaking a covenant called for a blood sacrifice for atonement. Custer was the blood sacrifice for the United States breaking the Sioux treaty. That, at least originally, was the meaning of the slogan.

Custer jokes, however, can barely be categorized, let alone sloganized. Indians say that Custer was well-dressed for the occasion. When the Sioux found his body after the battle, he had on an Arrow shirt.

Many stories are derived from the details of the battle itself. Custer is said to have boasted that he could ride through the entire Sioux nation with his Seventh Cavalry and he was half right. He got half-way through.

One story concerns the period immediately after Custer's contingent had been wiped out and the Sioux and Cheyennes were zeroing in on Major Reno and his troops several miles to the south of the Custer battlefield.

The Indians had Reno's troopers surrounded on a bluff. Water was scarce, ammunition was nearly exhausted, and it looked like the next attack would mean certain extinction.

One of the white soldiers quickly analyzed the situation and shed his clothes. He covered himself with mud, painted his face like an Indian, and began to creep toward the Indian lines.

A Cheyenne heard some rustling in the grass and was just about to shoot.

"Hey, chief," the soldier whispered, "don't shoot, I'm coming over to join you. I'm going to be on your side."

The warrior looked puzzled and asked the soldier why he wanted to change sides.

"Well," he replied, "better red than dead."

Custer's Last Words occupy a revered place in Indian humor. One source states that as he was falling mortally wounded he cried, "Take no prisoners!" Other versions, most of them off color, concentrate on where those ****

Indians are coming from. My favorite last saying pictures Custer on top of the hill looking at a multitude of warriors charging up the slope at him. He turns resignedly to his aide and says, "Well, it's better than going back to North Dakota."

Thought Questions

1. Compare and contrast the basic ideas of Powers' descriptions of Indians with the story of Chief Joseph.
2. How do Vine Deloria, Jr., and Chief Joseph compare as Indian voices?
3. Does the Alcatraz take-over represent a new period of Indian wars?
4. Compare Indian poetry to white American poetry.

six

AMERICAN FOREIGN POLICY:
From Isolation to
World Involvement

The United States has always had to deal with other nations. Foreign policy, or relations with other countries, has been an essential and changing aspect of our heritage. Initially, as an independent country, the United States had a weak bargaining position, and neutrality seemed the best policy. Although the Monroe Doctrine seemed an exception to that neutrality, it was not until the late 1800s that the United States started to become a leader in the world community. Despite the policy of neutrality, the United States went to war with England and Mexico, negotiated treaties, and relied heavily upon diplomacy in the 1800s. After the Spanish-American War and during the presidency of Theodore Roosevelt our foreign policy began to reflect imperialistic overtones.

Although the United States tried to remain generally aloof from world involvement during the 1920s and 1930s, a reaction to World War I, after World War II conditions necessitated new directions. The Truman Doctrine pledged our support to the free world in its fight against communism, and gave our foreign policy a whole new impetus. Since that time the struggle with communism has been evident in foreign and military aid to other nations. With the end of the Vietnam War and President Richard Nixon's visits to China and Russia, the direction of foreign policy must be reevaluated. What should the United States' role in foreign affairs be? The days of strict neutrality and isolation are impossible to recall. The United States must now consider all her domestic and foreign policy in terms of the world community.

I

Washington on Foreign Affairs*

American foreign policy was actually born during the presidency of George Washington. The first secretary of state, Thomas Jefferson, attempted to clarify United States boundaries, without jeopardizing its newly acquired independence. In dealing with other nations, Jefferson favored France who had signed a mutual aid treaty in 1778. When France and England went to war in 1793 Washington feared that the United States would be drawn into the war, so he issued a neutrality proclamation. This action was somewhat unpopular, as was the Jay Treaty with England in 1795. When Washington left office in 1796 he gave his famous farewell address. This reading from that address presents Washington's advice for future generations in foreign affairs.

Questions

1. What were Washington's general recommendations in foreign affairs?
2. Was Washington pledging a neutral or isolationist course?

It is our true policy to steer clear of permanent alliances with any portion of the foreign world, so far, I mean, as we are now at liberty to do it. For let me not be understood as capable of patronizing infidelity to existing engagements. I hold the maxim no less applicable to public than to private affairs that honesty is always the best policy. I repeat, therefore, let those engagements be observed in their genuine sense. But in my opinion it is unnecessary and would be unwise to extend them.

Taking care always to keep ourselves by suitable establishments on a respectable defensive posture, we may safely trust to temporary alliances for extraordinary emergencies.

*Source: James D. Richardson, ed., *A Compilation of the Messages and Papers of the Presidents* (Washington, D.C.: Government Printing Office, 1896), Volume I, pp. 221–23.

Harmony, liberal intercourse with all nations, are recommended by policy, humanity, and interest. But even our commercial policy should hold an equal and impartial hand, neither seeking nor granting exclusive favors or preference; . . . constantly keeping in view that it is folly in one nation to look for disinterested favors from another; that it must pay with a portion of its independence for whatever it may accept under that character; that by such acceptance it may place itself in the condition of having given equivalents for nominal favors, and yet of being reproached with ingratitude for not giving more. There can be no greater error than to expect or calculate upon real favors from nation to nation. It is an illusion which experience must cure, which a just pride ought to discard.

2

Wilson the Diplomat*

Presidents Theodore Roosevelt and William Howard Taft contributed heavily to American imperialistic tendencies. Roosevelt's admonition to walk softly and carry a big stick was characteristic of his foreign policy. Under his leadership the Panama Canal was built, the Roosevelt Corollary (that the made the United States the official guardian of the Western Hemisphere) was issued, and the Great White Fleet was sent around the world to demonstrate naval superiority. President Taft relied less on threats of military intervention and naval superiority and more on financial investments in foreign countries.

President Woodrow Wilson attempted to bring more morality to foreign affairs, but in many ways he was no different from Roosevelt or Taft. During his terms in office, he meddled directly in the internal politics of Mexico, Santo Domingo, and Haiti. His stand

Source: From *Wilson the Diplomatist* by Arthur Link (Baltimore: Johns Hopkins Press, 1954), pp. 9–14. Reprinted by permission of the author.

on neutrality, with the burgeoning war in Europe, was a difficult one to enforce and proved to be impossible to maintain. Wilson's idealistic solutions to world problems died one after another as they clashed with the harsh diplomacy of Europe and the United States Senate's refusal to ratify the Versailles Treaty that contained the League of Nations agreement. Noted historian Arthur Link describes the strengths and weaknesses of Wilson the diplomat in the following reading.

Questions

1. What were Wilson's strengths as diplomat?
2. What were his weaknesses?
3. Generally, how does Link evaluate Wilson as diplomat?

There is the temptation to conclude from this analysis of Wilson's observations during the decade 1898–1907 that, as one authority has said, he had demonstrated an understanding of the foreign relations of his country and considerable preparation for their conduct by the time he entered the White House.[1] Much, of course, depends upon the criteria that one applies. Compared to a Grant or a Harding, Wilson does indeed seem an eminent authority. On the other hand, to compare Wilson with a Jefferson or a John Quincy Adams is to point up some of the deficiencies in the latter-day President's intellectual and practical training for the difficult business of managing the foreign affairs of a great power.

The strengths and weaknesses in Wilson's unconscious preparation as a diplomatist will, I trust, become more fully evident as we proceed in this analysis, but it might be well to summarize them at this point. There was to his advantage the fact that he had done much serious thinking about general principles of politics and national ideals that transcended geographical boundaries. That is to say, Wilson came to the presidency equipped with a coherent and deeply rooted philosophy about the nature and ends of government, a philosophy that could be readily translated into the basis of a foreign policy. Also to his advantage was the fact of his awareness of the larger dimensions of the diplomatic revolution of the period and the impact of that revolution upon American political institutions.

Balanced on the debit side were certain obvious deficiencies in Wilson's thought and training in foreign affairs. The most serious of these was his

---

[1]Harley Notter, *The Origins of the Foreign Policy of Woodrow Wilson* (Baltimore, 1937), p. 145.

failure before 1913 to do any systematic thinking about the nature, complexity, and difficulties of foreign policy and his assumption that the main task of diplomacy was the simple one of translating national ideals into a larger program of action.

Secondly, there was Wilson's apparent ignorance of or unconcern with the elementary facts about the main thrusts of American diplomacy from 1901 to 1913 and about the tensions that were impelling Europe toward a general war during the same period. Even about those events on the international scene in which he evidenced a keen interest, the war with Spain and its immediate aftermath, much of Wilson's thinking was superficial and reflected more the faddish thought of the time than an astute understanding of what was taking place. Indeed, after the thrill of the war and of empire had quickly passed, Wilson apparently lost virtually all interest in affairs abroad. There were tremendous new developments in American foreign policy and furious partisan debates at home between 1901 and 1913. There were recurrent crises in Europe during the prolonged prelude to the war that would break out in 1914. Yet throughout this period, during which Wilson emerged as a preeminent political leader, he spoke and acted as if foreign problems did not exist. For example, during a brilliant campaign for the Democratic presidential nomination and for the presidency from 1911 to 1912, he never once mentioned a foreign issue that was not primarily a domestic concern.

A good argument can be made to the effect that Wilson was so absorbed in plans for Princeton from 1902 to 1910 and so engrossed in his political apprenticeship from 1910 to 1913 that he had neither time nor energy for a serious study of foreign policy. The argument has some merit, but we must also conclude that Wilson did not concern himself seriously with affairs abroad during the period 1901 to 1913 both because he was not interested and because he did not think that they were important enough to warrant any diversion from the mainstream of his thought. Therefore, Wilson was not being unduly self-deprecatory when he remarked before he went to Washington how ironical it would be if his administration had to deal chiefly with foreign affairs. He was simply recognizing the obvious fact of his primary concern with domestic issues and his superior training for leadership in solving them.

Regardless of the adequacy or inadequacy of his preparation, Wilson after 1913 faced foreign problems of greater magnitude than any president had confronted since the early years of the nineteenth century. Whether he responded wisely or unwisely to the mounting international challenges of the years from 1913 to 1920, he executed policies that were on the whole firmly grounded upon a consistent body of principles and assumptions that supplied motive power and shaped and governed policy in the fields of action. These principles and assumptions were deeply rooted in Wilson's general thinking before 1913 about cosmology, ethics, the nature and ends of government, and the role of his own country in the creative development of mankind; they were in turn enlarged and refined as Wilson sought to apply them in practical affairs after his inauguration. Determining and controlling, they gave both strength and weakness to the diplomatist in action.

The foundations of all of Wilson's political thinking were the religious and ethical beliefs and values that he inherited from the Christian tradition and from his own Presbyterian theology. In matters of basic Christian faith, Wilson was like a little child, never doubting, always believing, and drawing spiritual sustenance from Bible reading, church attendance, and prayer. Having derived his beliefs from the Shorter Catechism, his father's sermons, and the Presbyterian scholastics, Wilson was Calvinistic in theology. He believed in a sovereign God, just and stern as well as loving; in a moral universe, the laws of which ruled nations as well as men; in the supreme revelation and redemption of Jesus Christ; and in the Bible as the incomparable word of God and the rule of life. He was a predestinarian, not so much in his apparent belief in election as in his conviction that God controlled history and used men and nations in the unfolding of His plan according to His purposes. Few ministers of the gospel gave more eloquent voice to these beliefs than did Wilson in his day; to point out that there was nothing unique about them is not to detract from their underlying and pervasive importance.[2]

From such spiritual roots grew a sturdy tree of character, integrity, and concern for first principles in political action—in brief, all the components of the idealism that was the unifying force in Wilson's life. In the conduct of foreign affairs this idealism meant for him the subordination of immediate goals and material interests to superior ethical standards and the exaltation of moral and spiritual purposes. This is not to say that he ignored the existence and powerful operation of economic forces in international life. Indeed, for a brief period following the Spanish-American War he seemed almost to verge upon an economic determinism in his analysis of developments, both past and present, upon the international scene. As president, moreover, he was not unmindful of the necessities of a viable international economic life, of the material interests of Americans abroad, or of the economic rivalries that helped to produce conflict among nations. Even so, idealism was the main drive of Wilson's thinking about international relations. As he put it, foreign policy must not be defined in "terms of material interest," but should be "more concerned about human rights than about property rights."[3]

A second main theme in Wilson's political thinking with large consequences for his foreign policy was his belief in democracy as the most humane

---

[2]For examples of Wilson's religious addresses and writings, see "The Ministry and the Individual" and "The Bible and Progress," printed in Ray S. Baker and William E. Dodd (eds.), *The Public Papers of Woodrow Wilson, College and State* (2 vols.; New York, 1925), II, 178–87, 291–302; for a description and analysis, see Arthur S. Link, *Wilson: The New Freedom* (Princeton, N.J., 1956), pp. 64–65.

[3]For a rewarding amplification of the foregoing generalizations, see William Diamond, *The Economic Thought of Woodrow Wilson* (Baltimore, 1943), pp. 131–61.

and Christian form of government. From the beginning to the end of his adult career he studied, wrote about, and put into practice the essential aspects of democratic government, and it would be superfluous here to review his splendid synthesis of the Anglo-American democratic theories and traditions. More important for our purposes is an understanding of the way in which these assumptions helped to form his objectives and to determine his actions in the field of foreign affairs.

3

The Diplomacy of World War II*

World War II disturbed the calm of United States foreign policy and caused President Franklin D. Roosevelt to move from a policy of neutrality to active participation. U.S. diplomacy was essential in planning war and allied strategy, and in molding the postwar world. At Casablanca and Teheran Roosevelt, Churchill, and Stalin discussed war strategy and the future of Europe and the Far East. At Yalta they decided the future of Germany, the formation of the United Nations, and the Russian influence in Eastern Europe. When Harry S Truman replaced Roosevelt and attended the Potsdam Conference, the postwar world had emerged. Here is the text of the Teheran Conference and historian Gaddis Smith's description of the world that emerged from World War II.

Questions

TEHERAN

1. What was the general content of the report?
2. What were the goals and hopes discussed here?

*State Department Bulletin (Washington, D.C.: Government Printing Office), Vol. IX, p. 409; and Gaddis Smith, American Diplomacy during the Second World War, 1941–45. Copyright © 1965 by John Wiley & Sons, Inc. Reprinted by permission.

SMITH

1. How does Smith evaluate the postwar world?
2. What did Smith consider the prospects for the future?

The Teheran Conference

We—The President of the United States, the Prime Minister of Great Britain, and the Premier of the Soviet Union, have met these four days past, in this, the Capital of our Ally, Iran, and have shaped and confirmed our common policy.

We express our determination that our nations shall work together in war and in the peace that will follow.

As to war—our military staffs have joined in our round table discussions, and we have concerted our plans for the destruction of the German forces. We have reached complete agreement as to the scope and timing of the operations to be undertaken from the east, west and south.

The common understanding which we have here reached guarantees that victory will be ours.

And as to peace—we are sure that our concord will win an enduring Peace. We recognize fully the supreme responsibility resting upon us and all the United Nations to make a peace which will command the goodwill of the overwhelming mass of the peoples of the world and banish the scourge and terror of war for many generations.

With our Diplomatic advisors we have surveyed the problems of the future. We shall seek the cooperation and active participation of all nations, large and small, whose peoples in heart and mind are dedicated, as are our own peoples, to the elimination of tyranny and slavery, oppression and intolerance. We will welcome them, as they may choose to come, into a world family of Democratic Nations.

No power on earth can prevent our destroying the German armies by land, their U Boats by sea, and their war plants from the air.

Our attack will be relentless and increasing.

Emerging from these cordial conferences we look with confidence to the day when all peoples of the world may live free lives, untouched by tyranny, and according to their varying desires and their own consciences.

We came here with hope and determination. We leave here, friends in fact, in spirit and in purpose.

Gaddis Smith

In terms of the assumptions which had sustained the national war effort since the day of Pearl Harbor, victory lay gloriously complete. Hitler was dead and Germany lay powerless under Allied occupation. The Emperor's decision to surrender meant that the landings on Japan would be bloodless. Italy, ineffectual minor partner of the Axis, had withdrawn from the war two years before and, having repudiated fascism, was about to acquire a respected place among nations. The temptation was great during those happy August days of 1945 to dwell on the achievements of the nation in battle, on the home front, and around the diplomatic conference table. Americans, virtually unaided, had beaten Japan in the Pacific while providing the leadership and more than half the men for the attack on Hitler from the West. At the same time they had armed Britain, Russia, and China. Their diplomacy had preserved the great coalition, established the United Nations, and laid foundations for peace in Europe and Asia.

No informed American, however, could give in to that temptation. There was far too much evidence that the legacy of victory was not peace and prosperity for all mankind—as the Atlantic Charter had promised—but continued suffering, hatred, and threat of war. The United States directly and by supporting its allies had encompassed the unconditional defeat of the Axis enemy, but now found itself in a world where there was less national security than in 1941. Roosevelt and his advisers had correctly foreseen that genuine peace and security were impossible without firm Soviet-Western cooperation. They had followed tactics of conciliation and well-meaning appeasement of Russia during the war, but failed to win anything but a few paper agreements. By late summer 1945 even the paper agreements were in tatters. Little remained to conceal Soviet Russia's fundamental hostility to the non-Communist world.

For a few months longer American leaders in their public statements refrained from giving full voice to their somber conclusions, but privately most of them recognized that what was soon to be called "the Cold War" had begun. Behind the "Iron Curtain" the Russians were ruthlessly suppressing democracy, as it was understood in the West, and were erecting a cordon of Communist satellites: Poland, Hungary, Rumania, Bulgaria. Yugoslavia, if not a satellite under Tito, was closely tied to Moscow and a threat to peace through its territorial claims against Italy at the head of the Adriatic. Events in these countries were the subject of long and tedious argument at Potsdam. The United States and Britain complained that Russia was ignoring the Yalta agreements. Western observers in Russian-dominated areas were being denied freedom of movement and inquiry. Russia was acting unilaterally without the consultation promised at Yalta. Free elections were not being held; and (a minor complaint) American and British private property within the countries was being confiscated. Stalin and Molotov were so unmoved by these complaints that they scarcely bothered to justify Russia's behavior.

Germany, under four-power occupation, was already becoming a battleground in the Cold War rather than the symbol of Allied unity which the well-intentioned had hoped. President Truman at the Potsdam conference urged that Germany be treated as an economic unit, but Anglo-American efforts to work out genuinely uniform policies with Russia came to naught. In theory all three great powers had abandoned their wartime schemes for the dismemberment of Germany, but in fact the boundary dividing the Russian from the British and American zones had already severed the country. Furthermore, Russia had unilaterally turned over a large area of eastern Germany to Poland in defiance of Western protests. Berlin, an enclave in the Russian zone, was divided like Germany as a whole into four zones. Western access rights to the city had still not been defined by formal agreement. Austria, which by agreement was to be restored as an independent country, was like Germany divided into four zones of occupation (Vienna being treated in a manner similar to Berlin) and was also a medium of discord rather than cooperation.

Economically, all of Europe was prostrate. The United States was supplying food for temporary relief through the United Nations Relief and Rehabilitation Administration (UNRRA), but the American government and people had not yet faced the political implications of the possible spread of Communism into a dispirited and impoverished western Europe. Roosevelt had assumed that the American people would be unwilling to keep troops in Europe more than two years after victory or take on any long-term economic burdens. Although this assumption had not been publicly challenged by the late summer of 1945, an increasing number of observers were beginning to feel that American security demanded the very things which Roosevelt had assumed were impossible.

The legacy of victory was equally grim in Asia. There would be no friction with Russia in Japan because Truman had figuratively told Stalin to go to hell when he asked to share the control of the occupied country. Korea, however, was about to become a focal point of Soviet-American tension. Divided into occupation zones along the thirty-eighth parallel, it was in some respects an Asian equivalent of Germany. By 1950 Communist China had replaced Russia as the controlling power in North Korea and the United States found itself fighting a costly war simply to preserve the status quo of partition. Meanwhile, China's problems defied solution with the limited means which the United States was ready to apply. Few knowledgeable men really believed that exhortation would bring about the peaceful unification of Chiang Kai-shek's regime with the Chinese Communists. But for a nation unwilling to risk lives and large sums of money, exhortation was the only tactic available. It failed utterly. In 1949 the Chinese Communists gained complete control of the mainland when Chiang Kai-shek's Nationalist government retreated to Formosa, the crowded island which in accordance with the Cairo declaration of 1943 had been taken from Japan.

The early wartime assumption concerning Nationalist China's ability to bring leadership and stability to Asia was forgotten by 1945, but no new, workable premise had arisen in its place. In a manner, the determination to encourage the elimination of European colonialism from Asia had grown weaker without leading to a new policy for the colonial areas. The desire of American military leaders to retain unqualified national control for strategic reasons of islands in the Pacific was a major factor in this retreat from dogmatic anticolonialism. Thus, the United States emerged from the war with a vast collection of what were in effect Pacific island colonies, Okinawa being the largest and most important. On the other hand, the Philippines gained their independence in 1946 in accordance with earlier promises. Hong Kong was returned to British sovereignty, notwithstanding Roosevelt's frequent suggestions that it should be given to the Chinese. The British also regained sovereignty over Burma and Malaya, although both colonies were put on the road to independence as were the Netherlands East Indies. After the unsuccessful wartime intervention in British-Indian relations, the United States kept hands off India. The British Labour government moved quickly to grant the independence that had been promised but their best efforts were unable to prevent a Moslem-Hindu bloodbath or the partition of the country. Indochina, once considered by Roosevelt for trusteeship under Chinese administration, reverted to France. The French attempt to grant autonomy within the French Union to the different countries of Indochina led to a bloody colonial war and defeat of France despite the ironic military support of the United States.

In the Middle East the American wartime objectives of liquidating British and French authority had been largely achieved, but the results—war over Palestine, anti-Western nationalism in Egypt, Syria, Iraq, and Iran, and generally an increase in Soviet prestige—were not what American idealists had hoped. As in other areas of the world, the United States had encouraged the eradication of old regimes without being able to devise alternatives that served the national interest. Ultimately, the United States felt obliged to assume heavy economic and military commitments in the Middle East with mixed and less than satisfactory results.

Even Latin America, the one region which in 1945 seemed securely within the orbit of American beneficence, proved in a short time to be a source of anti-American discontent and, through ties with the Communist world, of direct insecurity of the United States.

Over this dismal, variegated globe lay the shadow of annihilation cast by the discovery of nuclear explosives. In August 1945 the American government did not know how to deal with this unprecedented fact of technology which had so suddenly changed all the old conditions in which nations sought through war and diplomacy to gain advantage over one another. Some Americans thought the United States should hold its secret and openly use its new power to coerce Russia. Others said that this course would lead to mutual destruction on the not-too-distant day when Russia had her own nuclear weapons. The second group said that the United States should voluntarily relinquish its atomic monopoly to an international authority. Actual policy as developed in subsequent months followed middle ground: a proposal to preserve the American monopoly of weapons until an international authority with adequate provision for inspection against violation was established. The Soviet Union, apparently suspecting a trick and hard at work on its own nuclear research, said no. The nuclear arms race was under way.

4

Kennedy and Johnson in the Western Hemisphere*

From the early 1960s foreign affairs have been changing dramatically. The old containment policy and the policies of Truman and Eisenhower are being carefully examined. Kennedy attempted innovation with the Peace Corps and the Alliance for Progress. He also met the Soviet challenge directly in the Cuban missile crisis, established a "hot line" phone with Russia, and signed the Nuclear Test Ban Treaty. The Vietnam War clouded Lyndon Johnson's foreign policy, as did the events of April, 1965, when Johnson sent marines into the Dominican Republic to stem a perceived communist threat. Nixon directly challenged the assumptions of containment policy, personally visited China and Russia, and ended the Vietnam War. New goals and directions in foreign policy are presently being implemented. Here the Senate gives power to Kennedy in the Cuban missile crisis and President Lyndon Johnson justifies his action in the Dominican Republic.

*Sources: *Senate Resolution 388,* 87th Cong., 2d sess., September 17, 1962; and *State Department Bulletin* (Washington, D.C.: Government Printing Office), LXII, pp. 744–45.

Questions

KENNEDY

1. What historical precedent did the Senate refer to?
2. What powers were given to Kennedy?

JOHNSON

1. How did Johnson explain the problems in the Dominican Republic?
2. How did he justify his action?

Kennedy

Whereas President James Monroe, announcing the Monroe Doctrine in 1823, declared to the Congress that we should consider any attempt on the part of European powers "to extend their system to any portion of this hemisphere as dangerous to our peace and safety."

Whereas in the Rio Treaty of 1947, the parties agreed that "an armed attack by any state against an American state shall be considered as an attack against all the American states, and, consequently, each one of the said contracting parties undertakes to assist in meeting in the exercise of the inherent right of individual or collective self-defense recognized by article 51 of the Charter of the United Nations."

Whereas the Foreign Ministers of the Organization of American States at Punta del Este in January 1962 unanimously declared: "The present Government of Cuba has identified itself with the principles of Marxist-Leninist ideology, has established a political, economic, and social system based on that doctrine, and accepts military assistance from extracontinental Communist powers, including even the threat of military intervention in America on the part of the Soviet Union";

Whereas since 1958 the international Communist movement has increasingly extended into Cuba its political, economic, and military sphere of influence: Now, therefore, be it

Resolved, That it is the sense of the Senate that the President of the United States is supported in his determination and possesses all necessary authority—

(a) to prevent by whatever means may be necessary, including the use of arms, the Castro regime from exporting its aggressive purposes to any part of this hemisphere by force or the threat of force;

(b) to prevent in Cuba the creation or use of an externally supported offensive military base capable of endangering the United States naval base at Guantanamo, free passage to the Panama Canal, United States missile and space preparations, or the security of this Nation and its citizens; and

(c) to work with other free citizens of this hemisphere and with freedom-loving Cuban refugees to support the legitimate aspirations of the people of Cuba for a return to self-determination.

Johnson

Meanwhile, all this time, from Saturday [April 24] to Wednesday [April 28], the danger was mounting. Even though we were deeply saddened by bloodshed and violence in a close and friendly neighbor, we had no desire to interfere in the affairs of a sister Republic.

On Wednesday afternoon [April 28] there was no longer any choice for the man who is your President. I was sitting in my little office reviewing the world situation with Secretary Rusk, Secretary McNamara, and Mr. McGeorge Bundy. Shortly after 3 o'clock I received a cable from our Ambassador [Bennett], and he said that things were in danger; he had been informed the chief of police and governmental authorities could no longer protect us. We immediately started the necessary conference calls to be prepared.

At 5:14, almost 2 hours later, we received a cable that was labeled "critic," a word that is reserved for only the most urgent and immediate matters of national security.

The cable reported that Dominican law enforcement and military officials had informed our Embassy that the situation was completely out of control, and that the police and the government could no longer give any guarantee concerning the safety of Americans or any foreign nationals.

Ambassador Bennett, who is one of our most experienced Foreign Service officers, went on in that cable to say that only an immediate landing of American forces could safeguard and protect the lives of thousands of Americans and thousands of other citizens of some 30 other countries. Ambassador Bennett urged your President to order an immediate landing.

In this situation hesitation and vacillation could mean death for many of our people, as well as many of the citizens of other lands.

I thought that we could not and we did not hesitate. Our forces, American forces, were ordered in immediately to protect American lives. They have done that. They have attacked no one, and although some of our servicemen gave their lives, not a single American civilian or the civilian of any other nation, as a result of this protection, lost their lives.

There may be those in our own country who say that such action was good but we should have waited, or we should have delayed, or we should have consulted further, or we should have called a meeting [of the Organization of American States]. But from the very beginning, the United States, at my instructions, had worked for a cease-fire beginning the Saturday the revolution took place. . . .

When that cable arrived, when our entire country team in the Dominican Republic, made up of nine men—one from the Army, Navy, and Air Force, our Ambassador . . . and others—said to your President unanimously: Mr. President, if you do not send forces immediately, men and women—Americans and those of other lands—will die in the streets—well, I knew there was no time to talk, to consult, or to delay. For in this situation delay itself would be decision—the decision to risk and to lose the lives of thousands of Americans and thousands of innocent people from all lands.

I want you to know that it is not a light or an easy matter to send our American boys to another country, but I do not think that the American people expect their President to hesitate or to vacillate in the face of danger, just because the decision is hard when life is in peril.

The revolutionary movement took a tragic turn. Communist leaders, many of them trained in Cuba, seeing a chance to increase disorder, to gain a foothold, joined the revolution. They took increasing control. And what began as a popular democratic revolution, committed to democracy and social justice, very shortly moved and was taken over and really seized and placed into the hands of a band of Communist conspirators.

Many of the original leaders of the rebellion . . . took refuge in foreign embassies because they had been superseded by other evil forces, and the Secretary General of the rebel government, Martínez Francisco, appealed for a cease-fire. But he was ignored. The revolution was now in other and dangerous hands.

When these new and ominous developments emerged, the OAS [Organization of American States] met again, and it met at the request of the United States. I am glad to say they responded wisely and decisively. A five-nation OAS team is now in the Dominican Republic, acting to achieve a cease-fire to insure the safety of innocent people, to restore normal conditions, and to open a path to democratic progress.

Thought Questions

1. How does Wilson's diplomacy compare with the diplomacy of World War II?
2. How do Kennedy and Johnson's foreign policies compare with the Monroe Doctrine?
3. Has the advice Washington gave in foreign affairs been followed?
4. Is the present foreign policy a good reflection of the past?

seven

AMERICAN ECONOMIC POLICY:
The Hamiltonian Tradition
Revisited

From the origins of America, money has moved people and government. In fact, economics could even be said to be responsible for the discovery of America. The expansion of European capitalism created an atmosphere of adventure for movement west. During the colonial period the mercantile theory—that the colony existed primarily for benefit of the mother country —was very evident, but its enforcement depended upon the European power involved. England, for example, followed a practice of salutary neglect toward its colonies. When the policy was changed to follow mercantilist lines, the American Revolution resulted.

Finances, one of the major problems of a new nation, continued to plague the growing country during the 1800s in the form of a series of severe economic depressions. Of course the expansion of industrialism after the Civil War caused a reevaluation of economic thinking and led to government intervention in the early 1900s. Prior to that time government had guided and watched economic fluctuations, but had never taken a direct role in controlling them. With the depression of 1929 the age of economic liberalism abruptly came to an end. Federal government policy and economic planning came to cooperate. The New Deal marked the birth of this pattern which has continued and expanded up to the present. For example, President Richard Nixon's wage-price freeze in the 1970s was in the best tradition of government economic leadership. The government now watches economic fluctuations carefully, while most Americans do the same to prices and their pocketbooks.

Alexander Hamilton: Pro and Con*

The American Revolution signaled the end of British economic domination of the thirteen colonies. Financially, the Articles of Confederation period was a disaster characterized by incidents of economic unrest such as Shays' rebellion. The Constitution gave government specific powers to tax, levy tariff, regulate commerce, and to exercise other powers. Under George Washington, finances loomed as one of the most immediate problems. The task of putting the infant government on its feet fell to Secretary of the Treasury Alexander Hamilton. Hamilton not only succeeded in getting congressional approval for assumption of state debts, funding of the national debt, and creation of a national bank, but also greatly influenced the policies of Washington. With his aristocratic outlook and emphasis on wealth, Hamilton incurred much wrath. The first reading expresses the sentiments of a Pennsylvania farmer toward Hamilton's funding scheme; the second presents an act for the creation of the first national bank.

Questions

FARMER

1. What are the arguments the farmer used against funding?
2. Does he believe that funding favors the rich?
3. Do his arguments make sense?

BANK BILL

1. How was the national bank established?
2. What were its limitations?

*Sources: *Pennsylvania Gazette*, January 27, 1790; and *Annals of Congress*, 1st Cong., 3rd sess., Appendix, pp. 2375–81.

3. Who were the subscribers and directors?
4. Is there any similarity with banks today?

A Farmer

Much has been said, we are told, by the Secretary of the Federal Treasury, in his report, in favor of the necessity of supporting *public credit.* But public credit cannot exist, at the expense of public and private *justice.* The Congress owe the balance of the certificates, above 2sh. 6d. in the pound, to their army. To gain a character, therefore, they commit a flagrant act of injustice. And with whom is this character to be gained? With Speculators, and British and Dutch Brokers. But with whom will it be lost? With their army, with the best whigs in the union, and with half the widows and orphans in the United States. But why do they attempt to restore their national character by *halves?* By redeeming their certificates at their nominal value, and not making up the losses sustained by widows and orphans by their paper money, they resemble a girl, who comes forward in a white sheet to do penance for a *second* bastard, without asking pardon of God and the congregation for her *first* breach of chastity. Public credit, therefore, at the expence of public and private justice, is folly and wickedness. The words are mere jingle, calculated only to catch weak people. But further, the proposed funding system is grossly oppressive upon the poor soldiers and officers of the American army. They must all pay taxes, to raise their certificates to their full value in the hands of the purchasers of them. Now is this right? It certainly is not. For then, instead of being paid by the United States for their services, or for their limbs, they are brought in debt to them: That is, an officer received a certificate of £200 instead of £1000 from them, and pays perhaps half the balance in taxes, for the benefit of the man to whom he sold it. Such injustice and oppression may be coloured over with fine words; but there is a time coming, when the pen of history will detect and expose the folly of the arguments in favor of the proposed funding system, as well as the iniquity. Instead of disgracing our country, by treating our army with so much ingratitude and injustice it would be far better to double the public debt, by paying the soldier and the Speculator the same sum.

The Congress under the old confederation, after having paid their army in depreciated paper money, made up to them the difference afterwards in what they called depreciation certificates. Shall the Congress under the new government deny them the same justice, by refusing to pay them the difference between two shillings and sixpence and twenty shillings?—Or shall they do worse—Shall they pay it to men who never earned it, and who have already received an interest on their purchases equal to the sum they cost them?

Should the balance still due to our army be paid to them, it would spread money through every county and township of the United States. If it is paid to the speculators, all the cash of the United States will soon center in our cities, and afterwards in England and Holland.

By the proposed funding system the interest of the original certificate holder is reduced to four per cent. Now is this just?—To take forty shillings a year from the just gains of one man, and add ten pounds a year to the unjust gains of another?—Is not this selling Justice—and the United States—at public vendue, to the highest bidder?

An Act to Incorporate the Subscribers to the Bank of the United States

Whereas it is conceived that the establishment of a bank for the United States, upon a foundation sufficiently extensive to answer the purposes intended thereby, and at the same time upon the principles which afford adequate security for an upright and prudent administration thereof, will be very conducive to the successful conducting of the national finances; will tend to give facility to the obtaining of loans, for the use of the Government, in sudden emergencies, and will be productive of considerable advantage to trade and industry in general:

Therefore,

Be it enacted, &c., That a Bank of the United States shall be established; the capital stock whereof shall not exceed ten millions of dollars, divided into twenty-five thousand shares, each share being four hundred dollars . . .

SEC. 2. *And be it further enacted,* That it shall be lawful for any person, co-partnership, or body politic, to subscribe for such or so many shares as he, she, or they shall think fit, not exceeding one thousand, except as shall be hereafter directed relatively to the United States; and that the sums respectively subscribed, except on behalf of the United States, shall be payable one-fourth in gold and silver, and three-fourths in that part of the public debt, which, according to the loan proposed in the fourth and fifteenth sections of the act, entitled "An act making provision for the debt of the United States," shall bear an accruing interest, at the time of payment of six per centum per annum, and shall also be payable in four equal parts, in the aforesaid ratio of specie to debt, at the distance of six calendar months from each other; the first whereof shall be paid at time of subscription.

SEC. 3. *And be it further enacted,* That all those who shall become subscribers to the said bank, their successors and assigns shall be, and are hereby created and made a corporation and body politic, by the name and style of "The President, Directors, and Company of the Bank of the United States;" and shall so continue until the fourth of March, one thousand eight hundred and eleven; and by the name shall be, and are hereby, made able and capable in law, to have, purchase, receive, possess, enjoy, and retain to them and their successors, lands, rents, tenements, hereditaments, goods, chattels, and effects of what kind, nature, or quality soever, to an amount not exceeding in the whole fifteen millions of dollars, including the amount of the capital stock aforesaid . . .

SEC. 4. *And be it further enacted,* That for the well ordering of the affairs of the said corporation there shall be twenty-five directors; of whom there shall be an election on the first Monday of January in each year, by the stockholders or proprietors of the capital stock of the said corporation, and by plurality of the votes actually given; and those who shall be duly chosen at any election, shall be capable of serving as directors, by virtue of such choice, until the end or expiration of the Monday of January next ensuing the time of such election, and no longer. . . .

SEC. 7. *And be it further enacted,* That the following rules, restrictions, limitations, and provisions shall form and be fundamental articles of the Constitution of the said corporation, viz:

I. The number of votes to which each stockholder shall be entitled, shall be according to the number of shares he shall hold, in the proportions following: that is to say, for one share, and not more than two shares, one vote; for every two shares above two, and not exceeding ten, one vote; for every four shares above ten, and not exceeding thirty, one vote; for every six shares above thirty, and not exceeding sixty, one vote; for every eight shares above sixty, and not exceeding one hundred, one vote; and for every ten shares above one hundred, one vote; but no person, co-partnership, or body politic shall be entitled to a greater number than thirty votes. And after the first election, no share or shares shall confer a right of suffrage, which shall not have been holden three calendar months previous to the day of election. Stockholders actually resident within the United States, and none other, may vote in elections by proxy.

II. Not more than three-fourths of the directors in office, exclusive of the president, shall be eligible for the next succeeding year; but the director, who shall be president at the time of an election, may always be re-elected.

III. None but a stockholder, being a citizen of the United States, shall be eligible as a director. . . .

VIII. The lands, tenements, and hereditaments which it shall be lawful for the said corporation to hold, shall be only such as shall be requisite for its immediate accommodation in relation to the convenient transacting of its business, and such as shall have been *bonafide* mortgaged to it by way of security, or conveyed to it in satisfaction of debts previously contracted in the course of its dealings, or purchased at sales upon judgments which shall have been obtained for such debts.

IX. The total amount of the debts, which the said corporation shall at any time owe, whether by bond, bill, note, or other contract, shall not exceed the sum of ten millions of dollars, over and above the moneys then actually deposited in the bank for safe-keeping, unless the contracting of any greater debt shall have been previously authorized by a law of the United States. . . .

X. The said corporations may sell any part of the public debt whereof its stock shall be composed, but shall not be at liberty to purchase any public debt whatsoever; nor shall directly or indirectly deal or trade in any thing, except bills of exchange, gold or silver bullion, or in the sale of goods really and truly pledged for money lent and not redeemed in due time; or of goods which shall be the produce of its lands. Neither shall the said corporation take more than at the rate of six per centum per annum, for or upon its loans or discounts.

XI. No loan shall be made by the said corporation, for the use or on account of the Government of the United States, to an amount exceeding one hundred thousand dollars, or of any particular State, to an amount exceeding fifty thousand dollars, or of any foreign prince or State, unless previously authorized by a law of the United States. . . .

XIII. The bills obligatory and of credit, under the seal of the said corporation, which shall be made to any person or persons, shall be assignable by endorsement thereupon, under the hand or hands of such person or persons, and of his, her, or their assignee or assignees, and so as absolutely to transfer and vest the property thereof in each and every assignee or assignees successively, and to enable such assignee or assignees to bring and maintain an action thereupon in his, or her, or their own name or names. . . .

XIV. Half-yearly dividends shall be made of so much of the profits of the bank as shall appear to the directors advisable; and once in every three years the directors shall lay before the stockholders, at a general meeting, for their information, an exact and particular statement of the debts which shall have remained unpaid after the expiration of the original credit, for a period of treble the term of that credit; and of the surplus of profit, if any, after deducting losses and dividends. . . .

XV. It shall be lawful for the directors aforesaid, to establish offices wheresoever they shall think fit within the United States, for the purposes of discount and deposite only, and upon the same terms, and in the same manner, as shall be practised at the bank; and to commit the management of the said offices, and the making of the said discounts, to such persons, under such agreements, and subject to such regulations as they shall deem proper; not being contrary to law, or to the constitution of the bank.

XVI. The officer at the head of the Treasury Department of the United States shall be furnished, from time to time, as often as he may require, not exceeding once a week, with statements of the amount of the capital stock of the said corporation, and of the debts due to the same; of the moneys deposited therein; of the notes in circulation, and of the cash in hand; and shall have a right to inspect such general accounts in the books of the bank as shall relate to the said statements. *Provided,* That this shall not be construed to imply a right of inspecting the account of any private individual or individuals with the bank. . . .

SEC. 10. *And be it further enacted,* That the bills or notes of the said corporation, originally made payable, or which shall have become payable on demand, in gold and silver coin, shall be receivable in all payments to the United States.

SEC. 11. *And be it further enacted,* That it shall be lawful for the President of the United States, at any time or times, within eighteen months after the first day of April next, to cause a subscription to be made to the stock of the said corporation, as part of the aforesaid capital stock of ten millions of dollars, on behalf of the United States, to an amount not exceeding two millions of dollars, to be paid out of the moneys which shall be borrowed by virtue of either of the acts, the one entitled "An act making provision for the debt of the United States;" and the other entitled "An act making provision for the reduction of the public debt;" borrowing of the bank an equal sum, to be applied to the purposes for which the said moneys shall have been procured, reimbursable in ten years by equal annual installments; or at any time sooner, or in any greater proportions that the Government may think fit.

SEC. 12. *And be it further enacted,* That no other bank shall be established by any future law of the United States, during the continuance of the corporation hereby created; for which the faith of the United States is hereby pledged.

2

The Farm Revolt*

The first half of the nineteenth century saw an intense struggle between President Andrew Jackson and the second national bank. In 1832 opponents of Jackson attempted to pass a bill to recharter the bank. The bill passed Congress, but was vetoed by Jackson, who argued that the bank existed for the wealthy and had little other value. The death of the bank in 1836 led to a national depression

*Source: From *The Age of the Economic Revolution, 1876–1900* by Carl N. Degler. Copyright © 1968 by Scott, Foresman and Company. Reprinted by permission of the publisher.

*in 1837. The Civil War, however, brought a great industrial boom
to the North and opened the era of big business.
The overriding economic philosophy of the late 1800s was favorable
to big business and moneyed interests, but particularly harmful to
the farmer. Although the farmer himself was undergoing an agricultural revolution, he found himself further and further out of touch
with that American dream of an agricultural nation. America was
becoming the land of cities and in turn the farmer's financial plight
was becoming more acute. Here historian Carl Degler talks of the
agricultural revolution, tenant farming, and the farm protest movement.*

Questions

1. What was the agricultural revolution?
2. Was it merely mechanical?
3. What was the situation of tenant farmers?
4. What was the farm protest movement and what were its demands?

Cash Crops: Development of Commercial Farming

NEW COMMERCIAL FARMER

The agricultural revolution was gradually transforming many farmers into businessmen, who devoted all their time, resources, and energy to the
raising of a commodity for profit. Admittedly, farmers had long been selling
some of their produce, but to a much greater extent they had farmed "for a
living"—that is, for subsistence. Never before had so many of them participated in the market, especially to the almost total extent that they did in the
last three decades of the nineteenth century. Although subsistence farm
families had sold some of their crops for money, they had relied primarily on
growing their own food, canning or preserving their own vegetables, baking
their own bread, and making their own clothes, as well as, perhaps their own
shoes and agricultural implements. But when agriculture became commercial,
many of these items, usually of much better quality, could be purchased from
stores and traveling merchants with the cash earned from the sale of one or
two staple crops, to which farmers devoted their full time and skill. Moreover,
with cash, the commercial farmers could partake of the amenities of life,
usually unavailable to the subsistence farmers. They could buy books, medi-
cines, better tools, finer clothes, trips to distant places, and a host of other
benefits. The considerably higher standard of living to be gained from com-

mercialization easily outweighed whatever objection farmers might have had to involvement in the market.

But there was another side to the lot of commercial farmers. By committing themselves almost entirely to production for the market, they became vulnerable to all the downward swings in the price curve. Unfortunately, after the middle 1870's, falling farm prices were characteristic of the American and world economy. Wheat which sold for $1.19 a bushel in 1881 brought only 49 cents in 1894; corn, priced at 63 cents a bushel in 1881, fell to 28 cents in 1890. At such prices, farmers grimly pointed out, it was cheaper to burn corn for fuel than to buy coal. It is true that prices in general fell during the same period. However, the prices of agricultural commodities always fell faster than the others, leaving the farmer in the position of Alice in Wonderland, producing "faster and faster" just to maintain the same economic position. The more successful he was in increasing production, the more supply outran demand and the lower the prices fell.

The productiveness of the American farmer was but one of several causes of the increasing supply of farm products, for the Communications Revolution was bringing into the world market producers in other lands, old and new. Canadian and Russian wheat, Argentine beef, Indian and Egyptian cotton, and Australian beef and wool now competed with American products.

GROWTH OF TENANT FARMING

Falling prices constituted one measure of the farmers' worsening condition; another was the report by the 1880 Census of widespread farm tenancy. Throughout most of their previous history, Americans had been proud of the broad distribution of landownership and the merely temporary role tenancy played in the life of the vast majority of farmers. The Census of 1880, however, reported that a quarter of America's farmers did not own the land on which they labored. A large proportion of the tenancy in the South, it is true, stemmed from the presence of former slaves who had never owned land, but the high level of tenancy in the northern states, where there were few Negroes in agriculture, showed that the heritage of slavery was not the whole explanation. Because of falling prices, many farmers obviously lost their land or were unable to purchase it. In Indiana, Illinois, Iowa, and Nebraska, for example, between 17 and 24 per cent of the farmers were tenants. As the century wore on, the situation only worsened; in 1900, a third of America's farmers were tenants.

ORGANIZATION AND PROTEST

Ordinarily in a free-enterprise economy, when an excess of production causes prices to fall disastrously, producers withdraw until the relationship between supply and demand is more favorable to them. That is what usually happens when there is a surplus of a manufactured commodity. But farmers were reluctant to leave their occupation. Unless a farmer actually abandoned his work, no action of his own could affect prices, whereas a large manufacturer might raise the price of his commodity by cutting production. Many farmers during this period of stress migrated to the cities, but not nearly as many as the low economic state of agriculture would have seemed to warrant.

Most farmers refused to act upon the danger signals of falling prices and instead sought ways that would enable them to stay on the land. As a result, during the last 30 years of the nineteenth century, farmers held meetings, issued protests, and formed organizations, even though previously they had always been distrustful of organization or collective action. But the falling prices brought about by the Economic Revolution threatened the farmer as nothing had before: organization seemed capable of meeting the danger.

There were two broad explanations for the decline of the farmers' income. One was overproduction. The other was a group of reasons that included high costs of credit, transportation, and farm equipment; and a shortage of currency leading to lower prices. The farmers based their protests almost entirely upon the second explanation and largely ignored the effects of overproduction. Yet subsequent history suggests that overproduction was in fact the principal cause for farm distress. The only times that farm income in the United States has risen significantly have been either when demand expanded, as in the first decade of the twentieth century, or when supply was cut by governmental action, as under the New Deal. Although there was some validity in the accusations of high interest rates and excessive transportation costs, these factors were not enough to account for the fall in the farmers' income at the end of the nineteenth century. Furthermore, recent research into the level of farm mortgage rates in the plains states suggests that interest rates were not excessive, considering the high risks to the lenders.

Since few farmers would admit that their own prodigious production lay at the root of their troubles, they emphasized the disadvantages that an independent producer faced in an age of large enterprise. They quickly grasped that in the marketplace the individual farmer was no match for the railroad companies, grain elevator operators, and agricultural machinery manufacturers, who were backed by vast resources and sometimes enjoyed a virtual monopoly. Consequently, in the last 30 years of the nineteenth century, the farmers concentrated not on limiting or controlling their production, which was probably beyond their power anyway, but on controlling and regulating the great business enterprises.

Short of curtailing production, there were only two ways in which the farmer could meet the problem of falling income. One was to try to raise the prices he received for his goods; the other was to cut his own costs of production in an effort to offset the fall in prices. Between 1870 and 1900, a variety of organizations were formed among farmers for achieving one or both of these goals.

THE GRANGE MOVEMENT

The earliest of the principal farmers' organizations was the Patrons of Husbandry, founded in 1867 by Oliver H. Kelley. In the beginning, the Grange, as this organization was popularly known, concentrated on educating farmers in better methods of cultivation. But inasmuch as such efforts to cut costs proved inadequate to meet the steady fall in farm income, the Grange in the early 1870's (with membership at a peak of 500,000) turned to other solutions. In order to reduce the costs of farm machinery, insurance premiums, interest on loans, and other items required by farmers, the Grangers formed cooperatives to supply these needs. None of the cooperative and other efforts proved very successful, but the talk and agitation aroused by the Grange meetings led to other activities by farmers, some of which, like political activity, the Grange would never officially sanction.

3

The Great Crash*

The Progressive Era in the first two decades of the twentieth century brought with it regulation of the economy. Laissez-faire economics was replaced by government regulation. During World War I business prospered, and after the war the Progressive Age abated. The 1920s ushered in an age of speculation in an atmosphere of general wartime prosperity.

The boom of the 1920s ended with the bust of 1929. By the end of the 1920s certain basic economic flaws began to show, but they

*Source: *New York Times,* June 16, 1931.

remained uncorrected. When the Great Depression deepened people turned to President Herbert Hoover, who believed that the depression would run its course, as earlier depressions had. In this reading he talks of economic reconstruction.

Questions

1. What was Hoover's plan for economic reconstruction?
2. Was it really a plan?
3. Was it realistic in view of what was happening?

We have many citizens insisting that we produce an advance 'plan' for the future development of the United States. They demand that we produce it right now. I presume the 'plan' idea is an infection from the slogan of the 'five-year-plan' through which Russia is struggling to redeem herself from the ten years of starvation and misery.

I am able to propose an American plan to you. We plan to take care of twenty million increase in population in the next twenty years. We plan to build for them four million new and better homes, thousands of new and still more beautiful city buildings, thousands of factories; to increase the capacity of our railways; to add thousands of miles of highways and waterways; to install twenty-five million electrical horsepower; to grow twenty per cent more farm products. We plan to provide new parks, schools, colleges, and churches for this twenty million people. We plan more leisure for men and women and better opportunities for its enjoyment.

We not only plan to provide for all the new generation, but we shall, by scientific research and invention, lift the standard of living and security of life to the whole people. We plan to secure a greater diffusion of wealth, a decrease in poverty and a great reduction in crime. And this plan will be carried out if we just keep on giving the American people a chance. Its impulsive force is in the character and spirit of our people. They have already done a better job for one hundred and twenty million people than any other nation in all history.

Some groups believe this plan can only be carried out by a fundamental, a revolutionary, change of method. Other groups believe that any system must be the outgrowth of the character of our race, a natural outgrowth of our traditions; that we have established certain ideals, over one hundred and fifty years, upon which we must build rather than destroy.

If we analyze the ideas which have been put forward for handling our great national plan, they fall into two groups. The first is whether we shall go on with our American system, which holds that the major purpose of a state is to protect the people and to give them equality of opportunity; that the basis of all happiness is in development of the individual, that the sum of progress can only be gauged by the progress of the individual, that we should steadily build up cooperation among the people themselves to these ends.

The other idea is that we shall, directly or indirectly, regiment the population into a bureaucracy to serve the state, that we should use force instead of cooperation in plans and thereby direct every man as to what he may or may not do.

These ideas present themselves in practical questions which we have to meet. Shall we abandon the philosophy and creed of our people for one hundred and fifty years by turning to a creed foreign to our people? Shall we establish a dole from the Federal Treasury? Shall we undertake federal ownership and operation of public utilities instead of the rigorous regulation of them to prevent imposition? Shall we protect our people from the lower standards of living of foreign countries? Shall the Government, except in temporary national emergencies, enter upon business processes in competition with its citizens? Shall we regiment our people by an extension of the arm of bureaucracy into a multitude of affairs?

Our immediate and paramount task as a people is to rout the forces of economic disruption and pessimism that have swept upon us.

The exacting duty of Government in these times is by use of its agencies and its influence to strengthen our economic institutions; by inspiring cooperation in the community to sustain good-will and to keep our country free of disorder and conflict; by cooperation with the people to assure that the deserving shall not suffer; and by the conduct of government to strengthen the foundations of a better and stronger national life. These have been the objectives of my administration in dealing with this the greatest crisis the world has ever known. I shall adhere to them.

4

The Nixon Freeze*

With the sweeping victory of Franklin Delano Roosevelt in 1932, the nation was ready for a "New Deal." What the New Deal meant in 1932 was not completely clear even to Roosevelt, but he knew that the federal government must have a greater responsibility for the nation's economic welfare and for the security of individual citizens. The economic cycle had to be watched, and even influenced and controlled. Most of Roosevelt's advisers agreed with his philosophy and believed that real economic recovery depended on effective centralized planning. Under Presidents John Kennedy and Lyndon Johnson government's involvement in the economy continued. Johnson in particular, with his plans for a Great Society, greatly increased the role of government. Kennedy, Johnson, and Nixon were all very worried by the possibility of a recession. Nixon, acting under the authority of the Economic Stabilization Act of 1970, issued a wage-price freeze in 1971 that introduced a new phase of government control. Franklin Roosevelt had used a measure like this with the National Industrial Recovery Act, but Nixon had gone a little further. In 1970 eight Republican members of the Joint Economic Committee issued their opposition to a price-wage freeze.

Questions

1. When did the government issue limitations before Nixon acted?
2. Were they successful?
3. What is the danger of ceilings on wages?
4. What *can* the administration do to stop runaway inflation?

From the Minority Views filed with the report of the Committee on the January 1970 Economic Report of the President, signed by the eight Republican Members of

*Source: *Congressional Digest,* Vol. 49, No. 10 (October 1970), pp. 6ff.

the 20-Member Joint Senate-House Committee. The Majority Report did not address itself in detail to the subject of wage and price controls.

"During the Joint Economic Committee's hearings on the President's economic report, it was suggested at several points that wage and price controls should be imposed in the year ahead. The most frequently mentioned proposal was a total wage and price freeze for at least 6 months.

"The Federal Government has found it necessary to impose general wage and price controls during only two critical periods in this Nation's history. The first was during World War II, a period of total national mobilization and defense demands on the domestic economy amounting to about half of GNP. The second period and the one more comparable to the present situation, was during the Korean war. We believe a recounting of that period of control would be valuable at the present time.

"The United States entered the Korean conflict in June 1950, and between that month and March 1951 the natural economic recovery from the 1948–49 recession, coupled with 'scare' buying in anticipation of wartime controls and shortages, forced wholesale prices up at an annual rate of 20 per cent and consumer prices at an annual rate of nearly 11 per cent. The economy's production was pushed toward its limits as manufacturing capacity utilization rose from 80 per cent to 96 per cent in the space of a year.

"Unlike the recent experience, immediate action was taken to make fiscal policy appropriately restrictive. Individual income taxes were raised twice, corporate income taxes three times and an excess profits tax imposed, all in slightly over a year. The entire Federal budget on a consolidated cash basis turned from a $2.2 billion deficit in fiscal 1950 to a $7.6 billion surplus in fiscal 1951. Monetary policy as well was tightened. The Federal Reserve raised reserve requirements twice in 1951, and the discount rate twice. The rate of growth of the money supply fell steadily from 5 per cent in 1951 to 1.6 per cent in 1953.

"In August 1950, Congress passed the Defense Production Act giving the President the power to impose direct controls on wages and prices, and in January 1951, the President activated these measures, which lasted until decontrol in March 1953. The price controls appear at first glance to have been quite effective. The wholesale price index actually fell during the 2 years of controls, while the consumer price index only registered a 4.6 per cent increase over the 2-year period. The success on the wage front was much less dramatic. Average hourly earnings rose 20 per cent from 1950 to 1953, and the rise in unit labor costs for the private nonfarm sector actually accelerated in 1951 after a decline over the previous 2 years.

"Although we cannot say with certainty, it is doubtful whether the price controls were responsible for restraining inflation. The prices of many commodities never really tested the ceilings. It has been noted that the wholesale price index actually fell during the control period, a result that cannot be laid to the ceilings. And the fact that, when controls were lifted in March 1953, there was nothing like the general price explosion that followed the lapsing of wartime controls after World War II would further indicate that little if any price inflation was suppressed by direct control.

"It seems much more reasonable to conclude that the restraint on demand exerted by substantial fiscal and monetary measures early in the war was the potent force. Aggregate demand was successfully restrained before inflation could really grow and take hold.

"The most that can be said for direct controls on wages and prices is that they treat the symptoms of inflation. Much of their appeal rests on their directness and apparent simplicity: if prices and wages are rising the best way to stop them is by direct regulation. Direct controls surely do not go to the cause of general inflation, whether it be excessive aggregate money demand relative to real supply or cost push pressures. If inflationary pressures are real, price controls only conceal or temporarily postpone inflation, but do not eliminate it. Instead of nominal price increases, inflation takes the form of declines in quality or the shift of transactions to black markets or the failure of industry to produce the kind and quality of goods the market demands.

"Ceilings on wages are also of limited effectiveness. They tend to produce evasions in the form of fictitious upgradings of workers, increases for particular groups to remove suddenly discovered 'inequities,' and the shift of demands for higher employees compensation from salaries and wages to other benefits: more paid holidays, longer vacations, higher pensions and sick benefits, rules promoting increased overtime and overtime rates.

"Price changes for goods and services have a legitimate role to play in our market economy. The free, competitive market is the most efficient allocator of resources that one could devise. Many Government programs, such as antitrust policies and the wage-price guidelines as originally formulated, are attempts to induce sectors which are not freely competitive to function in a competitive manner.

"The structure of relative prices and wages prevailing when controls are imposed may be optimum for that point in time, but frequent shifts in demand on the part of business, consumers, or Government can rapidly make that structure obsolete. If, because of direct controls, *relative* prices cannot shift to the new pattern of demand as they do in a market economy, there will certainly be shortages of some goods and services. In the normal market situation, prices of goods with increased demand would rise, signaling that more labor and capital resources should be devoted to their production. When relative prices cannot shift in this manner, producers have no indication they should shift resources from production of one good to another, nor any incentive to do so.

"In practice, there can be no such thing as an absolute wage and price 'freeze.' Exceptions have always been made, and should be made, for individual firms, workers, industries or sectors which, by some criterion or another, deserve special treatment. By the end of September 1951, 63 special regulations had been issued to relieve particular manufacturers and retailers during price control in the Korean war. And in August of that year, cost-of-living adjustments were authorized for all workers. The distortions in the economy caused by the exceptions bore heaviest on those who were not able to obtain relief, and the resulting inequities contributed nothing to economic stability.

"There are other inequities and rigidities inherent in the control system. For example, how fairly can wage controls treat workers who have succeeded in obtaining multiyear wage contracts with successive increases built in? And how can a price administrator determine the 'right' price for a new product? Certainly, the slow and laborious process of form-filing and documentation must discourage real invention and innovation. And what about those industries where productivity increases relatively faster than in others and are thus relatively unconstrained?

"Perhaps the greatest damage that direct controls do is hinder economic freedom. In a time when it is generally agreed that the flow of power over the last decade should be redirected from the national Government to the people, direct controls on wage and price decisions are particularly abhorrent. And just as we have found that there is no such thing as just a little inflation, wage and price controls beget further controls designed to make the inherently ineffective first round of controls work. And if controls appear to be restraining inflation, the cry will arise that they cannot be removed for fear of unleashing runaway prices and wages.

"We strongly oppose the imposition of wage and price controls to fight the current inflation. They are ineffective at best, and at worst distort the allocation of resources, penalize those with limited access to the market and breed contempt for Government and the observance of its laws. Our market economy has shown itself to be a powerful engine of economic progress and the shackles that wage and price controls would place on it during this critical period would seriously jeopardize our nation's economic advance.

"While rejecting wage and price controls in the present environment we do not necessarily rule out moral suasion by Government leaders. Nor do we reject the productivity standard embodied in the wage-price guideposts as originally formulated. We have always believed this standard could be a useful *guide* to wage and price behavior in markets where substantial monopoly power exists. What we have strongly objected to is the arbitrary and unfair manner in which they were imposed during the Johnson Administration.

"While rejecting the Johnson Administration guidepost policy, we do believe that this Administration has a responsibility to use its considerable powers of moral suasion and its ability to focus national attention on particular wage and price decisions to help stabilize the economy. The Administration has devoted considerable effort to several areas where price or wage pressures have seemed to be particularly excessive, notably the lumber, construction, and copper industries.

"We applaud these efforts to determine the causes of excessive cost pressures in these industries and to find agreeable alternatives. We are encouraged to hear from Secretary of Labor Schultz, 'The Administration is now considering proposals for establishing such evaluative and analytical capabilities on a more formal basis, not with the intention of intervening in the wage and price decisions of the market but to provide information on what underlies these decisions.' We believe this effort should be expanded to include all bottleneck industries and sectors where unusual monopoly power exists in business or labor.

"We recommend that the Administration immediately announce the inflationary implications of unusually significant wage and price decisions. The Council of Economic Advisers should calculate and make public how much each price increase adds to the wholesale or consumer price index, and indicate other prices which would be adversely affected by such an increase. It should publish specific arguments why a particular industry feels it necessary to raise its prices, and suggest Government studies of situations where particular bottlenecks or unusual supply and demand conditions exist.

"Similarly, on the wage front, the Council should publish the price implications of unusual collective bargaining agreements, including the timing of the wage increases under different assumptions, the productivity experience of workers in the industry, the industry's profit situation and whether industry officials feel the increases will necessitate price increases."

Thought Questions

1. Compare and contrast Hamilton's and Hoover's ideas of the role of government in the economy.
2. Is the Nixon Freeze consistent with the ideas of Alexander Hamilton on economics?
3. How has economic policy evolved since the colonial period?

eight

THE AMERICAN PRESIDENCY:
Personalities and Policies

The presidents have always had great influence on American society —both negatively and positively. The direction of American society has often been controlled by the one man who is the commander-in-chief and leader of domestic policies. But as times have changed so have the personalities and circumstances surrounding the presidency.

George Washington literally launched the American government, establishing many traditions that we still follow. By comparison John Adams was a less colorful and forceful president than Washington. Thomas Jefferson tried to bring democracy to the office, but found that the office frequently inhibits practice of one's beliefs. From the early 1800s to the Civil War Andrew Jackson stands out as one of the more noticeably energetic presidents even though his Indian policy is much criticized and his bank war led to a national depression. His image is almost more important than his accomplishments.

Abraham Lincoln is so shrouded in myth that it is hard to discern the real person. But he is considered by many to be the greatest president. From Lincoln to the twentieth century, the presidents are not very notable, probably because their accomplishments are not either. The names Theodore Roosevelt, Woodrow Wilson, Franklin Delano Roosevelt, and possibly Richard Nixon stand out, for one reason or another. Roosevelt and Wilson carried their brand of progressivism to new heights, while Franklin Roosevelt introduced his New Deal and made it national policy. Since World War II some presidents such as Harry Truman have been extremely strong in foreign affairs, while Lyndon Johnson accomplished much in domestic affairs. Richard Nixon ended the Vietnam War and changed both the direction and intent of domestic and foreign policy. All have done their part in adding to the color, reputation, and tradition of the presidency, as well as to America's place in the world.

I

The Myth of George Washington*

George Washington was elected president by Congress. He was neither a great politician nor an extrovert, but he was a good administrator able to get the government off to a good start. Domestically he helped solve the problems of civil liberties, finance, and the court system; in foreign affairs he avoided wars. It is true to say that he was sincere and honest, but with the scarcity of true information it is hard to say much more. Here historian Marcus Cunliffe describes one set of myths—Washington the copybook hero.

Questions

1. What does Cunliffe mean by "the copybook hero"?
2. What was the legend Weems perpetuated?
3. Because of these writers, what did Washington become?
4. Is it wrong to believe in Washington the legend?

Washington's life lay completely within the eighteenth century, though only just. But Washington as he has descended to us is largely a creation of the nineteenth-century English-speaking world, with its bustling, didactic, evangelical emphasis. This is the world of tracts and primers, of Chambers's *Miscellanies* and McGuffey's *Readers,* of Samuel Smiles and Horatio Alger, of mechanics' institutes and lyceum lectures, of autograph albums and gift annuals. Bazaars and bridges are opened, foundation stones laid, prizes and certificates distributed, drunkards admonished and rescued, slaves emancipated. It is, in the convenient term of David Riesman, the age of the "inner-directed" personality whose essential attributes are summed up in the titles

*Source: From *George Washington: Man and Monument* by Marcus Cunliffe. Copyright © 1958 by Marcus Cunliffe. Reprinted by arrangement with The New American Library, Inc., New York, New York.

of Smiles's various works—*Self-Help, Thrift, Duty, Character*—or in a short poem of Emerson's that is also called "Character."

> The stars set, but set not his hope:
> Stars rose; his faith was earlier up:
> Fixed on the enormous galaxy
> Deeper and older seemed his eye;
> And matched his sufferance sublime
> The taciturnity of time . . .

Character is the key word in the copybook view of George Washington, as we have already seen in the statement linking him with Shakespeare.[1] Lord Brougham is of the same opinion: "The test of the progress of mankind will be their appreciation of the character of Washington."

The enterprising Parson Weems, a Victorian before the Victorian era, was the first to fit Washington into what was to become the pattern of the century. His aim in writing a pamphlet biography of Washington was, Weems explained to a publisher in 1800, to bring out "his Great Virtues. 1 His Veneration for the Diety [*sic*], or Religious Principles. 2 His Patriotism. 3ᵈ His Magninimity [*sic*]. 4 his Industry. 5 his Temperance and Sobriety. 6. his Justice, &ᶜ &ᶜ." Here is the copybook canon. Weems was not quite as highminded as this statement might suggest, though there is no reason to doubt that he shared the general American veneration for Washington. As he told the same publisher, his proposal could win them "pence and popularity." At any rate, he did not hesitate to fabricate incidents, or to style himself "Rector" of the nonexistent parish of Mount Vernon. His pamphlet grew into a book, embodying stage by stage the famous false Weemsian anecdotes: Washington chopping down the cherry tree *("I can't tell a lie, Pa; you know I can't tell a lie. I did cut it with my hatchet."—Run to my arms, you dearest boy, cried his father in transports);* Washington upbraiding his schoolmates for fighting—an episode that gradually disappeared from the record, since later generations found it priggish *("You shall never, boys, have my consent to a practice so shocking! shocking even in slaves and dogs; then how utterly scandalous in little boys at school, who ought to look on one another as brothers");* young Washington throwing a stone across the Rappahannock *(It would be no easy matter to find a man, now-a-days, who could do it);* Washington's providential escape at Braddock's defeat *(A famous Indian warrior, who acted a leading part in that bloody tragedy, was often heard to swear, that "Washington was not born to be killed by a bullet! For . . . I had seventeen fair fires at him with my rifle, and after all could not bring him to the ground!");* Washington discovered—by a Quaker "of the respect-

---

[1] It is emphasized in 1843 by Daniel Webster, in an oration at Bunker Hill. America, he says, owes a considerable debt to the Old World. She has repaid it in large part by furnishing "to the world the character of Washington! And if our American institutions had done nothing else, that alone would have entitled them to the respect of mankind."

able family and name of Potts, if I mistake not"—praying at Valley Forge *(As he approached the spot . . . whom should be behold . . . but the commander in chief of the American armies on his knees at prayer!)*; and so on.

All through the book, as unremittingly as Horatio Alger was to thump home the message, Weems showed how "duty and advantage" went together. Thus, kindness to his elder brother brought George the Mount Vernon estate when his brother died childless save for one ailing infant; and exemplary conduct subsequently won him the hand of the widow Custis, whose "*wealth* was equal, at least, to one hundred thousand dollars!" The homily was irresistible; by 1825 Weems's biography had gone through forty editions, and forty more were to appear in due course. The cherry-tree story—eventually incorporated in McGuffey's highly popular *Readers*—became a special favorite in copybook lore. Invention was even added to invention in Morrison Heady's little life of Washington, *The Farmer Boy, and How He Became Commander-in-Chief* (1863). Heady describes how a Negro boy was blamed for cutting down the tree, and how young George saved him from a flogging by confession to the crime. Indeed, in the secular hagiology of the period—the equivalent of Saint Lawrence with his gridiron, or Saint Catherine with her wheel—Washington and the tree joined the company of Newton and William Tell with their respective apples, Watt with his kettle, Bruce with his spider, Columbus with his egg, King Alfred with his cakes, Philip Sidney with his water bottle.

But Washington's whole career was pressed into service, not merely one episode. The expense accounts that he kept during the Revolutionary War were printed in facsimile, as proof of his patriotic frugality and business efficiency. His religious opinions were recast, by Weems and others, into the nineteenth-century mold. One tale has it that he left the Anglican Church for Presbyterianism. According to another fable, he secretly joined the Baptists. It is unnecessary to emphasize that all such notions, whether they originated in the fertile mind of Weems or elsewhere, were untrue in detail and unhistorical in a larger way. Weems and his successors were not concerned with what they would have thought of as scholastic pedantry. Their object, quite deliberately, was to point a moral and adorn a tale. They agreed with the words of Henry Lee, in praise of Weems (and quoted on Weems's title page): "No biographer deserves more applause than he whose chief purpose is to entice the young mind to the affectionate love of virtue, by personifying it in the character most dear to these states." Or, as Horatio Hastings Weld said in his *Pictorial Life of George Washington* (1845): "The first word of infancy should be mother, the second father, the third WASHINGTON." We may feel that Weems and the rest of the copybook moralizers must share some of the blame for blurring our image of Washington. In their defense, however, we should add that they did not mean to turn Washington into a plaster saint. They were well aware of this tendency. "In most of the elegant orations pronounced to his praise," wrote Weems, "you see nothing of Washington below *the clouds* . . . 'tis only Washington the HERO, and the Demigod . . . Washington the *sun beam* in council, or the *storm* in war." Weems wanted to humanize him, as well as present him as a copybook character. Certainly there is not much of the marmoreal in Weems's racy narrative; with its aid, he managed to impose his apocryphal Washington on a whole nation for a whole century. Weems would no doubt claim that he could not have done so if people had not wished to believe that this was the truth. Washington's family motto was *Exitus acta probat;* to suit himself and vindicate his fictions, Weems might mistranslate this as "The end justifies the means." At any rate, what he depicted was Washington as the man without faults, and with all the nineteenth-century virtues, from courage to punctuality, from modesty to thrift —and all within human compass, and all crowned by success.

2

Abraham Lincoln: The Myth and the Man*

Abraham Lincoln's election in 1860 caused several southern states to secede from the Union and led to the Civil War. Because there has been so much written on Lincoln there is more mythology and legend surrounding him than anyone else. The fact is that he was a wartime president who led the North to victory. His leadership during the war and his plans for reconstruction help to make him one of the important presidents. In this reading historian David Donald considers Lincoln a folk hero.

Questions

1. What are the major characteristics of Lincoln the folk hero?
2. How can one tell truth from reality in regard to Lincoln the hero?
3. Why has Lincoln been made a legend?

Lincoln was saved from this kind of deification by a different stream of tradition, frequently Western in origin and more truly folkloristic in quality. The grotesque hero—the Gargantua or the Till Eulenspiegel—is one of the oldest and most familiar patterns in folk literature. In America the type had been already exemplified by such favorites as Davy Crockett, Mike Fink, and Paul Bunyan. Of a like cut was the myth of Lincoln as frontier hero. This Lincoln of "folk say" was the practical joker, the teller of tall and lusty tales. Stupendously strong, he was also marvelously lazy. A true romantic, he pined over the grave of Ann Rutledge, but he also lampooned one woman who refused him and jilted another who accepted. He was Old Abe, a Westerner, and his long flapping arms were not the wings of an angel.

This folk pattern of Lincoln as frontier hero had been sketched in outline before his death. After his assassination the details were filled in. Many of the stories in the strong Western tradition can be traced back to Herndon, Lincoln's law partner, who has been called the "master myth-maker" of Lincoln folklore. Herndon did not invent the legends, but his singular personality made him peculiarly receptive to this type of Western mythology. Herndon was born in Kentucky, and, as an early German traveler put it, "the Kentuckian is a peculiar man." Moody, erratic, loquacious, addicted to high-flown "philosophical" language, but with a fondness for earthy stories, Herndon had shortly after his partner's death decided to write a biography of Lincoln. From the very outset he had in mind showing Lincoln as a Western character, shaped by the "power of mud, flowers, & mind" which he had encountered in the pioneer Northwest. Deliberately he sought to emphasize those factors which would distinguish Lincoln as a Westerner from his Eastern contemporaries. He proposed to exhibit "the type" of the "original western and south-western pioneer— . . . at times . . . somewhat open, candid, sincere, energetic, spontaneous, trusting, tolerant, brave and generous."

Seeking information about Lincoln, Herndon interviewed older settlers in central Illinois and southern Indiana at just the time when the outlines of the folk portrait were becoming firmly established. From his notes emerged the essentially fictitious picture of a semilegendary frontier hero. The stories Herndon collected fall into patterns familiar to the student of American folklore. Some remembered Lincoln as a ring-tailed roarer of the Davy Crockett type, who would wave a whisky bottle over his head to drive back his foes, shouting that "he was the big buck at the lick." There were tales of the Paul Bunyan variety, describing how Lincoln would "frequently take a barrel of whiskey by the chimes and lift it up to his face as if to drink out of bunghole," a feat that "he could accomplish with greatest ease."

This was the Lincoln who chastely wooed Ann Rutledge and, when she died, pined sadly over her grave. "My heart," he was supposed to have said, "lies buried there." More in the frontier tradition was his courtship of Mary Owens, a well-educated Kentucky lady who refused his hand. Afterward Lincoln described her as "weather-beaten," "oversize," and lacking teeth. Of a like pattern were the tales Herndon accumulated of Lincoln's domestic unhappiness with Mary Todd, for the henpecked husband is one of the oldest comic types and was a favorite in the Western joke books of the day. Herndon also collected irreligious or, as he called them, "infidel" statements attributed to Lincoln; the folk hero is frequently anticlerical.

Many of these tales probably had a grain of historical truth, and their evolution exhibits the familiar developments of folk literature. "If a man has been well known for special powers," Robert Price has pointed out in his examination of the Johnny Appleseed traditions, "folk fancies soon seize upon particular instances of these powers, begin to enhance them into facts of remarkable quality, and then proceed, as the desire for greater color grows, to invent still others that will markedly emphasize the quality admired." As the historical personage becomes absorbed in the myth, "the whole cycle of his birth, youth, education, loves, mating, maturity, and death becomes significant and grows increasingly in color and particular detail." On a rather sophisticated plane, the Lincoln of Western legend represented a true folk-hero type.

The folkloristic quality of these stories is sometimes overlooked. When Herndon visited in Indiana, he was told of verses that Lincoln had written to celebrate the wedding of his sister:

> When Adam was created
> He dwelt in Eden's shade,
> As Moses has recorded,
> And soon a bride was made.

(The poem continues for seven additional stanzas.) Dr. Milo M. Quaife has traced this ballad back to early English folk verse and has shown that it was introduced into America before the Revolutionary War. In the process of being handed down, it somehow became identified in the minds of backwoods Hoosiers with Lincoln; it was related to Herndon as such; he published the verses in his Lincoln biography; and the poem is not infrequently cited as Lincoln's original composition. Of the making of myths there is no end.

The process of evolving Western legends about Lincoln neither began nor ended with Herndon. Gossip, imagination, delayed recollection, and hearsay have all continued to multiply "Lincoln" stories. Sometimes the results of this accumulation of "folk say" are amusing. One can take, for example, a less familiar episode in Lincoln's early career—his projected duel with James Shields. The actual facts of the affair are easily ascertained. In 1842 Mary Todd and Julia Jayne published anonymously in the *Sangamo Journal* some satirical verses about Shields, then Illinois state auditor. That hot-tempered Irishman demanded of the editor the names of the writers, and Lincoln, to protect the ladies, offered to take the blame. After some stilted correspondence and much dashing back and forth of seconds, a duel with broadswords was arranged. Ultimately, however, explanations and apologies were made, and actual combat was averted. The affair remained a sore memory to Lincoln, and he disliked hearing the episode referred to. The whole affair is summarized in any good Lincoln biography.

As this same tale comes down in folklore, the whole emphasis is altered. It becomes an illustration of Lincoln the humorist and the practical joker. The duel had an amusing origin, according to one old settler who had heard another old-timer tell the story:

> Lawyer Shields and Julia Jayne were seated together at the supper table. Across the table from them sat Abe and Mary Todd. By and by the lawyer squeezed Julia's hand. In those days, you know, a pin was a woman's weapon. Julia used it when Shields squeezed her hand. And that made him scream. . . . Lincoln, who was a laughing fellow, hawhawed right out loud, much to the embarrassment of Shields. Well to make a long story short, Shield[s] issued a duel challenge to Abe.

Another version gives a play-by-play account of the duel that never happened. "Shields fired and missed," says this "eyewitness," speaking of an encounter that was to have been fought with broadswords. "Lincoln then took steady aim and fired. A blotch of read [*sic*] appeared on the breast of Shields who fell to the ground thinking he was mortally wounded, but in fact was unhurt. Lincoln's gun was loaded with pokeberries."

To treat such statements simply as exaggerated reminiscences is to miss their significance. They are really folk stories. Seldom do they have an identifiable author, for the narrator is recounting what "they said." The very pattern of the statement is significant; "to make a long story short" is a frequent formula to conclude a folk tale. The Shields episode is only one less widely known incident about which a surprisingly large amount of folklore has accumulated. The body of tradition concerning Lincoln's courtship, his marriage, or his law practice is much more voluminous. And there is an extensive cycle of ribald and Rabelaisian stories attributed to Lincoln, for the most part unprintable and now almost forgotten.

3

FDR and the New Deal*

The presidents of the late 1800s presided over an age dominated by business and frequently reflected the interest of politics in business. Although presidents like Grover Cleveland and Chester Arthur have been largely forgotten today, Grover Cleveland was actually considered one of the best presidents of the late 1800s. He attempted to change the direction of government and remove politics from the hands of business. He even felt that the public office was a public trust and tried to give it some prestige. With the twentieth century a change in government impetus began. During the terms of Roosevelt, William Howard Taft, and Woodrow Wilson, an era of Progressivism made government the guardian of individual American welfare. This era, however, seemed to abate with the golden days of the 1920s.

The Jazz Age of the 1920s seemed to run itself without a president. Harding died in office; Coolidge was reelected on the slogan of Keep Cool with Coolidge; but Hoover was faced with a national depression. Hoover was the most capable administrator of the three, but his rugged individualism philosophy could not deal with a fierce urban depression. His defeat in 1932 was not much of a surprise to many Americans who voted for a change. Roosevelt, with his New Deal, brought that change. The New Deal stabilized the depression and brought about some of the most revolutionary changes in government since the adoption of the Constitution. Here is Roosevelt's famous first inaugural address.

Questions

1. What problems does Roosevelt address himself to?
2. How is he trying to instill a sense of security in the people?

*Source: *Inaugural Addresses,* (Washington, D.C.: Government Printing Office, 1933), pp. 235–39.

3. What were the problems in world affairs?
4. What was his philosophy of government?
5. Was he really promising a New Deal?

I am certain that my fellow Americans expect that on my induction into the Presidency I will address them with a candor and a decision which the present situation of our Nation impels. This is preeminently the time to speak the truth, the whole truth, frankly and boldly. Nor need we shrink from honestly facing conditions in our country to-day. This great Nation will endure as it has endured, will revive and will prosper. So, first of all, let me assert my firm belief that the only thing we have to fear is fear itself— nameless, unreasoning, unjustified terror which paralyzes needed efforts to convert retreat into advance. In every dark hour of our national life a leadership of frankness and vigor has met with that understanding and support of the people themselves which is essential to victory. I am convinced that you will again give that support to leadership in these critical days.

In such a spirit on my part and on yours we face our common difficulties. They concern, thank God, only material things. Values have shrunken to fantastic levels; taxes have risen; our ability to pay has fallen; government of all kinds is faced by serious curtailment of income; the means of exchange are frozen in the currents of trade; the withered leaves of industrial enterprise lie on every side; farmers find no markets for their produce; the savings of many years in thousands of families are gone.

More important, a host of unemployed citizens face the grim problem of existence, and an equally great number toil with little return. Only a foolish optimist can deny the dark realities of the moment.

Yet our distress comes from no failure of substance. We are stricken by no plague of locusts. Compared with the perils which our forefathers conquered because they believed and were not afraid, we have still much to be thankful for. Nature still offers her bounty and human efforts have multiplied it. Plenty is at our doorstep, but a generous use of it languishes in the very sight of the supply. Primarily this is because the rulers of the exchange of mankind's goods have failed, through their own stubbornness and their own incompetence, have admitted their failure, and abdicated. Practices of the unscrupulous money changers stand indicted in the court of public opinion, rejected by the hearts and minds of men.

True they have tried, but their efforts have been cast in the pattern of an outworn tradition. Faced by failure of credit they have proposed only the lending of more money. Stripped of the lure of profit by which to induce our people to follow their false leadership, they have resorted to exhortations, pleading tearfully for restored confidence. They know only the rules of a generation of self-seekers. They have no vision, and when there is no vision the people perish.

The money changers have fled from their high seats in the temple of our civilization. We may now restore that temple to the ancient truths. The measure of the restoration lies in the extent to which we apply social values more noble than mere monetary profit.

Happiness lies not in the mere possession of money; it lies in the joy of achievement, in the thrill of creative effort. The joy and moral stimulation of work no longer must be forgotten in the mad chase of evanescent profits. These dark days will be worth all they cost us if they teach us that our true destiny is not to be ministered unto but to minister to ourselves and to our fellow men.

Recognition of the falsity of material wealth as the standard of success goes hand in hand with the abandonment of the false belief that public office and high political position are to be valued only by the standards of pride of place and personal profit; and there must be an end to a conduct in banking and in business which too often has given to a sacred trust the likeness of callous and selfish wrongdoing. Small wonder that confidence languishes, for it thrives only on honesty, on honor, on the sacredness of obligations, on faithful protection, on unselfish performance; without them it can not live.

Restoration calls, however, not for changes in ethics alone. This Nation asks for action, and action now.

Our greatest primary task is to put people to work. This is no unsolvable problem if we face it wisely and courageously. It can be accomplished in part by direct recruiting by the Government itself, treating the task as we would treat the emergency of a war, but at the same time, through this employment, accomplishing greatly needed projects to stimulate and reorganize the use of our natural resources.

Hand in hand with this we must frankly recognize the overbalance of population in our industrial centers and, by engaging on a national scale in a redistribution, endeavor to provide a better use of the land for those best fitted for the land. The task can be helped by definite efforts to raise the values of agricultural products and with this the power to purchase the output of our cities. It can be helped by preventing realistically the tragedy of the growing loss through foreclosure of our small homes and our farms. It can be helped by insistence that the Federal, State, and local governments act forthwith on the demand that their cost be drastically reduced. It can be helped by the unifying of relief activities which to-day are often scattered, uneconomical, and unequal. It can be helped by national planning for and supervision of all forms of transportation and of communications and other utilities which have a definitely public character. There are many ways in which it can be helped, but it can never be helped merely by talking about it. We must act and act quickly.

Finally, in our progress toward a resumption of work we require two safeguards against a return of the evils of the old order; there must be a strict supervision of all banking and credits and investments; there must be an end to speculation with other people's money, and there must be provision for an adequate but sound currency.

There are the lines of attack. I shall presently urge upon a new Congress in special session detailed measures for their fulfillment, and I shall seek the immediate assistance of the several States.

Through this program of action we address ourselves to putting our own national house in order and making income balance outgo. Our international trade relations, though vastly important, are in point of time and necessity secondary to the establishment of a sound national economy. I favor as a practical policy the putting of first things first. I shall spare no effort to restore world trade by international economic readjustment, but the emergency at home can not wait on that accomplishment.

The basic thought that guides these specific means of national recovery is not narrowly nationalistic. It is the insistence, as a first consideration, upon the interdependence of the various elements in all parts of the United States —a recognition of the old and permanently important manifestation of the American spirit of the pioneer. It is the way to recovery. It is the immediate way. It is the strongest assurance the recovery will endure.

In the field of world policy I would dedicate this Nation to the policy of the good neighbor—the neighbor who resolutely respects himself and, because he does so, respects the rights of others—the neighbor who respects his obligations and respects the sanctity of his agreements in and with a world of neighbors.

If I read the temper of our people correctly, we now realize as we have never realized before our interdependence on each other; that we can not merely take but we must give as well; that if we are to go forward, we must move as a trained and loyal army willing to sacrifice for the good of a common discipline, because without such discipline no progress is made, no leadership becomes effective. We are, I know, ready and willing to submit our lives and property to such discipline, because it makes possible a leadership which aims at a larger good. This I propose to offer, pledging that the larger purposes will bind upon us all as a sacred obligation with a unity of duty hitherto evoked only in time of armed strife.

With this pledge taken, I assume unhesitatingly the leadership of this great army of our people dedicated to a disciplined attack upon our common problems.

Action in this image and to this end is feasible under the form of government which we have inherited from our ancestors. Our Constitution is so simple and practical that it is possible always to meet extraordinary needs by changes in emphasis and arrangement without loss of essential form. That is why our constitutional system has proved itself the most superbly enduring political mechanism the modern world has produced. It has met every stress of vast expansion of territory, of foreign wars, of bitter internal strife, of world relations.

It is to be hoped that the normal balance of executive and legislative authority may be wholly adequate to meet the unprecedented task before us. But it may be that an unprecedented demand and need for undelayed action may call for temporary departure from that normal balance of public procedure.

I am prepared under my constitutional duty to recommend the measures that a stricken nation in the midst of a stricken world may require. These measures, or such other measures as the Congress may build out of its experience and wisdom, I shall seek, within my constitutional authority, to bring to speedy adoption.

But in the event that the Congress shall fail to take one of these two courses, and in the event that the national emergency is still critical, I shall not evade the clear course of duty that will then confront me. I shall ask the Congress for the one remaining instrument to meet the crisis—broad Executive power to wage a war against the emergency, as great as the power that would be given to me if we were in fact invaded by a foreign foe.

For the trust reposed in me I will return the courage and the devotion that befit the time. I can do no less.

We face the arduous days that lie before us in the warm courage of the national unity; with the clear consciousness of seeking old and precious moral values; with the clean satisfaction that comes from the stern performance of duty by old and young alike. We aim at the assurance of a rounded and permanent national life.

We do not distrust the future of essential democracy. The people of the United States have not failed. In their need they have registered a mandate that they want direct, vigorous action. They have asked for discipline and direction under leadership. They have made me the present instrument of their wishes. In the spirit of the gift I take it.

In this dedication of a Nation we humbly ask the blessing of God. May He protect each and every one of us. May He guide me in the days to come.

4

Richard Nixon and the Future*

The election of Richard Nixon in 1968 again brought a change to the direction of American government. Nixon finally kept his promise to end the Vietnam War in 1973, and personally visited the People's Republic of China and the U.S.S.R. in hopes of changing the old containment policy. In domestic affairs he faced student demonstrations, rising food prices, and the Watergate hearings. Here in an interview with CBS News he comments on the presidency.

Questions

1. What changes does Nixon feel are taking place in society?
2. What does he see as the national mood?
3. What does he think of the future?

Television Interview for CBS Morning News, August 31, 1970

Question. Do you find it easier to concentrate here than in the East?

The President. It depends on what the subject is. I think the main advantage of a place like this and Camp David and Florida, all of which I use, is that moving from place to place changes the perspective, so that you aren't in a rut, you don't think in a way that is noncreative. Of course, that doesn't mean that if you are hemmed in, in one place, that it is impossible to create.

I have found that generally when I write a speech or something like that, I have to sit in one place, and usually this is not too pleasant. You get out—all this business that you write better when you are looking out at the ocean—

*Source: *Public Papers of the Presidency of Richard Nixon* (Washington, D.C.: Government Printing Office, 1971), pp. 691–94.

Q. That is not true?

The President. Not at all true. A beautiful place is a place to, well, to clear the mind, and there needs to be a pause in all the heavy concentration. But when it comes to making important decisions or it comes to writing something that has to be precise, there is no substitute for just sitting in a bare room—a reporter does it with a typewriter—and that is to sit and think and have no distraction. That is the way it affects me.

Q. You have your advisers here, you have your Cabinet members, you have your Counsellors here. I wonder if you feel you can get away here from that isolation booth that you were talking about yourself?

The President. It is particularly good for them, for one thing. I mean, staff people are terribly overburdened, Cabinet people and the rest. They, of course, more than I, have no control over their schedules. They have to go to the cocktail parties and dinners and so forth, and they move in the same circle; they talk to the same people.

Now, out here, of course, they tend to—but whether it is Kissinger or Ehrlichman or Haldeman or Finch or any of these people, when they come to California or Florida, they break out of that; they break out of the usual patterns.

Q. Are you able to break out and feel less isolated here, do you think?

The President. Yes, I do, because I know different people in different places. And, of course, when I am in a place like Camp David, then I break out because I am really by myself there. People are around and I can use them, but when you are sitting in an office—it is always a compulsion to be on the phone and have somebody in. In other words, you have got to have a schedule. That is particularly true when you are in Washington.

Q. I was just going to ask you a kind of a personal question. I am coming from Saigon, Cambodia, and other points east to move to Washington. What kind of advice would you have for a returning American coming back after 14 years, as to what to look for in the United States?

I am just wondering what would be your suggestions to somebody like myself as to what to watch for in the United States, as an amateur American coming back to one's own country?

The President. Well, I would by all means not spend too long a time in Washington. What your tendency will be is to come back and sit down in Washington and be surrounded by your friends in the media and, of course, the political world, and so forth. That will not give you a perspective that is really broad enough.

It is very important to get that perspective because they are the people who affect millions of others around the country. I would get on a plane or in an automobile and drive around the country and get some feel of it.

I think some of the reporters these days who are doing that are doing a lot for themselves and a lot for good reporting. Take a fellow like Dave Broder.[1] He has been moving around the country. He goes to places like Tennessee and Evansville and Oregon, as you know, and, writes his reports, and that has been a custom for a couple of others.

That is what I would do, if I were you. Don't just come to Washington and have whatever views you do have either completely changed or just driven in.

I think my conviction—and I base that not on any recent discovery, but after having been in Washington as a Congressman, as a Senator, and as a Vice President, and also having lived in New York for 6 years and in California—is that this is a very diverse country, which is all to the good, and it is very important to get around and circulate.

We tend to generalize about youth, generalize about the race problem, generalize about what people think of the political issues, in all respects, and many times the generalizations are correct. I think one of the reasons sometimes those who report the news may sometimes miss what the national mood is is that they are talking too much among themselves—and by that I mean people who think like them, who read the same things.

Q. What is the national mood now, do you think, Mr. President, going into this fall, this school year?

The President. I am unable to give an answer to that yet. I can answer it better within a month. One thing I know is that moods change in a very volatile way these days. That is another factor that is new in American politics because of television, instant news, instant appraisal of events; you will find that there is a very great change. A very great change may take place before you know it.

You take Gallup's polls which he prints from time to time on what is the number one issue. You will find that that changes dramatically almost month to month. Usually changes occur over a period of 3 or 4 years. That is the other thing. Don't ever assume that what you think today is the big issue is going to be the big issue tomorrow.

I constantly have to tell my staff, "Keep checking, checking with Congressmen, Senators, but also with people generally in the country."

Of course, that is one of the benefits you get from the mail. The mail's only usefulness is not the number but the moods, the changes that occur.

For example, naturally, the overriding interest in the war, the war in Southeast Asia, the possibilities of becoming involved in something in the Mideast, all of these are concerns that will always be number one or number two. In other words, the great issues are basically war and peace, the pocketbook and all of its ramifications—that is prices, taxes, Government spending, and the rest—and finally coming up very hard and fast and going up and down,

[1]David S. Broder, a reporter for the *Washington Post.*

depending upon what the latest news story is, is the whole issue related to order and justice—

Q. Civil disturbances?

The President. Civil disturbances, but in a much broader context, and I include in that the problem—let's put it this way: The problem of race, race problems, those are not new. First, we have them in very great degree because of the history in this country. But they are all over the world, and they are among races. You don't have to look at the United States; you can find them in Britain; you will find them in Southeast Asia.

Q. Within the same countries?

The President. Within the same countries and between various peoples. Race problems are not new and neither is the generation gap. That is not new.

What is the major concern today is how those problems will be handled, whether they will be handled in an orderly process, under our constitutional procedures, which we have usually recognized in the past should be the way, or whether people will resort to and whether society will generally accept, at least be resigned to, resorting to means outside the constitutional processes. This is the great issue of our time.

Q. What do you see in the future? Do you see a long period of civil disturbance, a long testing period?

The President. We are keeping our fingers crossed, but I think that it is not insignificant to note that, despite all the dire predictions, this summer has not been the hot summer that we had expected. It has been terribly hot from the standpoint of the weather, as you know. Yet, after the tragic experiences of 2 years ago, last summer and this summer have been less.

Q. I was thinking of the revolutionaries as much as anything.

The President. The revolutionaries is something else, because that is something which is a new and growing development in the United States and all over the world. Again, we have got to see this in terms not just of our own problems. That is why when we look at America's problems we say, "It is something we do." It may be. We may be contributing to it—our society.

But every foreign leader that I have talked to, in which there is supposed to be a free society, has the same problem. You have got it in the Philippines; you have it in Japan. You have got it, of course, in every industrial country of Eastern Europe and all over Latin America.

Q. In your visit throughout Southeast Asia last year, this is one of the things you discovered. You said, Mr. President, that two of the issues are the Middle East and the other being Southeast Asia, in the mail and in general response patterns that you feel about the United States. What are you saying in reply to those, for example, about the chances for something developing in the way of peace in Southeast Asia and the Middle East?

The President. There is nothing new to report in that respect, except that we are continuing our support of the ceasefire initiative in the Mideast, recognizing that it is fraught with difficulties on both sides. But, on the other

hand, when we consider that initiative, what we have to recognize is, as difficult as it is, look how much worse it would be if it had not been started.
Q. What about the chances of peace in Southeast Asia?
The President. As far as Southeast Asia is concerned, there again, we, of course, are waiting the beginning of some discussions in Paris with Xuan Thuy[2] returning.

Thought Questions

1. Compare and contrast the myths concerning Washington and Lincoln.
2. Compare and contrast the philosophies of government of Franklin D. Roosevelt and Richard Nixon.
3. How do the presidents view America?
4. How has the office of the presidency evolved from the time of Washington?

[2]Xuan Thuy was the chief North Vietnamese delegate at the Paris peace talks.

nine

AFRO-AMERICANS:
From Slaves to Black Panthers

The black experience in America has been long and often painful. Blacks accompanied the early Spanish to the New World and were the basis of the labor force throughout the colonial period. It is not known exactly whether those blacks that arrived in Jamestown, Virginia, in 1619 were servants or slaves, but it made little difference, for by the late 1600s the majority of blacks in America were slaves. Prior to the Revolution, blacks worked in both North and South. By 1800 slavery was gone from the North. It is believed that slavery would have died out in the South too if Eli Whitney had not invented a cotton gin that made slavery profitable on cotton plantations. From 1800 to 1860 the number of southern slaves grew to more than four million—four million people enslaved in a cruel labor system that submerged their humanity beneath the needs of property.

Slavery was no doubt an underlying factor in the coming of the Civil War. After the war the Thirteenth, Fourteenth, and Fifteenth Amendments made the slave free, but only legally. The North had no plans to transform the slave to citizen, and with the end of Reconstruction in 1877, blacks were left at the mercy of the South. The Ku Klux Klan, Jim Crow laws, voting restrictions, and increased violence kept Southern blacks in an inferior position. Even the courts helped to relegate blacks to second class status.

Black protest was born with the twentieth century. There were black protestors prior to the 1900s, but they were really voices crying alone in the wilderness. William E. B. DuBois, for example, was an intellectual who preached immediate political and social equality—but "immediate" did not come. World War I saw a great exodus of blacks from the South to the northern cities and the birth of northern ghettoes. Leaders such as Marcus Garvey tried to instill black pride into these urban dwellers, but found much apathy and resistance. During the 1920s and 1930s blacks were relatively quiet; they were suffering more from the Great Depression than most Americans.

With World War II conditions changed; President Truman encouraged equal treatment for blacks in the armed forces. And the blacks themselves were on the move. The Montgomery Bus Boycott began the Civil Rights Movement in 1955. It had gained a great deal of impetus from the 1954 desegregation decision, but now movement leaders such as Martin Luther King, Jr., were talking of mass demonstrations and nonviolent protest. New organizations formed, such as the Student Nonviolent Coordinating Committee, to give new answers to black questions. Eventually more radical groups such as the Black Muslims and Black Panthers were born. But quick changes without solutions to problems caused trouble. The summer race riots of the 1960s used violence to instigate social change, sadly often accomplishing faster results, and more official wrath, than passive resistance and mass protest.

By the late 1960s a black consciousness movement was making the white world more and more aware of blacks. Still many problems remained. What the future holds for social and political equality for everyone is very difficult to tell.

I

The Slave Experience*

The slaves brought to the North and South formed the basis of the country's labor system. Since there was relatively little humanitarian concern during this era, little was done to improve slaves' lot. But with the Revolution and the fact that many blacks fought on the American side, slavery died out in the North. The Constitution outlawed the slave trade after 1808; many feel that slavery would have ended in the South also. But the cotton gin made slavery extremely profitable, and it flourished until stopped by the Civil War.

During the 1800s there were actually three classes of blacks in America: plantation slaves, urban slaves, and free blacks. These three readings cross-section life in the antebellum United States. In the first reading is Sojourner Truth on life in the North; the second reading presents a black spiritual; and the third comes from the Confessions of Nat Turner.

Questions

SOJOURNER TRUTH

1. What is the significance of this episode?
2. What was Truth trying to do?
3. Does this story indicate discrimination and prejudice in the North?

GO DOWN, MOSES

1. How does this story of Moses apply to the slave experience?
2. Was this a happy story?

*Sources: Sojourner Truth, *The Narrative of Sojourner Truth* (Boston, 1875), pp. 184–87. *The Confessions of Nat Turner* (Boston, 1831), pp. 6ff.

NAT TURNER

1. Why did Turner call himself a prophet?
2. How did religion influence his thinking?

Sojourner Truth

While Sojourner was engaged in the hospital, she often had occasion to procure articles from various parts of the city for the sick soldiers, and would sometimes be obliged to walk a long distance, carrying her burdens upon her arm. She would gladly have availed herself of the street cars; but, although there was on each track one car called the Jim Crow car, nominally for the accommodation of colored people, yet should they succeed in getting on at all they would seldom have more than the privilege of standing, as the seats were usually filled with white folks. Unwilling to submit to this state of things, she complained to the president of the street railroad, who ordered the Jim Crow car to be taken off. A law was now passed giving the colored people equal car privileges with the white.

Not long after this, Sojourner, having occasion to ride, signaled the car, but neither conductor nor driver noticed her. Soon another followed, and she raised her hand again, but they also turned away. She then gave three tremendous yelps, "I want to ride! *I want to ride!!* I WANT TO RIDE!!!" Consternation seized the passing crowd—people, carriages, go-carts of every description stood still. The car was effectually blocked up, and before it could move on, Sojourner had jumped aboard. Then there arose a great shout from the crowd, "Ha! ha! ha!! She has beaten him," &c. The angry conductor told her to go forward where the horses were, or he would put her out. Quietly seating herself, she informed him that she was a passenger. "Go forward where the horses are, or I will throw you out," said he in a menacing voice. She told him that she was neither a Marylander nor a Virginian to fear his threats; but was from the Empire State of New York, and knew the laws as well as he did.

Several soldiers were in the car, and when other passengers came in, they related the circumstance and said, "You ought to have heard that old woman talk to the conductor." Sojourner rode farther than she needed to go; for a ride was so rare a privilege that she determined to make the most of it. She left the car feeling very happy, and said, "Bless God! I have had a ride."

Returning one day from the Orphan's Home at Georgetown, she hastened to reach a car; but they paid no attention to her signal, and kept ringing a bell that they might not hear her. She ran after it, and when it stopped to take other passengers, she succeeded in overtaking it and, getting in, said to the conductor, "It is a shame to make a lady run so." He told her if she said another word, he would put her off the car, and came forward as if to execute his threat. She replied, "If you attempt that, it will cost you more than your car and horses are worth." A gentleman of dignified and commanding manner, wearing a general's uniform, interfered in her behalf, and the conductor gave her no further trouble.

At another time, she was sent to Georgetown to obtain a nurse for the hospital, which being accomplished, they went to the station and took seats in an empty car, but had not proceeded far before two ladies came in, and seating themselves opposite the colored woman began a whispered conversation, frequently casting scornful glances at the latter. The nurse, for the first time in her life finding herself in one sense on a level with white folks and being much abashed, hung her poor old head nearly down to her lap; but Sojourner, nothing daunted, looked fearlessly about. At length one of the ladies called out, in a weak, faint voice, "Conductor, conductor, does niggers ride in these cars?" He hesitatingly answered, "Ye yea-yes," to which she responded, " 'Tis a shame and a disgrace. They ought to have a nigger car on the track." Sojourner remarked, "Of course colored people ride in the cars. Street cars are designed for poor white, and colored, folks, and will take them 2 or 3 miles for sixpence. Then ask for a nigger car!! Carriages are for ladies and gentlemen." Promptly acting upon this hint, they arose to leave. "Ah!" said Sojourner, "now they are going to take a carriage. Good by, ladies."

Mrs. Laura Haviland, a widely known philanthropist, spent several months in the same hospital and sometimes went about the city with Sojourner to procure necessaries for the invalids. Returning one day, being much fatigued, Mrs. Haviland proposed to take a car although she was well aware that a white person was seldom allowed to ride if accompanied by a black one. "As Mrs. Haviland signaled the car," says Sojourner, "I stepped one side as if to continue my walk and when it stopped I ran and jumped aboard. The conductor pushed me back, saying, 'Get out of the way and let this lady come in.' Whoop! said I, I am a lady too. We met with no further opposition till we were obliged to change cars. A man coming out as we were going into the next car, asked the conductor if 'niggers were allowed to ride.' The conductor grabbed me by the shoulder and jerking me around, ordered me to get out. I told him I would not. Mrs. Haviland took hold of my other arm and said, 'Don't put her out.' The conductor asked if I belonged to her. 'No,' replied Mrs. Haviland, 'She belongs to humanity.' 'Then take her and go,' said he, and giving me another push slammed me against the door. I told him I would let him know whether he could shove me about like a dog, and said to Mrs. Haviland, Take the number of this car.

"At this, the man looked alarmed, and gave us no more trouble. When we arrived at the hospital, the surgeons were called in to examine my shoulder and found that a bone was misplaced. I complained to the president of the road, who advised me to arrest the man for assault and battery. The Bureau furnished me a lawyer, and the fellow lost his situation. It created a great sensation, and before the trial was ended, the inside of the cars looked like pepper and salt; and I felt, like Poll Parrot, "Jack, I am riding." A little circumstance will show how great a change a few weeks had produced: A lady saw some colored women looking wistfully toward a car, when the conductor, halting, said, 'Walk in, ladies.' Now they who had so lately cursed me for wanting to ride, could stop for black as well as white, and could even condescend to say, 'Walk in, ladies.' "

Go Down, Moses

Go down, Moses,
'Way down in Egypt land,
Tell ole Pharaoh,
To let my people go.
Go down, Moses,
'Way down in Egypt land,
Tell ole Pharaoh,
To let my people go.
When Israel was in Egypt land,
Let my people go,
Oppressed so hard they could not stand,
Let my people go,
Thus spoke the Lord, bold Moses said,
Let my people go,
If not I'll smite your first-born dead,
Let my people go.
Go down, Moses,
'Way down in Egypt land,
Tell ole Pharaoh,
To let my people go.

Nat Turner

Sir,—You have asked me to give a history of the motives which induced me to undertake the late insurrection, as you call it—To do so I must go back to the days of my infancy, and even before I was born. I was thirty-one years of age the 2d of October last, and born the property of Benj. Turner, of this county. In my childhood a circumstance occurred which made an indelible impression on my mind, and laid the ground work of that enthusiasm, which has terminated so fatally to many, both white and black, and for which I am about to atone at the gallows. It is here necessary to relate this circumstance —trifling as it may seem, it was the commencement of that belief which has grown with time, and even now, sir, in this dungeon, helpless and forsaken as I am, I cannot divest myself of. Being at play with other children, when three or four years old, I was telling them something, which my mother overhearing, said it had happened before I was born—I stuck to my story, however, and related some things which went, in her opinion, to confirm it

—others being called on were greatly astonished, knowing that these things had happened, and caused them to say in my hearing, I surely would be a prophet, as the Lord had shewn me things that had happened before my birth. And my father and mother strengthened me in this my first impression, saying in my presence, I was intended for some great purpose, which they had always thought from certain marks on my head and breast—[a parcel of excrescences which I believe are not at all uncommon, particularly among negroes, as I have seen several with the same. In this case he has either cut them off or they have nearly disappeared]—My grandmother, who was very religious, and to whom I was much attached—my master, who belonged to the church, and other religious persons who visited the house, and whom I often saw at prayers, noticing the singularity of my manners, I suppose, and my uncommon intelligence for a child, remarked I had too much sense to be raised, and if I was, I would never be of any service to any one as a slave— To a mind like mine, restless, inquisitive and observant of every thing that was passing, it is easy to suppose that religion was the subject to which it would be directed, and although this subject principally occupied my thoughts—there was nothing that I saw or heard of to which my attention was not directed—The manner in which I learned to read and write, not only had great influence on my own mind, as I acquired it with the most perfect ease, so much so, that I have no recollection whatever of learning the alphabet —but to the astonishment of the family, one day, when a book was shewn me to keep me from crying, I began spelling the names of different objects —this was a source of wonder to all in the neighborhood, particularly the blacks—and this learning was constantly improved at all opportunities— when I got large enough to go to work, while employed, I was reflecting on many things that would present themselves to my imagination, and whenever an opportunity occurred of looking at a book, when the school children were getting their lessons, I would find many things that the fertility of my own imagination had depicted to me before; all my time, not devoted to my master's service, was spent either in prayer, or in making experiments in casting different things in moulds made of earth, in attempting to make paper, gun-powder, and many other experiments, that although I could not perfect, yet convinced me of its practicability if I had the means. I was not addicted to stealing in my youth, nor have ever been—Yet such was the confidence of the negroes in the neighborhood, even at this early period of my life, in my superior judgment, that they would often carry me with them when they were going on a roguery, to plan for them. Growing up among them, with this confidence in my superior judgment, and when this, in their opinions, was perfected by Divine inspiration, from the circumstances already alluded to in my infancy, and which belief was ever afterwards zealously inculcated by the austerity of my life and manners, which became the subject of remark by white and black. Having soon discovered to be great, I must appear so, and therefore studiously avoided mixing in society, and wrapped myself in mystery, devoting my time to fasting and prayer—By this time, having arrived to man's estate, and hearing the scriptures commented on at meetings, I was struck with that particular passage which says: "Seek ye the kingdom of Heaven and all things shall be added unto you." I reflected much on this passage, and prayed daily for light on this subject—As I was praying one day at my plough, the spirit spoke to me, saying "Seek ye the kingdom of Heaven and all things shall be added unto you." *Question*—what do you mean by the Spirit. *Ans.* The Spirit that spoke to the prophets in former days—and I was greatly astonished, and for two years prayed continually, whenever my duty would permit—and then again I had the same revelation, which fully confirmed me in the impression that I was ordained for some great purpose in the hands of the Almighty. Several years rolled round, in which many events occurred to strengthen me in this my belief. At this time I reverted in my mind to the remarks made of me in my childhood, and the things that had been shewn me—and as it had been said of me in my childhood by those by whom I had been taught to pray, both white and black, and in whom I had the greatest confidence, that I had too much sense to be raised, and if I was, I would never be of any use to any one as a slave. Now finding I had arrived to man's estate, and was a slave, and these revelations being made known to me, I began to direct my attention to this great object, to fulfil the purpose of which, by this time, I felt assured I was intended. Knowing the influence I had obtained over the minds of my fellow servants, (not by the means of conjuring and such like tricks—for to them I always spoke of such things with contempt) but by the communion of the Spirit whose revelations I often communicated to them, and they believed and said my wisdom came from God. I now began to prepare them for my purpose, by telling them something was about to happen that would terminate in fulfilling the great promise that had been made to me—About this time I was placed under an overseer, from whom I ran away—and after remaining in the woods thirty days, I returned, to the astonishment of the negroes on the plantation, who thought I had made my escape to some other part of the country, as my father had done before. But the reason of my return was, that the Spirit appeared to me and said I had my wishes directed to the things of this world, and not to the kingdom of Heaven, and that I should return to the service of my earthly master—"For he who knoweth his Master's will, and doeth it not, shall be beaten with many stripes, and thus have I chastened you." And the negroes found fault, and murmured against me, saying that if they had my sense they would not serve any master in the world. And about this time I had a vision—and I saw white spirits and black spirits engaged in battle, and the sun was darkened —the thunder rolled in the Heavens, and blood flowed in streams—and I heard a voice saying, "Such is your luck, such you are called to see, and let it come rough or smooth, you must surely bear it." I now withdrew myself as much as my situation would permit, from the intercourse of my fellow servants, for the avowed purpose of serving the Spirit more fully—and it appeared to me, and reminded me of the things it had already shown me, and that it would then reveal to me the knowledge of the elements, the revolution of the planets, the operation of tides, and changes of the seasons. After this revelation in the year 1825, and the knowledge of the elements being made known to me, I sought more than ever to obtain true holiness before the great day of judgment should appear, and then I began to receive the true knowledge of faith. And from the first steps of righteousness until the last, was I made perfect; and the Holy Ghost was with me, and said, "Behold me as I stand in the Heavens"—and I looked and saw the forms of men in different attitudes—and there were lights in the sky to which the children of darkness gave other names than what they really were—for they were the lights of the Saviour's hands, stretched forth from east to west, even as they were extended on the cross on Calvary for the redemption of sinners. And I wondered greatly at these miracles, and prayed to be informed of a certainty of the meaning thereof—and shortly afterwards, while laboring in the field, I discovered drops of blood on the corn as though it were dew from heaven—and I communicated it to many, both white and black, in the neighborhood—and I then found on the leaves in the woods hieroglyphic characters, and numbers, with the forms of men in different attitudes, portrayed in blood, and representing the figures I had seen before in the heavens. And now the Holy Ghost had revealed itself to me, and made plain the miracles it had shown me—For as the blood of Christ had been shed on this earth, and had ascended to heaven for the salvation of sinners, and was now returning to earth again in the form of dew—and as the leaves on the trees bore the impression of figures I had seen in the heavens, it was plain to me that the Saviour was about to lay down the yoke he had borne for the sins of men, and the great day of judgment was at hand. . . .

Booker T. Washington*

During the late 1800s blacks lacked a spokesman. Frederick Douglass had spoken for many blacks during the Civil War, but with his passing and the nation's general indifference to black people's plight, the nation became involved with industrial expansion. Booker T. Washington appeared in the midst of increasing violence and discrimination. A leader who had worked his way from slavery to brick laying to teaching, he eventually was placed in charge of Tuskegee Institute and became a leading black voice. In 1895 Booker T. Washington expressed his feelings about blacks in a famous speech called the Atlanta Exposition Address.

Questions

1. How does he view the situation of blacks in America?
2. What are his solutions?
3. Why does he reject militancy?
4. How can he be called an "Uncle Tom"—a sort of racial compromiser?

Not only this, but the opportunity here afforded will awaken among us a new era of industrial progress. Ignorant and inexperienced, it is not strange that in the first years of our new life we began at the top instead of at the bottom; that a seat in Congress or the state legislature was more sought than real estate or industrial skill; that the political convention of stump speaking had more attractions than starting a dairy farm or truck garden.

A ship lost at sea for many days suddenly sighted a friendly vessel. From the mast of the unfortunate vessel was seen a signal, "Water, water; we die of thirst!" The answer from the friendly vessel at once came back, "Cast down your bucket where you are." A second time the signal, "Water, water; send us water!" ran up from the distressed vessel, and was answered, "Cast down

*Booker T. Washington, *Up from Slavery* (Boston, 1901), pp. 217ff.

your bucket where you are." And a third and fourth signal for water was answered, "Cast down your bucket where you are." The captain of the distressed vessel, at last heeding the injunction, cast down his bucket, and it came up full of fresh, sparkling water from the mouth of the Amazon River. To those of my race who depend on bettering their condition in a foreign land or who underestimate the importance of cultivating friendly relations with the Southern white man, who is their next-door neighbour, I would say: "Cast down your bucket where you are"—cast it down in making friends in every manly way of the people of all races by whom we are surrounded.

Cast it down in agriculture, mechanics, in commerce, in domestic service, and in the professions. And in this connection it is well to bear in mind that whatever other sins the South may be called to bear, when it comes to business, pure and simple, it is in the South that the Negro is given a man's chance in the commercial world, and in nothing is this Exposition more eloquent than in emphasizing this chance. Our greatest danger is that in the great leap from slavery to freedom we may overlook the fact that the masses of us are to live by the productions of our hands, and fail to keep in mind that we shall prosper in proportion as we learn to dignify and glorify common labour and put brains and skill into the common occupations of life; shall prosper in proportion as we learn to draw the line between the superficial and the substantial, the ornamental gewgaws of life and the useful. No race can prosper till it learns that there is as much dignity in tilling a field as in writing a poem. It is at the bottom of life we must begin, and not at the top. Nor should we permit our grievances to overshadow our opportunities.

To those of the white race who look to the incoming of those of foreign birth and strange tongue and habits for the prosperity of the South, were I permitted I would repeat what I say to my own race, "Cast down your bucket where you are." Cast it down among the eight millions of Negroes whose habits you know, whose fidelity and love you have tested in days when to have proved treacherous meant the ruin of your firesides. Cast down your bucket among these people who have, without strikes and labour wars, tilled your fields, cleared your forests, builded your railroads and cities, and brought forth treasures from the bowels of the earth, and helped make possible this magnificent representation of the progress of the South. Casting down your bucket among my people, helping and encouraging them as you are doing on these grounds, and to education of head, hand, and heart, you will find that they will buy your surplus land, make blossom the waste places in your fields, and run your factories. While doing this, you can be sure in the future, as in the past, that you and your families will be surrounded by the most patient, faithful, law-abiding, and unresentful people that the world has seen. As we have proved our loyalty to you in the past, in nursing your children, watching by the sickbed of your mothers and fathers, and often following them with tear-dimmed eyes to their graves, so in the future, in our humble way, we shall stand by you with a devotion that no foreigner can approach, ready to lay down our lives, if need be, in defence of yours, interlacing our industrial, commercial, civil, and religious life with yours in a way that shall make the interests of both races one. In all things that are purely social we can be as separate as the fingers, yet one as the hand in all things essential to mutual progress.

There is no defence or security for any of us except in the highest intelligence and development of all. If anywhere there are efforts tending to curtail the fullest growth of the Negro, let these efforts be turned into stimulating, encouraging, and making him the most useful and intelligent citizen. Effort or means so invested will pay a thousand per cent interest. These efforts will be twice blessed—"blessing him that gives and him that takes."

There is no escape through law of man or God from the inevitable:—

> The laws of changeless justice bind
> Oppressor with oppressed;
> And close as sin and suffering joined
> We march to fate abreast.

Nearly sixteen millions of hands will aid you in pulling the load upward, or they will pull against you the load downward. We shall constitute one-third and more of the ignorance and crime of the South, or one-third its intelligence and progress; we shall contribute one-third to the business and industrial prosperity of the South, or we shall prove a veritable body of death, stagnating, depressing, retarding every effort to advance the body politic.

Gentlemen of the Exposition, as we present to you our humble effort at an exhibition of our progress, you must not expect overmuch. Starting thirty years ago with ownership here and there in a few quilts and pumpkins and chickens (gathered from miscellaneous sources), remember the path that has led from these to the inventions and production of agricultural implements, buggies, steam-engines, newspapers, books, statuary, carving, paintings, the management of drug-stores and banks, has not been trodden without contact with thorns and thistles. While we take pride in what we exhibit as a result of our independent efforts, we do not for a moment forget that our part in this exhibition would fall far short of your expectations but for the constant help that has come to our educational life, not only from the Southern states, but especially from Northern philanthropists, who have made their gifts a constant stream of blessing and encouragement.

The wisest among my race understand that the agitation of questions of social equality is the extremest folly, and that progress in the enjoyment of all the privileges that will come to us must be the result of severe and constant struggle rather than an artificial forcing. No race that has anything to contribute to the markets of the world is long in any degree ostracized. It is important and right that all privileges of the law be ours, but it is vastly more important that we be prepared for the exercises of these privileges. The opportunity to earn a dollar in a factory just now is worth infinitely more than the opportunity to spend a dollar in an opera-house.

3

The Birth of the Civil Rights Movement*

The black protest movement, though active throughout the 1920s, 30s, and 40s, never really accomplished much. Marcus Garvey tried to instill racial pride in the black masses of the urban ghettoes by advocating racial separatism and a back-to-Africa movement. But he was deported from the United States. With the end of World War II Presidents Franklin Roosevelt and Harry Truman attempted through executive action to bring more equality into the armed forces. Their actions, plus the Supreme Court decision of 1954 (Brown v. Board of Education) *and the Montgomery Bus Boycott of 1955, brought full-blown life to the Civil Rights Movement. Here Louis E. Lomax describes the origins of that movement.*

Questions

1. What were the demands of the Montgomery Improvement Association?
2. How did the revolt start?
3. What were the results of the boycott?
4. How did this movement account for the rise of King?

"Lord, child," a Mississippi woman once said to me, "we colored people ain't nothing but a bundle of resentments and sufferings going somewhere to explode."

The explosion—and no one would have then taken it for that—came on December 1, 1955, the day Mrs. Rosa Parks boarded the Cleveland Avenue bus in Montgomery, Alabama. And the Negro revolt is properly dated from the moment Mrs. Parks said "No" to the bus driver's demand that she get up and let a white man have her seat.

There have been scores of attempts to discover why Mrs. Parks refused to move. The local white power structure insisted that the NAACP had put her

*Source: From pp. 81–86 in *The Negro Revolt* by Louis E. Lomax. Copyright © 1962 by Louis E. Lomax. By permission of Harper & Row, Publishers, Inc.

up to it, but this charge was quickly disproved. The extremists spread the word that Mrs. Parks was a Communist agent, that the whole thing had been hatched in the Kremlin; that rumor collapsed under the weight of its own preposterousness. The truth is that Mrs. Parks was a part of the deepening mood of despair and disillusionment that gripped the American Negro after World War II. She had been an official in the Montgomery NAACP; Mrs. Parks was an alert woman, a dedicated Negro and fully aware of the continuing injustices Negroes all over the nation were enduring. The only way to account for Mrs. Parks is to say she was a part of the times; that, at long last, her cup ran over.

Word of Mrs. Parks' arrest swept the Negro community. By nightfall an *ad hoc* committee of Negro women was calling for action; they telephoned their clergymen and other civic leaders and demanded that a boycott of the busses be called. On Friday evening, little more than twenty-four hours after Mrs. Parks' arrest, the largest gathering of local Negro leaders ever assembled met to map a plan of action. The meeting almost broke up before it started because the chairman, Reverend L. Roy Bennett, was so angry about the arrest that he didn't wish to tolerate discussion from the floor. "It is time to act," he shouted. "Let's act!"

Calmer heads prevailed, however, and, after several members had asked questions about the wisdom of the action, it was decided to call a bus boycott for the following Monday morning, three days away. This meant that word had to be gotten to the seventeen thousand Negroes—75 percent of the bus-riding population—that they were to walk to work on Monday morning. The clergymen promised to take to their pulpits Sunday and spread the word; but there was still the monumental task of mimeographing and distributing printed material among Montgomery's fifty thousand Negro citizens. A young Baptist minister, Dr. Martin Luther King, accepted that task.

As the busses moved through the Negro section on Monday morning, they were empty. The boycott was on. So was the Negro revolt. That night, hundreds of Negroes jammed a church for a mass meeting to formalize the boycott and the organization that was to direct it. Martin Luther King, a man who, three weeks earlier, had rejected the presidency of the local NAACP because he felt he was too new in town, was elected president.

Formed into the Montgomery Improvement Association, the group did not ask for the end of segregated seating. Rather they asked that:

1. Negro bus riders be given courteous treatment.
2. All bus riders be seated on a first-come, first-served basis; that Negroes would sit from the back toward the front, the white passengers from the front toward the rear.
3. Negro drivers be hired on routes that served predominantly Negro sections.

The program was much too mild for the local NAACP and that organization refused to enter the boycott, principally because the demands did not ask for the outright end of segregated seating.

The white reaction was bitter. First, the bus company officials proved absolutely intransigent. Second, charged with racist emotions, white gangs began terrorizing Negroes and committing acts of violence; Martin Luther King and other leaders of the protest were jailed on various charges. Despite these acts the protest continued; and because of these acts King and the other Negro spokesmen decided to redirect their forces and attack segregated seating per se. This, of course, led to increased violence, but it also brought the NAACP into the Montgomery story. On May 11, 1956, Robert Carter, legal counsel for the NAACP, argued the case before the Federal District Court. On June 4, six months after Mrs. Parks' arrest, the Court ruled against segregated seating on municipal busses. Four months later, the United States Supreme Court upheld that decision and bus segregation came to an end in Montgomery.

"Praise the Lord," one Negro woman shouted, "God has spoke from Washington, D.C."

Their God had indeed spoken, and He had talked about more than segregated busses. The Montgomery struggle had involved fifty thousand Negroes; it sprang up overnight out of deep resentment over a situation that had aggrieved the local community for almost two decades. As they walked to work or organized car pools, Montgomery Negroes struck back for cursings, slappings and jailings that had been their daily fare for more years than they had courage to remember. They at first did not ask for integration; they only wanted decent treatment. When even this was denied, they struck for more, and got it.

Meanwhile, the Montgomery story inspired Negroes in other Southern cities who had been bearing the same cross for years. King, along with clergymen from other Southern cities, formed the Southern Christian Leadership Conference and made segregated bus conditions their prime target. The Tallahassee, Florida, and Birmingham, Alabama, stories that grew out of this are now history along with Montgomery.

Montgomery was the launching pad for Martin Luther King; he soared into orbit before he himself realized what had happened. Once he had a quiet moment to reflect and assess his life, it was too late. He had gained international fame, the applause of the world was ringing in his ears, eighteen million Negroes were calling him "Savior," and world ethicists were comparing him to Gandhi and Thoreau.

This was heady stuff for a twenty-seven-year-old whose main ambition had been to become a great preacher. Now, some six years later, Martin Luther King is a somewhat troubled man. He left Montgomery, his work undone; the busses are integrated, but the schools are not; neither are the parks, playgounds or any other public facilities. And one of the questions now plaguing social scientists is why such a deep-rooted movement as the

Montgomery boycott resulted in nothing more than the integration of the busses.

Martin Luther King left Montgomery and returned to his home, Atlanta, where he became associate pastor, along with his father, of Ebenezer Baptist Church and settled down as executive head of the Southern Christian Leadership Conference. It was about as difficult for Martin King to go home again as it was for Thomas Wolfe. The established Negro leadership in Atlanta was wary about his return, and there are those who say that King returned under a truce agreement which calls for him to concentrate, by and large, on national matters and leave local affairs to the entrenched Negro power structure.

Whatever the uneasiness of his return Martin King has been in Atlanta for two years now, and the organization which he heads from there has become a major force in the Negro revolt. Dr. King is, by far, the most popular Negro in America today and it is all but impossible to assess him, his leadership and his organization, without incurring the wrath of thousands, Negro and white, who call his named blessed. Although I am among those who venerate Martin King, I happen to believe he is quite human. He was created by the Negro revolt and it could well be that he will be destroyed by it. The French Revolution ended in victory, with the beheading of those who started it; the Negro revolt could go the same path, for there is something about a revolution that makes it impatient with the strong and the powerful.

The honeymoon between Dr. King and others close to the Negro revolt is over; for the first time since Montgomery criticism of Dr. King is now appearing in print, and comes from, of all people, the Negro students. His crime seems to be that he has not gone to jail enough to merit the badge of continuing leadership. Students are not only idealistic, they are impatient. Then again they could be right; not that Dr. King's jail record is not impressive, but rather that there may be something lacking in the leadership Dr. King and his organization have given. The students are not the only ones who speak critically of Martin King, although none of Dr. King's adult critics will allow themselves to be quoted. In *Harper's Magazine* of February, 1961, writer James Baldwin talked of "The Dangerous Road Ahead for Martin Luther King." When pressed to state just what Martin King's future was, Baldwin halted, pirouetted, and then took refuge in a quote from William James to the effect that "all futures are rough."

The problem facing Martin Luther King is created by his admirers, who would make of him more than he is and therefore obscure what he is in so much controversy that his real merit is almost impossible to determine. The first thing any accurate appraisal of Martin King must do, then, is to establish clearly just what he *is;* and this can best be done by listing the things he *is not.*

Martin Luther King is not an administrator.

Thought Questions

1. Is Booker T. Washington an "Uncle Tom"?
2. Was the Civil Rights Movement a reaction to white racism?
3. Are the ideas of Nat Turner and Booker T. Washington still relevant today?

ten

INDUSTRIALIZATION:
From Colonial Industry
to Corporate State

America is run like a big and impersonal corporation; the chains of command are as evident in government, as in a large corporation from the executive to the mail clerk. Yet America has not always accepted the corporate state idea. There was a time when America was a land of farms and to be a successful farmer was the height of the American dream.

During the colonial period, industry and the factory system as we know it today were virtually nonexistent. Industries were part of the economic scene, but in the sense that many products were made at home or by village artisans. After the American Revolution and the English industrial revolution, Americans such as Samuel Slater and Francis Cabot Lowell began to set up factories. By the time of Jackson, the factory was part of urban life and "sweat shop" conditions were evident too. There were virtually no labor unions so management reigned tyrannical and absolute. With the Civil War, industry expanded even more and big business became an accepted part of life in America.

The period from the Civil War to the 1900s is referred to as the Industrial Age. The invention of phonographs, telephones, and other mechanical devices hastened the rapid industrialization of America. Monopolies and capitalists became commonplace. The "gospel of wealth" was the bible of the age. Business was in politics and politics was in business. In this age of Carnegies and Rockefellers government policy was laissez-faire (hands-off). Reaction to this age of uncontrolled competition came with the Progressive Era in the twentieth century. Progressivism was an attempt to restore decent competition and dignity to American life. It succeeded fairly well in regulating, not destroying, monopoly and in bringing justice to more Americans. But the Progressive Era ended in the 1920s, a great boom time during which corporate executives and the ad men came into their own. Rampant speculation led directly to the disastrous crash of 1929.

At first business supported Franklin Roosevelt's New Deal, but with the return of prosperity, they opposed many of his "restrictive" policies. Yet Roosevelt accepted the fact that big business would remain and could not be replaced completely. During both World Wars business boomed under government control and supervision. And after World War II corporations, advertising men, and vast capitalization became even more evident. Today Americans live with corporations, subsidiary corporations, interlocking businesses—whether they want to or not.

Alexander Hamilton on Manufacturing*

Generally colonial industry remained small and backward, and was even outlawed by British law. At the time of the American Revolution, America was feeling the results of the English Industrial Revolution. The promotion of manufacturing became a popular cause and was stimulated on the national level by Alexander Hamilton. In 1799 Hamilton issued his now famous "Report on the Subject of Manufactures," in which he not only described the current status of manufacturing but also recommended expansion in the industrial area. Although no great changes immediately followed his report, America in the 1800s finally followed the ideas of Hamilton. Here is part of his speech on manufactures.

Questions

1. What was the value of manufacturing to America?
2. What were the essential conditions for starting a manufacturing establishment?
3. Why should America become an industrial nation?
4. Are Hamilton's reasons for manufacturing still relevant today?

. . . II. But, without contending for the superior productiveness of manufacturing industry, it may conduce to a better judgment of the policy which ought to be pursued respecting its encouragement, to contemplate the subject under some additional aspects, tending not only to confirm the idea that this kind of industry has been improperly represented as unproductive in itself, but to evince, in addition, that the establishment and diffusion of manufactures have the effect of rendering the total mass of useful and productive labor, in a community, greater than it would otherwise be. . . .

*Source: John C. Hamilton, ed., *The Works of Alexander Hamilton* (New York: Charles S. Francis and Co., 1850), Vol. II, pp. 64ff.

. . . Whether the value of the produce of the labor of the farmer be somewhat more or less than that of the artificer, is not material to the main scope of the argument, which, hitherto, has only aimed at showing that the one, as well as the other, occasions a positive augmentation of the total produce and revenue of the society.

It is now proper to proceed a step further, and to enumerate the principal circumstances from which it may be inferred that manufacturing establishments not only occasion a positive augmentation of the produce and revenue of the society, but that they contribute essentially to rendering them greater than they could possibly be without such establishments. These circumstances are:

1. The division of labor.
2. An extension of the use of machinery.
3. Additional employment to classes of the community not ordinarily engaged in the business.
4. The promoting of emigration from foreign countries.
5. The furnishing greater scope for the diversity of talents and dispositions, which discriminate men from each other.
6. The affording a more ample and various field for enterprise.
7. The creating, in some instances, a new, and securing, in all, a more certain and steady demand for the surplus produce of the soil.

Each of these circumstances has a considerable influence upon the total mass of industrious effort in a community; together, they add to it a degree of energy and effect which is not easily conceived. . . .

1. *As to the division of labor* . . . the mere separation of the occupation of the cultivator from that of the artificer, has the effect of augmenting the productive powers of labor, and with them, the total mass of the produce or revenue of a country. . . .

2. *As to an extension of the use of machinery* . . . It is an artificial force brought in aid of the natural force of man; and, to all the purposes of labor, is an increase of hands, an accession of strength, unencumbered too by the expense of maintaining the laborer. . . .

4. *As to the promoting of emigration from foreign countries* . . . Manufacturers who, listening to the powerful invitations of a better price for their fabrics or their labor, of greater cheapness of provisions and raw materials, of an exemption from the chief part of the taxes, burthens, and restraints which they endure in the Old World, of greater personal independence and consequence, under the operation of a more equal government, and of what is far more precious than mere religious toleration, a perfect equality of religious privileges, would probably flock from Europe to the United States, to pursue their own trades or professions, if they were once made sensible of the advantages they would enjoy. . . .

6. *As to the affording a more ample and various field for enterprise.* This also is of greater consequence in the general scale of national exertion than might, perhaps, on a superficial view be supposed, and has effects not altogether dissimilar from those of the circumstance last noticed (i.e., opening a wider scope to diversity of talents and temperament). To cherish and stimulate the activity of the human mind, by multiplying the objects of enterprise, is not among the least considerable of the expedients by which the wealth of a nation may be promoted. . . .

The spirit of enterprise, useful and prolific as it is, must necessarily be contracted or expanded, in proportion to the simplicity or variety of the occupations and productions which are to be found in a society. It must be less in a nation of mere cultivators, than in a nation of cultivators and merchants; less in a nation of cultivators and merchants, than in a nation of cultivators, artificers, and merchants.

7. *As to the creating, in some instances, a new, and securing in all, a more certain and steady demand* . . . It is evident that the exertions of the husbandman will be steady or fluctuating, vigorous or feeble, in proportion to the steadiness or fluctuation, adequateness or inadequateness, of the markets on which he must depend for the vent of the surplus which may be produced by his labor; and that such surplus, in the ordinary course of things, will be greater or less in the same proportion.

For the purpose of this vent, a domestic market is greatly to be preferred to a foreign one; because it is, in the nature of things, far more to be relied upon.

It is a primary object of the policy of nations, to be able to supply themselves with subsistence from their own soils; and manufacturing nations, as far as circumstances permit, endeavor to procure from the same source the raw materials necessary for their own fabrics. This disposition, urged by the spirit of monopoly, is sometimes even carried to an injudicious extreme . . . the effect of which is, that the manufacturing nations abridge the natural advantages of their situation, through an unwillingness to permit the agricultural countries to enjoy the advantages of theirs, and sacrifice the interests of a mutually beneficial intercourse to the vain project of selling every thing and buying nothing.

But it is also a consequence of the policy which has been noted, that the foreign demand for the produces of agricultural countries is, in a great degree rather casual and occasional, than certain or constant. . . .

Considering how fast and how much the progress of new settlements in the United States must increase the surplus produce of the soil, and weighing seriously the tendency of the system which prevails among most of the commercial nations of Europe, whatever dependence may be placed on the force of natural circumstances to counteract the effects of an artificial policy, there appear strong reasons to regard the foreign demand for that surplus as too uncertain a reliance, and to desire a substitute for it in an extensive domestic market.

To secure such a market there is no other expedient than to promote manufacturing establishments. . . .

It merits particular observation, that the multiplication of manufactories not only furnishes a market for those articles which have been accustomed to be produced in abundance in a country, but it likewise creates a demand for such as were either unknown or produced in inconsiderable quantities. The bowels as well as the surface of the earth are ransacked for articles which were before neglected. Animals, plants, and minerals acquire a utility and a value which were before unexplored.

The foregoing considerations seem sufficient to establish, as general propositions, that it is the interest of nations to diversify the industrious pursuits of the individuals who compose them; that the establishment of manufactures is calculated not only to increase the general stock of useful and productive labor, but even to improve the state of agriculture in particular. . . .

2

Another View of the Gospel of Wealth*

The Civil War boosted the American industrial revolution tremendously. Farming was still the primary American occupation, but by the end of the Civil War the United States was becoming one of the leading manufacturing countries of the world. With this age of enterprise came the "gospel of wealth," a philosophy which saw wealth as a worthwhile goal to be attained at all costs and poverty as an evil. The government's role in the scheme was merely to protect the system of wealth.

The captains of industry were frequently called robber barons by their critics for their fraudulent and high-handed business practices. By the late 1800s their empires had grown and they were control-

*Source: Charles S. Pierce, "Evolutionary Love," *The Monist,* January, 1893, pp. 178–82.

ling broader segments of the economy. The more powerful they became, the more Americans began to react against them. Here Charles S. Pierce, one of the leading thinkers of the time, talks of the philosophy of the age.

Questions

1. What was the basis of Pierce's criticism?
2. What is the "gospel of greed"?
3. Does Pierce seem to present an accurate evaluation of the age?

The nineteenth century is now fast sinking into the grave, and we all begin to review its doings and to think what character it is destined to bear as compared with other centuries in the minds of future historians. It will be called, I guess, the Economical Century; for political economy has more direct relations with all the branches of its activity than has any other science. Well, political economy has its formula of redemption, too. It is this: Intelligence in the service of greed ensures the justest prices, the fairest contracts, the most enlightened conduct of all the dealings between men, and leads to the *summum bonum,* food in plenty and perfect comfort. Food for whom? Why, for the greedy master of intelligence. I do not mean to say that this is one of the legitimate conclusions of political economy, the scientific character of which I fully acknowledge. But the study of doctrines, themselves true, will often temporarily encourage generalisations extremely false, as the study of physics has encouraged necessitarianism. What I say, then, is that the great attention paid to economical questions during our century has induced an exaggeration of the beneficial effects of greed and of the unfortunate results of sentiment, until there has resulted a philosophy which comes unwittingly to this, that greed is the great agent in the elevation of the human race and in the evolution of the universe.

I open a handbook of political economy,—the most typical and middling one I have at hand,—and there find some remarks of which I will here make a brief analysis. I omit qualifications, sops thrown to Cerberus, phrases to placate Christian prejudice, trappings which serve to hide from author and reader alike the ugly nakedness of the greed-god. But I have surveyed my position. The author enumerates "three motives to human action":

The love of self;
The love of a limited class having common interests and feelings with one's self;
The love of mankind at large.

Remark, at the outset, what obsequious title is bestowed on greed,—"the love of self." Love! The second motive *is* love. In place of "a limited class" put "certain persons," and you have a fair description. Taking "class" in the old-fashioned sense, a weak kind of love is described. In the sequel, there seems to be some haziness as to the delimitation of his motive. By the love of mankind at large, the author does not mean that deep, subconscious passion that is properly so called; but merely public-spirit, perhaps little more than a fidget about pushing ideas. The author proceeds to a comparative estimate of the worth of these motives. Greed, says he, but using, of course, another word, "is not so great an evil as is commonly supposed. . . . Every man can promote his own interests a great deal more effectively than he can promote any one else's, or than any one else can promote his." Besides, as he remarks on another page, the more miserly a man is, the more good he does. The second motive "is the most dangerous one to which society is exposed." Love is all very pretty: "no higher or purer source of human happiness exists." (Ahem!) But it is a "source of enduring injury," and, in short, should be overruled by something wiser. What is this wiser motive? We shall see.

As for public-spirit, it is rendered nugatory by the "difficulties in the way of its effective operation." For example, it might suggest putting checks upon the fecundity of the poor and the vicious; and "no measure of repression would be too severe," in the case of criminals. The hint is broad. But unfortunately, you cannot induce legislatures to take such measures, owing to the pestiferous "tender sentiments of man towards man." It thus appears that public-spirit, or Benthamism, is not strong enough to be the effective tutor of love (I am skipping to another page), which must therefore be handed over to "the motives which animate men in the pursuit of wealth," in which alone we can confide, and which "are in the highest degree beneficent."[1] Yes, in the "highest degree" without exception are they beneficent to the being upon whom all their blessings are poured out, namely, the Self, whose "sole object," says the writer, in accumulating wealth is his individual "sustenance and enjoyment." Plainly, the author holds the notion that some other motive might be in a higher degree beneficent even for the man's self to be a paradox wanting in good sense. He seeks to gloze and modify his doctrine; but he lets the perspicacious reader see what his animating principle is; and when, holding the opinions I have repeated, he at the same time acknowledges that society could not exist upon a basis of intelligent greed alone, he simply pigeon-holes himself as one of the eclectics of inharmonious opinions. He wants his mammon flavored with a *soupçon* of god.

The economists accuse those to whom the enunciation of their atrocious villainies communicates a thrill of horror of being *sentimentalists.* It may be so: I willingly confess to having some tincture of sentimentalism in me, God be thanked! Ever since the French Revolution brought this leaning of thought

---

[1] How can a writer have any respect for science, as such, who is capable of confounding with the scientific propositions of political economy, which have nothing to say concerning what is "beneficent," such brummagem generalisations as this?

into ill-repute,—and not altogether undeservedly, I must admit, true, beautiful, and good as that great movement was,—it has been the tradition to picture sentimentalists as persons incapable of logical thought and unwilling to look facts in the eyes. This tradition may be classed with the French tradition that an Englishman says *godam* at every second sentence, the English tradition that an American talks about "Britishers," and the American tradition that a Frenchman carries forms of etiquette to an inconvenient extreme, in short with all those traditions which survive simply because the men who use their eyes and ears are few and far between. Doubtless some excuse there was for all those opinions in days gone by; and sentimentalism, when it was the fashionable amusement to spend one's evenings in a flood of tears over a woeful performance on a candle-litten stage, sometimes made itself a little ridiculous. But what after all is sentimentalism? It is an *ism,* a doctrine, namely, the doctrine that great respect should be paid to the natural judgments of the sensible heart. This is what sentimentalism precisely is; and I entreat the reader to consider whether to contemn it is not of all blasphemies the most degrading. Yet the nineteenth century has steadily contemned it, because it brought about the Reign of Terror. That it did so is true. Still, the whole question is one of *how much.* The reign of terror was very bad; but now the Gradgrind banner has been this century long flaunting in the face of heaven, with an insolence to provoke the very skies to scowl and rumble. Soon a flash and quick peal will shake economists quite out of their complacency, too late. The twentieth century, in its latter half, shall surely see the deluge-tempest burst upon the social order,—to clear upon a world as deep in ruin as that greed-philosophy has long plunged it into guilt. No post-thermidorian high jinks then!

So a miser is a beneficent power in a community, is he? With the same reason precisely, only in a much higher degree, you might pronounce the Wall Street sharp to be a good angel, who takes money from heedless persons not likely to guard it properly, who wrecks feeble enterprises better stopped, and who administers wholesome lessons to unwary scientific men, by passing worthless checks upon them,—as you did, the other day, to me, my millionaire Master in glomery, when you thought you saw your way to using my process without paying for it, and of so bequeathing to your children something to boast of their father about,—and who by a thousand wiles puts money at the service of intelligent greed, in his own person. Bernard Mandeville, in his "Fable of the Bees," maintains that private vices of all descriptions are public benefits, and proves it, too, quite as cogently as the economist proves his point concerning the miser. He even argues, with no slight force, that but for vice civilisation would never have existed. In the same spirit, it has been strongly maintained and is to-day widely believed that all acts of charity and benevolence, private and public, go seriously to degrade the human race.

The "Origin of Species" of Darwin merely extends politico-economical views of progress to the entire realm of animal and vegetable life. The vast majority of our contemporary naturalists hold the opinion that the true cause of those exquisite and marvellous adaptations of nature for which, when I was a boy, men used to extol the divine wisdom is that creatures are so crowded together that those of them that happen to have the slightest advantage force those less pushing into situations unfavorable to multiplication or even kill them before they reach the age of reproduction. Among animals, the mere mechanical individualism is vastly reënforced as a power making for good by the animal's ruthless greed. As Darwin puts it on his title-page, it is the struggle for existence; and he should have added for his motto: Every individual for himself, and the Devil take the hindmost! Jesus, in his sermon on the Mount, expressed a different opinion.

Here, then, is the issue. The gospel of Christ says that progress comes from every individual merging his individuality in sympathy with his neighbors. On the other side, the conviction of the nineteenth century is that progress takes place by virtue of every individual's striving for himself with all his might and trampling his neighbor under foot whenever he gets a chance to do so. This may accurately be called the Gospel of Greed.

3

The Overlords of Business*

The age of big business was in part created by geniuses of business like John Rockefeller and Andrew Carnegie, but by the late 1890s the corporations were almost independent, and the magnates were losing individual control. To the fore came financial capitalism, where the banker with large amounts of available capital became the dominant figure. Industrialists turned to bankers for advice and capitalization. Still, individuals such as John Pierpont Morgan were important in the new stage of capitalism. In this reading,

*Source: From pp. 70–73 in *Lords of Creation* by Frederick Lewis Allen. Copyright © 1935 by Frederick Lewis Allen. By permission of Harper & Row, Publishers, Inc.

*journalist Frederick Lewis Allen describes the overlords of business
in the early 1900s.*

Questions

1. What is an overlord?
2. Was Keene a typical overlord?
3. What was the crisis of 1903?
4. How did Allen describe the overlords? Was he critical of them?

The pell-mell rush to form huge industrial consolidations and to speculate
in their securities—a rush which did not slacken for long until late in 1902
—had distressing after-effects. Although a sharp recovery followed the
Northern Pacific panic, the spree was bound in time to bring a headache, and
so it did: during the latter part of 1902 and the whole of 1903, Wall Street
and the other financial centers suffered from a malady correctly ascribed by
Pierpont Morgan to "undigested securities." (James J. Hill, improving on
Morgan's phrase, remarked that the securities which caused the trouble were
"indigestible," and many of them surely were.)

Too much stock and too many bonds had been issued. Not only had the
formation of each holding company called for the sale of quantities of stock
to the investing public, but when a railroad company or a manufacturing
company had purchased control of another concern to further the ambitions
of the men in control (as when the Northern Pacific acquired the Burlington
for Morgan and Hill, or the Union Pacific acquired the Southern Pacific for
Harriman) this had usually meant the sale of a new issue of stock or of bonds,
thus adding to the supply of securities outstanding without adding to the
physical properties. At last the purchasing power of the possible buyers of
securities was exhausted and they could take no more.

The exhaustion was intensified by the effects of the depredations of professional speculators and stock-market manipulators throughout the boom. The
fine art of organizing pools to buy and sell securities in hugh bulk on the
Stock Exchange and thus push stock prices up and down, taking profits along
the way from the pockets of unorganized and unlucky speculators, had never
before attained such perfection.

For example, let us watch James R. Keene in action. (Keene was the man
whom the Morgan syndicate engaged to distribute the shares of the Steel
Corporation by manipulation on the Exchange.) According to an entry made
by Clarence Barron in his journal in 1900, Keene managed the pool formed
by the brokerage house of Moore and Schley to manipulate the stock of the
"whisky trust," and when the pool was organized "the question came up as
to whether individual members of the pool could also operate on their own

account. Mr. Keene said, 'Certainly, operate all you want to; buy it and sell it; . . . but just understand that I will get the best of you all in the business and I invite you to trade with me.' Then Mr. Keene began. . . . Ten thousand shares went out one day and were bought back the next day. He began moving it so many shares a day up and down, and kept swinging it back and forth—some days it was twenty thousand shares a day, again it was ten thousand shares a day. Then when the whole public was trading in whisky [stock] with a great big swing to the market, Keene gave them the whole business, possibly went short fifty thousand shares himself, and landed the entire stock of the pool on the public."

Other speculators operated with equal power and assurance. Barron quotes Herman Sielcken, the "coffee king," as saying early in 1904 of his manipulation of a commodity market, "I can put coffee down again just as easily as I put it down once before." And as for the operations of the most potent group of all speculators of those days, the "Standard Oil crowd" led by William Rockefeller and Henry H. Rogers, who made millions by promoting the Amalgamated Copper Company and by pushing the price of its stock up to 130 and down to 60 again, listen to the testimony of Henry Clews, who, far from being a radical critic, was an enraptured believer in Wall Street as a national institution.

Clews wrote in 1900: "At his best, Jay Gould was also compelled to face the chance of failure [in his stock-market manipulations]. Commodore Vanderbilt, though he often had the Street in the palm of his hand, was often driven into a corner where he had to do battle for his life; and so it had been with every great speculator, or combination of speculators, until the men who control the Standard Oil took hold. With them, manipulation has ceased to be speculation. Their resources are so vast that they need only concentrate on any given property in order to do with it what they please. . . . With them the process is gradual, thorough, and steady, with never a waver or break. How much money this group of men have made, it is impossible even to estimate . . . and there is an utter absence of chance that is terrible to contemplate."

So long had operators of this type enjoyed a field day that the supply of victims was bound ultimately to run short. By 1903 the crisis became acute. Syndicates which had been formed to launch new corporations found themselves with unsold securities piled upon their shelves. Market manipulators who had loaded up with stock in the hope of dumping it later into the laps of eager investors found the eagerness gone, stock-market prices sagging, and their loans from the banks frozen. So over-generous had been the capitalization of most of the new giants of industry that a period of sustained prosperity would be necessary to squeeze the water out of them; and when the pace of business lagged a little and the strain on credit began to become oppressive, earnings declined, dividends were passed, some of the crazier of the new combinations went to the wall, and the stock market had a series of sinking spells.

Fortunately this crisis of 1903 was a "rich men's panic," and not to any large extent a poor men's panic too. The momentum of industry was still strong, and the speculative excesses and consequent financial indigestion were generally limited to the professional promoters and speculators. The little investor, the occasional speculator, had been singed, or at least scared, in the Northern Pacific panic, and had learned a measure of discretion; and after all he did not then constitute a very numerous species. It must be remembered that even at the height of the hysteria of 1901 the total of daily transactions on the New York Stock Exchange had barely exceeded three million shares, as against frequent daily totals of five or six or seven million shares in 1928 and after. The number of men who were staking their accumulated savings on the rise of the market was probably hardly a tenth of the number who were to do so in the bull market of the nineteen-twenties. Few newspapers printed daily tables of stock prices. Investing in common stock was still considered somewhat hazardous for all but astute business men, and outside of the Wall Street area, speculation on borrowed money was still generally considered a form of legitimized gambling rather than a form of prudent "participation in American prosperity." The rich men's panic caused some spectacular failures and annihilated many a Wall Street plunger; but it checked only briefly the onward march of American industry. . . .

4

The Status Seekers*

Today as a truly affluent society, we are eating, drinking, and anxiously consuming more than any other nation on earth. And a wealthy elite control the corporate life of America. Vance Packard, in his book The Status Seekers, *talks of these American leaders of wealth.*

Questions

1. What is the general behavior of these people? How do they differ from the masses?
2. What are their habits of speech and drink?
3. Do you know people like this?

"The upper classes LIVE in a HOUSE . . . use the TOILET, the PORCH, LIBRARY or PLAYROOM. The middle classes RESIDE in a HOME . . . use the LAVATORY, the VERANDA, DEN or RUMPUS ROOM."—E. DIGBY BALTZELL, University of Pennsylvania.

While Americans are ceremoniously egalitarian in their more conspicuous behavior patterns, they reflect, sometimes wittingly and often unwittingly, their class status by the nuances of their demeanor, speech, taste, drinking and dining patterns, and favored pastimes.

In the matter of demeanor, the upper-class ideal is one of cool, poised reserve. This demeanor serves the double purpose of rebuffing pretenders and demonstrating one's own competence to carry the torch of gentility. The model for genteel behavior is the pre-World War II British aristocrat, who wore a wooden mask and, in the male version, cultivated a mustache to hide any emotional twitchings at the mouth when the owner was under stress.

The stiff upper lip must be maintained regardless of the provocations. Some months ago, I happened to attend a very proper upper-class tea. The guests included members of several old, moneyed families, a university dean, etc. The hostess exuded cool elegance. In the midst of the tea sipping her young son burst in excitedly to exhibit a mongrel pup he had just bought for $2 at an auction. The hostess, presumably, was appalled by his intrusion and by the long-term implications of his impulsive purchase. But she smiled, murmured "How nice," and went on talking to a guest. The flustered pup, meanwhile, lost bowel control in the middle of the Persian rug. In a lower white-collar home, such an untoward incident would have occasioned gasps, blushes, and howls of embarrassed merriment. At this tea, the incident seemingly passed almost unnoticed. Guests continued chatting on unrelated subjects. The hostess acted as if this was the most natural thing in the world to happen at a party, raised a window, calmly asked her son to please remove all traces of the pup, and went on chatting about the forthcoming marriage of one of her guests' daughters.

In speech, too, the upper-class members copy the British model, at least to the extent of striving for a cool, precise diction, and by pronouncing the "a" of tomato with an "ah." The British upper-class members still have such a distinctive form of speech that, not long ago, a nationwide argument developed over claims that the Royal Navy, in its screening of officer candidates, was favoring candidates with upper-class accents, other things being equal. *The Evening Standard* headlined one article: "Is There a Sound Barrier against Your Son?" and added that "It might hang on a dropped 'h.' "

With Americans, choice of words is more indicative of status than accent, although the New England boarding schools nurturing future upper-class boys have long fostered the Harvard, or Proper Bostonian, accent. In general, both the upper classes and the lower classes in America tend to be more forthright and matter-of-fact in calling a spade a spade (for example: organs of the body, sexual terms, excretory functions, etc.) than people in between, members of the semi-upper and limited-success classes. In this respect, at least, we are reminded of Lord Melbourne's lament: "The higher and lower classes, there's some good in them, but the middle classes are all affectation and conceit and pretense and concealment."

Persons who feel secure in their high status can display their self-assurance by using unpretentious language. Old Bostonians are notably blunt (often to the point of rudeness) in their language. A well-established society matron of Dallas and Southampton gave the appropriate upper-class answer when asked about the "secrets" of her success in entertaining. She responded, according to *The New York Times*, with: "Why, I just give them peanuts and whisky."

Sociologist E. Digby Baltzell of the University of Pennsylvania has compiled a table of upper-class and middle-class usage of language as he found it while making a study of Philadelphia's elite. Here are a few examples:

Upper Class	*Middle Class*
Wash	Launder
Sofa	Davenport
Long dress	Formal gown
Dinner jacket	Tuxedo
Rich	Wealthy
Hello	Pleased to meet you
What?	Pardon?
I feel sick	I feel ill

Also, I might add, as you move from the upper class to those somewhat below, sweat becomes perspiration, pants become trousers, jobs become positions, legs become limbs, and people "go to business" instead of "go to work."

When members of different classes address each other, we see a recognition of the differences in the language used. Ostensibly, we use first names with each other because first-naming is symbolic of equality. Actually, it is a little more complicated. Anyone is uncomfortable if his expectations are not met, and a social inferior expects his superior to act superior. However, it must be done in a nice, democratic way. The superior calls the inferior, democratically, by the first name; but the inferior shows deference in responding by addressing the superior more formally. Amy Vanderbilt, the etiquette authority, for example, advises me that even though the wife of a boss may address the wife of a subordinate by her first name, the subordinate's wife should not address the wife of the boss by her first name until invited to do so.

A sociologist, investigating salutations in shipyards, discovered that, while supervisors invariably addressed workers by their first names, the workers only addressed each other by their first names. They addressed their foreman as "Brown," and front-office supervisors who came through the yard as "Mister Brown," and often took their caps off while doing it. One worker, when addressed formally as "Mister _____" by the investigating sociologist who had got to know him quite well, confessed that it embarrassed him to be so addressed. "It's like you were making fun of me somehow, pretending I'm more important than I am."

Experts in communications are finding that the maintenance of good communication between different levels, as between management and workers, is far more difficult than assumed. Meanings become lost or distorted, especially when workers try to communicate upward. One investigator makes the figurative point that communication between management and workers is filtered by a funnel with the large end facing upward. The workers, he said, must try to get their thoughts "through the small end of the funnel. Sometimes the results are fantastic."

Our very modes of communication, furthermore, differ from class to class. This is seen in a study made of responses of people in Arkansas when they tried to relate to investigators what had happened when a tornado struck their community. The interviews were gathered by the National Opinion Research Center. A comparison was made between responses from an "upper group" (some college education and an income of at least $4,000) and those of a "lower group," composed of people with little schooling and income. The sheer problem the lower-class person encountered in trying to communicate across class lines his tale to the college-trained investigator was in itself a strain. Aside from language difficulties, communication was complicated by the fact that the lower-class person had different rules for ordering his speech and thought.

The lower-class narrator related the events of the tornado entirely in terms of his own perspective. His story was like a movie made with a single, fast-moving, and sometimes bouncing, camera. Other people came into the story only as he encountered them. His account was vivid and exciting, but often, to the listener, fragmented and hard to follow. (Example: "We run over there to see about them, and they was all right.") In contrast, the narrator from the upper group is more like the director of a movie who is commanding several cameras, as he tries to give the listener the big picture of what happened. He tells what other people did, what organizations did, and even what other towns did. His account becomes so generalized and full of classifying, however, that it is less concrete and vivid than the lower-class account.

Now we turn to other areas of behavior where characteristic class patterns emerge.

DRINKING HABITS

Social Research, Inc., made a comparative study of patrons of twenty-two cocktail lounges and twenty-four taverns in the Chicago area, and found that they represented different worlds socially.

The cocktail lounge is primarily an upper-middle-class institution serving primarily mixed drinks made of hard liquor, and operating in a commercial district primarily between the hours of 12 to 8 P.M. In contrast, the tavern is a neighborhood social center, and operates from early morning till late at night. Its patrons are almost entirely from what I call the supporting classes, the lower three. As you go down the scale, the number of hours that people who frequent drinking establishments spend in those establishments increases. Upper-lower-class people (essentially working class) who frequent taverns spend fourteen to twenty-three hours a week there. Pierre Martineau has made the interesting observation that many taverns catering to this group use, as a name for the establishment, a title combining the names of the proprietor and his wife. Examples: "Vie & Ed's," "Fran & Bill's," "Curley & Helen's."

As might be surmised from the foregoing, patrons of the tavern see the tavern as a place where they can obtain social and psychological satisfactions —and not just a fast drink. Most of the patrons live within two blocks of the tavern. Each tavern has its own social system. "Regulars" come in at the same time every day; they have their own rules about who is acceptable as a member of their in-group, and what constitutes proper and improper behavior in a tavern.

Each tavern caters not only to a specific social class but often to a special group within that class. Many of the taverns studied turned out to have a clientele consisting almost entirely of either Old Poles, New Poles, Italians, hillbillies, or Germans. One of the taverns catering to Polish-Americans had on its walls posters announcing events of interest to Polish-Americans, such as meetings of Polish-American war veterans, and the juke box offered primarily polkas. This tavern's proprietor said of a nearby tavern, "No, the tavern across the street is not like this one . . . all hillbillies over there . . . never come in here—don't want them in here. . . . We never have any trouble, and we don't want any. . . . They stay in their places. . . . No, they just learn fast when they move in here that this is not a place for them."

That hillbilly tavern across the street, catering to recent white immigrants from the South, featured on its juke box rock 'n' roll, hillbilly, and Western music. While the big drink in the Polish tavern is beer, the big drink with the hillbillies is a "shot" of whisky.

In general, however, the preferred drink of tavern habitués is beer. A glass of beer can be nursed a long time and further, it is less likely to threaten self-control. Pierre Martineau, in mentioning this fact, referred to beer as a "drink of control." He went on to say that the tavern customer, usually a solid workingman, has a "terrible fear of getting out of control and getting fired." You find the least concern about self-control, he added, at the top of the social structure. People there don't worry when they drink. They can do no wrong. This may explain something I noticed in Northeast City. The most notorious lush in town was a playboy who had inherited his father's wealth. Many people reported having seen him sloppy drunk in public.

Thought Questions

1. Is Frederick Allen as critical of the captains of industry as Pierce?
2. Compare and contrast the ideas of Hamilton and Pierce on wealth. Are they similar at all or completely different?
3. How do you relate the status seekers to past businessmen?
4. What major ideas in manufacturing grew during the time from the colonial age to the present?

eleven

LABOR IN AMERICA:
Challenge to Industrialization

Labor is and has always been essential to the functioning of our nation, but the type of labor and its conditions have changed radically since early America. During the colonial period workers were servants, slaves, or skilled artisans. Land was cheap and labor was generally scarce. There was virtually no working class as we know it today. There were some labor disturbances but the relationship between worker and employer was not formalized. After the American Revolution there were some local labor unions and even violent strikes. Although these organizations and their strikes hurt the *initial* growth of unions, the courts did more damage in ruling that unions were combinations in restraint of trade. The factory system and its concurrent social evils increased the demand for organization, but by the Civil War there were still few unions.

The period from the Civil War to the beginning of the twentieth century saw the growth of large national unions that continued to be involved in bitter strikes. The 1870s were particularly notable for labor violence and strife. The Knights of Labor became the first successful national labor union, but the void it left was soon filled by the American Federation of Labor. The AFL's conservative policies helped it survive the violence and depression of the 1890s and become the leading national labor union in the early twentieth century.

The workers of America gained a great deal during the Progressive Period, and labor unions grew in strength and power. But the AFL still did not meet the demands of all workers, and some dissidents formed the Industrial Workers of the World, who appeared unpatriotic during World War I and disappeared soon after. In the 1920s the government remained pro-business and labor unions were generally hurt, although many workers shared in the general economic prosperity. The passage of the Norris–La Guardia Act in 1932 and the Wagner Act in 1935 brought labor the recognition that it had been fighting for so many years. In many ways labor unions became equal partners with business. Strikes, however, continued.

Workers in industrial jobs still felt that the AFL more clearly reflected the demands of skilled workers, so the Congress of Industrial Organization was formed, waging a bitter struggle with its rival union until the two powers finally united in the 1950s. During World War II labor played a decisive role in war production and worked closely with business and government. After the war labor suffered a temporary setback with the passage of the Taft-Hartley Act, a bill which minimized the power of labor and gave the president emergency strike-breaking power. But labor had become powerful enough to fight big business, and remains a potent economic and political force.

Life in the Factory*

In the early 1800s there was little unionization among factory workers, but trade unions were evident. Life in the factory was generally hard. Factory workers toiled long hours and often found their lives almost controlled by factory owners. Whether you worked with your entire family in the Fall River system or you, as a young girl, worked in the Waltham system, the same abuses were evident. Here is a description of the young factory women of Lowell, Massachusetts.

Questions

1. What are the specific abuses described in this article?
2. Analyze the hours and conditions of work.
3. What were conditions in the dormitories?
4. Is the author critical of this system of labor?
5. Compare and contrast similar work then and today.

We have lately visited the cities of Lowell [Mass.] and Manchester [N.H.] and have had an opportunity of examining the factory system more closely than before. We had distrusted the accounts which we had heard from persons engaged in the labor reform now beginning to agitate New England. We could scarcely credit the statements made in relation to the exhausting nature of the labor in the mills, and to the manner in which the young women—the operatives—lived in their boardinghouses, six sleeping in a room, poorly ventilated.

We went through many of the mills, talked particularly to a large number of the operatives, and ate at their boardinghouses, on purpose to ascertain by personal inspection the facts of the case. We assure our readers that very little information is possessed, and no correct judgment formed, by the public at large, of our factory system, which is the first germ of the industrial or commercial feudalism that is to spread over our land. . . .

In Lowell live between seven and eight thousand young women, who are generally daughters of farmers of the different states of New England. Some

*Source: *The Harbinger*, November 14, 1836.

of them are members of families that were rich in the generation before. . . .

The operatives work thirteen hours a day in the summer time, and from daylight to dark in the winter. At half past four in the morning the factory bell rings, and at five the girls must be in the mills. A clerk, placed at watch, observes those who are a few minutes behind the time, and effectual means are taken to stimulate to punctuality. This is the morning commencement of the industrial discipline (should we not rather say industrial tyranny?) which is established in these associations of this moral and Christian community.

At seven the girls are allowed thirty minutes for breakfast, and at noon thirty minutes more for dinner, except during the first quarter of the year, when the time is extended to forty-five minutes. But within this time they must hurry to their boardinghouses and return to the factory, and that through the hot sun or the rain or the cold. A meal eaten under such circumstances must be quite unfavorable to digestion and health, as any medical man will inform us. At seven o'clock in the evening the factory bell sounds the close of the day's work.

Thus thirteen hours per day of close attention and monotonous labor are exacted from the young women in these manufactories. . . . So fatigued—we should say, exhausted and worn out, but we wish to speak of the system in the simplest language—are numbers of girls that they go to bed soon after their evening meal, and endeavor by a comparatively long sleep to resuscitate their weakened frames for the toil of the coming day.

When capital has got thirteen hours of labor daily out of a being, it can get nothing more. It would be a poor speculation in an industrial point of view to own the operative; for the trouble and expense of providing for times of sickness and old age would more than counterbalance the difference between the price of wages and the expense of board and clothing. The far greater number of fortunes accumulated by the North in comparison with the South shows that hireling labor is more profitable for capital than slave labor.

Now let us examine the nature of the labor itself, and the conditions under which it is performed. Enter with us into the large rooms, when the looms are at work. The largest that we saw is in the Amoskeag Mills at Manchester. . . . The din and clatter of these five hundred looms, under full operation, struck us on first entering as something frightful and infernal, for it seemed such an atrocious violation of one of the faculties of the human soul, the sense of hearing. After a while we became somewhat inured to it, and by speaking quite close to the ear of an operative and quite loud, we could hold a conversation and make the inquiries we wished.

The girls attend upon an average three looms; many attend four, but this requires a very active person, and the most unremitting care. However, a great many do it. Attention to two is as much as should be demanded of an operative. This gives us some idea of the application required during the thirteen hours of daily labor. The atmosphere of such a room cannot of course be pure; on the contrary, it is charged with cotton filaments and dust, which, we are told, are very injurious to the lungs.

On entering the room, although the day was warm, we remarked that the windows were down. We asked the reason, and a young woman answered very naïvely, and without seeming to be in the least aware that this privation of fresh air was anything else than perfectly natural, that "when the wind blew, the threads did not work well." After we had been in the room for fifteen or twenty minutes, we found ourselves, as did the persons who accompanied us, in quite a perspiration, produced by a certain moisture which we observed in the air, as well as by the heat. . . .

The young women sleep upon an average six in a room, three beds to a room. There is no privacy, no retirement, here. It is almost impossible to read or write alone, as the parlor is full and so many sleep in the same chamber. A young woman remarked to us that if she had a letter to write, she did it on the head of a bandbox, sitting on a trunk, as there was no space for a table.

So live and toil the young women of our country in the boardinghouses and manufactories which the rich and influential of our land have built for them.

2

The Baltimore Railroad Strike of 1877*

William Sylvia tried to form a national labor union of all workers in the 1860s, but with his death the union failed. In the 1870s the violence from the Tompkins Square riot to the miners and railroad strikes demonstrated the frustrations of American laborers everywhere. The height of the violence occurred during a series of railroad strikes in Baltimore and Pittsburgh in 1877. In Baltimore the strikers found themselves at war with the strong militia, while in Pittsburgh the howling mob left the railway station in ruins and turned to destroy the city itself. Generally public sentiment was strongly against both of these strikes. This reading from Robert V. Bruce's book 1877: Year of Violence *describes the end of the Baltimore strike.*

*Source: From *1877: Year of Violence* by Robert V. Bruce (Chicago: Quadrangle Books, 1970), pp. 109–14. Reprinted by permission.

Questions

1. What was the incident described between the troops and the strikers?
2. What brought an end to the strike?
3. Was it an uneasy peace?
4. What can be realized about the extent of the strike?

At nine o'clock police cleared all civilians, excepting officials, from the depot building proper. Under orders from General Herbert, Company C fixed its bayonets and charged a mob which had forced its way northward halfway along the platform to a point above Barre Street. Flying stones knocked out two militia men, who were taken to King's private car at the rear of the troop train. The mob fell back from the platform and made a stand in the yards. Reinforced by Company K, the militia charged again. They were ordered back after meeting pistol fire as well as brickbats from a mob of several thousand. The defiant mob tore up tracks and demonstrated before the depot on Camden Street. Anxious to stretch the civil power to its limit before invoking further military force, Governor Carroll asked Mayor Latrobe to summon all available city police. By ten, Baltimore police were present in force guarding the depot and the yards. Vice-President King made a telegraphic report to John Garrett, adding: "It is said to be the fiercest mob ever known in Baltimore."

By now 15,000 people were massed around the depot. Again a strange silence had fallen, broken by the tramp of feet and occasional yells from boys in the crowd. Suddenly the sound of a fire alarm stirred the crowd, and people pointed to three flaming passenger cars. Woodwork on a locomotive took fire, and the south end of the passenger platform blazed up. Firemen arrived, laid hoses and started up their pumps. Some rioters attacked one of the fire engines, cutting its hose and quenching its fire. Police exchanged pistol shots with the attackers and drove them back, wounding several. Rumors swept the mob: first, that all railroad property was to be burned; then, that rioters meant to burn out the whole city. (People well remembered the fate of Chicago six years before.)

When he saw the flames and heard the rumors, Carroll immediately wired President Hayes that the rioters had got beyond the state's power to control, that they had "taken possession of the Baltimore and Ohio Railroad depot, set fire to same, and driven off all firemen who attempted to extinguish the flames," and that in Maryland's name, he must now call upon the United States government for military aid. Without troubling this time to ask questions, Hayes promptly authorized Federal intervention. That night Secretary McCrary ordered General William Barry, commanding Fort McHenry, to report to Governor Carroll with all available men and to act under Carroll's orders in quelling the riot. Three companies were also ordered to Baltimore from stations in New York Harbor.

Even before these orders had been received, Carroll had discovered that the rumors were false, that the fires were out and the crowd was drifting away. By one o'clock in the morning of the twenty-first, most police had been withdrawn from the depot and the militia had bedded down within. Carroll notified McCrary that order had returned and United States troops would not be needed right away. "There is," he added, however, "increasing lawlessness at Cumberland and as I will not be able to send a force from here I may be obliged to ask the Government for aid." In all these transactions, Carroll behaved rather less like the rider than like the balky steed, equally galled by thorns to the front and spurs to the rear.

Carroll let his original request stand; and on Saturday afternoon, in a proclamation replete with whereases, Hayes officially brought Maryland alongside West Virginia within the fold of Federal protection. Giving General Barry command of Baltimore operations, Hayes sent that knightly major general, Winfield Scott Hancock, commander of the Military Division of the Atlantic, to confer with Governor Carroll on the situation—unofficially, in fact, to take chief command of what was rapidly assuming the form of a major campaign.

The sunlight of Saturday morning seemed to have driven off the fears of Friday night. Baltimore had apparently, in Emerson's phrase, let off its peccant humors. The crowds that filled Baltimore Street that morning came as sight-seers. They stood in pleasurable awe before Chenoweth's Saloon, the Dime Restaurant, the Sixth Regiment Armory, pointing out smashed panes, bullet scars and spots that could be blood. Merchants boarded up windows and locked doors, not in fear of tumult, but in disgust with such unprofitable notoriety; for those who gawked did not buy. Calm surrounded the B. & O. depot, more calm, indeed, than ever before in its history. In what its foes considered a mere petty spite of all the world, the B. & O. had stopped passenger trains, which the strikers (if not the Friday rioters) had never molested. Along the whole line east of the Ohio River not a wheel turned that day.

Around noontime, nevertheless, fears revived. City authorities closed all saloons (the Murphy temperance movement had not taken hold in Baltimore). "There is a horrible feeling with the populace, which will result in a fearful riot tonight," King warned Garrett. Carroll, suddenly glad that Federal troops were now at his command, asked General Barry to call and confer "on the subject of keeping the peace in this city tonight." "It may," he said nervously, "be extremely important for the safety of the city that a show of force should be made." At ten-thirty Friday night, independently of Carroll's application to Hayes, the War Department had sent a guard of Federal troops from Fort McHenry to the B. & O.'s great harbor terminal at Locust Point, on the collector of customs' insistence that the riot endangered the United States (and B. & O.) bonded warehouses there; and the Treasury Department had sent a revenue cutter, guns shotted with grape, to fend off possible rioters at the same place. This, and the earlier dispatch of troops to Martinsburg, left Barry with no infantry at all and only enough artillerymen to serve three guns. Ever since late Friday night the sending of troops from New York Harbor stations had been dizzily on and off, off and on, to the confusion of their commanders. Now it was finally on. At Barry's call the War Department ordered the New York detachments to entrain. The Navy sent 100 marines from the Washington Navy Yard.

Around Camden Station all remained quiet until dusk. Men of the Fifth Regiment walked guard about the depot building. Had those of the now-hated Sixth shown themselves, they would have baited trouble; and, anyway, two-thirds of them had sneaked out, changed to civilian clothes in a near-by saloon and gone home. Knots of angry men began to appear in the circles of dim gaslight under the street lamps. Fifty police in blue uniforms and shiny badges formed a cordon around the station. "Herbert reports turbulent crowd at station," wired Carroll to Barry; "bring your men and guns . . . the Marines are expected every moment." Before Barry's men got there, the crowd broke through the police cordon. Pistol fire erupted, mostly from the police, who aimed low to avoid fatalities, but some also from a gang of thirty boys equipped with old-fashioned pepperbox revolvers. More than a score of rioters limped away wounded, two of them dangerously and one of these a boy of fifteen. Suddenly, by a well-ordered plan, the police moved into the crowd, each officer selecting and collaring a man. The riot collapsed limply. Guardsmen with fixed bayonets herded the prisoners—with accidental irony—into the gentlemen's waiting room. Locked in, and increased by succeeding batches to about 100, they raved with comic impotence, sang and swore in chorus, pounded on the door and broke off bench legs for bludgeons, all to no purpose. Arraigned next day, most were held over for hearings on Wednesday. Thus the expected "fearful riot" turned into anticlimax.

At York and Light streets that night, "South Baltimore roughs," canalmen and some miners engaged a police squad in a brief scuffle until police reinforcements came. After yells, pistol shots and the sound of running feet, the skirmish ended with the police in possession not only of the field but also of fifty more candidates for the magistrates' attention.

Except for an apparently incendiary fire which destroyed a lumberyard, the only other excitement of the night occurred at Mount Clare Station elsewhere in the city. At ten o'clock about 100 rioters attacked the foundry, but were routed by a volley from twenty-five police armed with Springfield rifles. Near by, four hours later, flame and smoke burst from a train of petroleum cars. "Quiet as death" till then, the night suddenly rang with the shouts of a mob on an embankment overlooking the track. In the face of threats and missiles, police and a B. & O. passenger brakeman uncoupled the burning cars and pushed the others out of danger, saving all but seven. The mob gave up and dispersed.

To be self-sustaining, a popular frenzy must develop progressively greater sensations. Momentum must be more than maintained, it must be increased. This had not happened in Baltimore. After the lethal march of Friday night Saturday's mere scuffles forecast peace on Sunday; and so it turned out.

So it would probably have turned out even if Federal troops had stayed away. The arrival of those troops only reinforced an ordinance of human nature. Coming from Washington, the Marines reached Camden Station just before Saturday midnight, arriving first, as in popular tradition (even though a little after the crisis had passed). Some of them were sent to patrol the yards at Mount Clare after the police had dispersed the crowd. Just after midnight Barry's artillery, three three-inch rifles, were planted at Howard and Camden streets. Sunday morning brought regulars from New York and from Fortress Monroe, Virginia. To avoid "an unnecessary march through the city," most were taken directly from Canton Street Station by Tug to Fort McHenry. One detachment of 100 men went on to President Street Station and marched thence to the Sixth Regiment Armory. Along the way stones were thrown experimentally and then, when the troops stoically ignored them, more boldly and accurately. At last, one stone dropped a soldier. "Halt!" shouted Brigadier General Henry Abbott. "Fix bayonets! Forward march!" Almost before the commands were out of Abbott's mouth, the crowd had fled; and the rest of the march was peaceful. Taking the hint, however, General Abbott borrowed a suit of civilian clothes from Colonel Peters before calling on General Hancock at Barnum's Hotel. And when late that night, Governor Carroll ordered all troops and arms transferred from the Sixth's armory to the Fifth's, General Abbott contrived to carry off the movement before daylight "and thus avoid bloodshed."

So peace had come to Baltimore. By Sunday night, some 500 Federal troops, including the Marines, were stationed in the city. The B. & O. was running passenger trains again and without incident—though the strike against freight service remained unbroken.

That day a Baltimorean wrote his wife that the killing of citizens had been "universally condemned," and that Colonel Peters of the Sixth Regiment "would be mobbed if he should venture upon the streets." Also writing privately, the United States District Attorney blamed "the folly and incompetency of the authorities in sounding the fire alarm to call out the militia," compounded by a demoralization of the Sixth Regiment, "consisting largely of overgrown boys."

"I want you to state," said the chairman of a strikers' committee to a *Philadelphia Inquirer* reporter, "that we had nothing to do with this outbreak. Not one of our men was in it. . . . When we found there was going to be trouble we passed the word among our men to keep out of it, and nearly every one of them went home and stayed there." The *Inquirer* printed the statement; and most other newspapers did the strikers similar justice, though many charged them with indirect responsibility.

On the score of indirect guilt, the public had other ideas. That Sunday a friend wrote John Garrett that "believing your life and property to be in danger," he would if desired "endeavor to raise a sufficient force" to protect them. A full week after the riot, a visiting New York politician wrote home that "the poor misguided laborers will, as must always be the case, be the greatest sufferers—But I hope that the lesson will not be lost on the managers of our great trunk roads who are indirectly (at least) responsible for a great deal of the mischief done." John W. Garrett, added the letter writer, "keeps himself entirely out of sight. No one has seen or heard from him for days. He is most bitterly denounced by all classes of society, and will I think be forced to retire from the Presidency of the Company."

Thus ran Baltimore opinion. But in the rest of the nation by that time (for whatever consolation it may have afforded John Garrett) the Sixth Regiment's bloody march had sunk out of mind beneath the terrible, almost incredible tidings from Pittsburgh.

3

Samuel Gompers on Labor*

The first successful national labor union was the Knights of Labor, formed from a secret society of tailors. It was a union for all workers, both skilled and unskilled, and with its humanitarian goals, it attempted to change the entire structure of American labor. Both Uriah Stephens and Terrence Powderly contributed to the decline of the Knights in the late 1880s. While the Knights did not last after the early 1890s, one of its early rivals, the American Federation of Labor, has continued to the present. This union for skilled workers was molded and led in the beginning by Samuel Gompers. Gompers believed in a practical approach to unionism. That modus

*Source: Samuel Gompers, *What Does Labor Want?* (New York, 1893), pp. 6–10.

operandi plus his conservative policies in the 1890s led to the AFL's survival. In this brief article, Gompers tried to define what labor wants.

Questions

1. What does labor want?
2. What is the conflict between the laborers and the capitalists?
3. Does Gompers give a reasonable answer?

What does labor want? It wants the earth and the fulness thereof. There is nothing too precious, there is nothing too beautiful, too lofty, too ennobling, unless it is within the scope and comprehension of labor's aspirations and wants.

Modern society . . . is based on one simple fact, the practical separation of the capitalistic class from the great mass of the industrious.

The separation between the capitalistic class and the laboring mass is not so much a difference in industrial rank as it is a difference in social status, placing the laborers in a position involving a degradation of mind and body.

A distinction scarcely noticed earlier has become a veritable chasm, economic, social and moral. On each side of this seemingly impassable chasm we see the hostile camps of the rich and poor. On one side, a class in possession of all the tools and means of labor; on the other an immense mass begging for the opportunity to labor. In the mansion the soft notes betokening ease and security; in the tenement, the stifled wail of drudgery and poverty, the arrogance of the rich ever mounting in proportion to the debasement of the poor. . . .

The capitalist class had its origins in force and fraud, that it has maintained and extended its brutal sway more or less directly through the agency of specified legislation, most ferocious and barbarous, but always in cynical disregard of all law save its own arbitrary will. . . .

This class of parasites devours incomes derived from many sources, from the stunted babies employed in the mills, mines and factories to the lessees of the gambling halls and the profits of fashionable brothels; from the lands which the labor of others had made valuable; from the royalties on coal and other miners beneath the surface and from rent of houses above the surface.

The Industrial Workers of the World*

With the demise of the Knights of Labor, the needs of unskilled workers were not being met, for the AFL allowed only skilled workers among its members. In 1915 the Industrial Workers of the World was formed to meet this need; it was basically a revolutionary union opposed to capitalistic control. While the union had little success nationally, it did organize many chapters in the West. The union opposed American entrance into World War I and the war itself. This seemingly unpatriotic stand led to prosecution of union members, raids on union officers, and the eventual end of the union itself. Here are two selections from the IWW newspaper Solidarity. *The first is the poem "Comrades" by Lawrence Tully; "The Deadly Parallel" is an antiwar tract.*

Questions

"COMRADES"

1. What was the poem trying to say?
2. How does it apply to American labor?

"THE DEADLY PARALLEL"

1. What is the deadly parallel?
2. How does this article express the IWW feelings on the war?
3. Is this a radical stand?

Comrades

I went into the Reichstag
My comrades there to see.
They sat in all their pomp and power
And broad humanity.

*Source: Lawrence Tully, "Comrades," Solidarity, October 10, 1914; and "The Deadly Parallel," Solidarity, March 24, 1917.

It was Comrade this and Comrade that
And "Comrade, you are first."
And "Comrade, let me help you,
Ere with eloquence you burst."

And then a man rose up in front
And "Comrades," says, says he,
"We're gathered here this blessed day,
To consider our army."

"Our Comrades, 'cross the Channel,
They're arming to the teeth,
We must grab them by their hairy throats,
We must shake them off their feet."

It was Comrade this and Comrade that
And "Comrade, let me shake,"
And "Comrade, you're a poltroon
When the Fatherland's at stake."

I walked the streets of Paris
And I hadn't walked so far,
Ere the thought was born within me:
The nation's going to war.

Beneath a spluttering torch-light,
For the day was turning dark,
A Red was loudly shouting,
And I stopped to hear him bark.

It was Comrade this and Comrade that,
"But our German comrades! God!
We must bayonet them and burn them
We must plant them neath the sod."

For, Comrades, you're my brother,
No matter what your 'ality,
But you're a hissing, crawling serpent,
When it comes to boundary.

I stood upon the battle field
And watched the spitting flow
Of life-blood from the Saxon
And his stalwart Teuton foe.

And Comrade this and Comrade that
Had drenched themselves again;
They had done their masters' bidding,
And were numbered 'mongst the slain.

Now many words could type this sheet
Of what I saw cross the sea,
But what's the use of wording
When it comes to you and me.

For Comrade this and Comrade that
It sounded very fine
The bomb has burst beneath you,
You are swallowed in a mine.
And the cant that turned to cannon,
And the handclasp that was mailed

Will record unto ages
The philosophy that failed.

The Deadly Parallel: A Declaration

We, the Industrial Workers of the World, in convention assembled, hereby reaffirm our adherence to the principles of Industrial Unionism, and rededicate ourselves to the unflinching prosecution of the struggle for the abolition of wage slavery, and the realization of our ideals in Industrial Democracy.

With the European war for conquest and exploitation raging and destroying the lives, class consciousness, and unity of the workers, and the ever growing agitation for military preparedness clouding the main issues, and delaying the realization of our ultimate aim with patriotic, and therefore, capitalistic aspirations, we openly declare ourselves determined opponents of all nationalistic sectionalism or patriotism, and the militarism preached and supported by our one enemy, the Capitalist Class. We condemn all wars, and, for the prevention of such, we proclaim the anti-militarist propaganda in time of peace, thus promoting class solidarity among the workers of the entire world, and, in time of war, the general strike in all industries.

We extend assurances of both moral and material support to all the workers who suffer at the hands of the Capitalist Class for their adhesion to the principles, and call on all workers to unite themselves with us, that the reign of the exploiters may cease and this earth be made fair through the establishment of the Industrial Democracy.

Pledge Given to Nation by American Federation of Labor.

We, the officers of the national and international trades unions of America in national conference assembled, in the capital of our nation, hereby pledge ourselves in peace or in war, in stress or in storm, to stand unreservedly by the standards of liberty and the safety and preservation of the institutions and ideals of our republic.

In this solemn hour of our nation's life, it is our earnest hope that our republic may be safeguarded in its unswerving desire to peace; that our people may be spared the horrors and the burdens of war; that they may have the opportunity to cultivate and develop the arts of peace, human brotherhood and a higher civilization.

But, despite all our endeavors and hopes, should our country be drawn into the maelstrom of the European conflict, we, with these ideals of liberty and justice herein declared, as the indispensable basis for national policies, offer our services to our country in every field of activity to defend, safeguard and preserve the republic of the United States of America against its enemies, whosoever they may be, and we call upon our fellow workers and fellow citizens in the holy name of labor, justice, freedom and humanity to devotedly and patriotically give like service.

6

Politics and Labor*

After World War I, John L. Lewis began his drive for industrial unionism in the mass production industries, while Walter Reuther actively recruited members for his United Auto Workers and used the sitdown technique to assure collective bargaining. The Congress of Industrial Organizations emerged out of the struggle within the American Federation of Labor over industrial unions. Although the two unions merged again in 1955, their bitter internecine wars hurt the cause of organized labor.

Since the New Deal, labor has become more and more cognizant of the value of political support and political favors. And presidents have become more aware of the power of labor and the problem of increasing automation. In this selection historian Thomas R. Brooks describes the relations between labor and politics in the late 1950s and early 1960s.

Questions

1. What was the relationship between Eisenhower and organized labor?
2. Did Kennedy change this relationship?
3. What does the future look like for organized labor?

The air of expectancy that surrounded the beginnings of the Kennedy Administration had a decided piquancy for organized labor. For eight years the unions had longed for a friend in the White House. Harassed by the renewed recalcitrance of management and apprehensive over the economic downturn, they worked very hard to elect John F. Kennedy, whose bona fides

*Source: From *Toil and Trouble: A History of American Labor* by Thomas R. Brooks. Copyright © 1964 by Thomas R. Brooks. Reprinted by permission of the publisher, Delacorte Press.

as a friend of labor were exemplary. But the fruits of victory are not always of an unmixed sweetness. The alliance between organized labor and the Kennedy Administration was an uneasy one indeed.

For the last four or five years of the Eisenhower Administration the unions had floundered in a morass of self-pity and frustration. It was not possible, they argued, to increase their membership when the National Labor Relations Board was loaded against labor, when union resolutions welcoming the Supreme Court decision on school desegregation hampered their activities in the South, and when white-collar workers were being scared off by the exposures of the Senate Select Committee on Improper Activities in the Labor or Management Field, headed by Senator John F. McClellan. But whatever the causes, the blunt fact was that the high expectations of great activity and even greater achievements raised by the merger of the American Federation of Labor and the Congress of Industrial Organizations in 1955 were never realized.

Although the unions, as a result of the McClellan hearings, adopted a Code of Ethical Practices and cleansed themselves of much of labor racketeering, they were unable to avoid Congressional action. In 1959, Congress passed the Landrum-Griffin Act, which embodied recommendations developed out of the Senate Select Committee's findings. The act, among other things, barred known criminals from union office; required filing of reports disclosing union financial activity and the operation of welfare funds; and spelled out a "Bill of Rights" for union members, protecting their rights to freedom of expression, assembly and to a hearing in disciplinary proceedings. The passage of the act was appropriately symbolic of labor's fall from grace.

The blame, until the 1960 election, could be lodged at President Eisenhower's door. But the election of John F. Kennedy placed the responsibility squarely on the shoulders of labor itself. President Kennedy was without question a friend of the unions, and he also knew more about labor—its strengths as well as its weaknesses—than any other current elected public official and certainly more than any previous President. Franklin D. Roosevelt was intuitively sympathetic to the workers and supported their efforts to organize, but he did not have Kennedy's detailed knowledge of unions. Harry S Truman received his labor education, so to speak, in office. Kennedy, by contrast, came to the Presidency after twelve years of intensive legislative experience in labor affairs—including an instructive term of service on the McClellan Committee.

This knowledgeability lay behind the caution that President Kennedy exercised in his appointment of Arthur J. Goldberg as Secretary of Labor. In December, AFL-CIO president George Meany had arrived at Kennedy's Georgetown residence with the names of five elected union officials, all of whom had the Federation's approval as candidates for the cabinet post. Kennedy, however, in the light of his experience on the McClellan Committee, well knew that he could not appoint a labor executive to administer the reform provisions of the Landrum-Griffin Act; he chose, instead, a man who was *from* the unions but not *of* them. As special counsel to the AFL-CIO's Ethical Practices Committee, Arthur J. Goldberg had won recognition and respect—both from the public and from the Kennedy brothers—for his independence of union bossism. To be sure, many union officials would have liked to disown Goldberg altogether for his part in the cleaning up of corruption inside the labor movement and in the expulsion of the Teamsters from the AFL-CIO. But they dared not do so. Goldberg was the perfect appointee for an administration basically friendly to the unions but only too aware of their failings and vices.

When the President appointed Goldberg to the Supreme Court, the unions did not bother to press the suit of a favored candidate. President Kennedy appointed W. Willard Wirtz, Goldberg's Undersecretary of Labor, to the Cabinet post. It was an appointment more in keeping with the Administration's relationship with the unions. Wirtz is an attorney specialist in labor arbitration. With the Government's greater involvement in collective bargaining as a third party, Wirtz' expertise makes him a natural for the post. Actually, unionists were much relieved by his appointment. There is a decided feeling that organized labor can do better with a Labor Secretary from outside union ranks. "We can put pressure on Wirtz," an AFL-CIO official declared, "that we could never bring to bear on Goldberg!"

However unhappy the unions were over these developments, their feelings were assuaged by the efforts of the Democrats to make the labor law less burdensome to the unions—particularly such weaker unions as the Textile Workers—and so help organized labor rather than obstruct it. The Republican 3–2 majority on the National Labor Relations Board was upset by President Kennedy early in his Administration.

The present board, naturally, cannot set aside the law; it can be, and has been, considerably more liberal in its interpretations. In doing so, it has relied heavily upon the original idea behind the Wagner Act that the public interest is served by strengthening weak unions *vis-à-vis* strong employers until a more or less even balance is achieved. This, for example, is what the board had in mind in the Deering, Milliken, Inc.–Darlington case decided in 1962. One of the nation's largest textile chains was ordered to pay back wages to 500 workers who had lost their jobs when an affiliated mill shut down in 1956 after its workers had voted to be represented by the United Textile Workers. In previous cases, the NLRB had held that it is an unfair labor practice for a company to shut down to avoid dealing with a union. The question in the Deering case was whether or not a chain could be held accountable for such an action on the part of a subsidiary. The NLRB not only held the chain responsible for back pay but also required it to reinstate the discharged workers if it should reopen the Darlington operation. The company also must offer them first crack at available jobs at other mills in the area and pay travel and moving expenses. Although the close 3-to-2 NLRB decision was immediately challenged by the company and may remain before the courts for another year, the unions have welcomed it as an aid to organizing in textiles and in the South. "It is a breakthrough," says a United Textile Workers spokesman, "as far as fear among Southern textile workers is concerned. We can now tell the guys in the mill that Uncle Sam is behind him."

With NLRB decisions running in this direction, employers in segments of the economy where unions are weak can expect new organizing efforts. If these are successful, it will be the real measure of labor gains under the Kennedy and Johnson Administrations.

The tragic death of President Kennedy has not changed the fundamental relationship between the unions and the Democratic Administration in Washington. Union leaders quickly rallied to the support of President Lyndon B. Johnson. There is, however, a subtle difference in relations that may strengthen the unions' political position. The late President had the votes of the rank-and-file trade unionists; President Johnson has had to woo their vote. It remains to be seen if this process will result in a push to the left on the new Administration.

For all this, however, the present crisis in the labor movement can only be dealt with by the unions themselves, and unless they act, they cannot avoid a serious and continuing decline in power and prestige. Unions, like any other social institution, must either grow or atrophy—and this means expanding their membership while also adjusting to the new conditions that economic development has inevitably brought about. The character of the American labor movement in the 1960s is bound to change—as a result of automation, the growth of white-collar employment both within manufacturing and outside it, the increasing importance of skilled workmen, and the decline of the unskilled and semi-skilled. Whether or not organized labor can meet the challenges inherent in these developments depends to a large extent on its capacity to take drastic action in a number of vital areas.

The AFL-CIO is in fairly good condition for facing the 1960s. The McClellan era is at an end, and there are signs that the Federation intends to put its newly developed strength as a national labor organization to active use. It has set up a central investment policy agency to advise its constituents on investing their vast reserves (pension funds and the like). It has shown a renewed interest in recruiting untapped groups, in particular the white-collar workers and the unorganized in small plants scattered throughout industrial centers such as Los Angeles, Philadelphia and the Winston-Salem, North Carolina area.

Thought Questions

1. How has the position of labor changed since the colonial period?
2. Compare and contrast the ideas of Samuel Gompers and the Industrial Workers of the World.
3. What factors involved in the railroad strike sounded like modern labor disputes?
4. Are there any similar ideas and themes in the evolution of labor in American history?

twelve

MEXICAN-AMERICANS:
From Cortés to La Raza

Mexican-American history began when the Spanish came to the southwestern part of the United States, long before the thirteen English colonies along the Atlantic seaboard were founded. As the Mexican-American influence in the United States has frequently been historically submerged beneath the English heritage, so many modern Mexican-Americans have also been submerged beneath the Anglo culture. But the day of Tio Taco is dead; Mexican-Americans are beginning to regain their inherent importance through organizations, protests, and education.

In the early 1800s the Mexicans revolted against the Spanish and took control of Mexico and its northern colonies, which at that time were California, Arizona, Texas, and New Mexico. At the same time that Americans began to move into Texas, and after the Texas Revolution and Mexican War, Mexico was no longer in control of the borderlands. The United States now governed the inhabitants. In general, the Americans there looked upon themselves as the conquerors and the Mexicans as conquered people. Eventually much of the original land held by Mexicans was taken and given to Americans. This issue is partly the cause of the mutual animosity that developed between these two peoples, particularly in Texas.

The twentieth century saw a migration of Mexicans to the United States to meet the American demand for cheap labor. These migrants moved north in large numbers, settling voluntarily in large urban communities which today form the nucleus of the modern Mexican-American population. Immigration fluctuated during the 1920s and 1930s, as boom and depression affected the employment market. The New Deal brought some economic improvements for the Mexican-American population, but not many. Immigration restrictions after World War II created the bracero program—contract laborers from Mexico. The bracero program, coupled with illegal immigration, continued into the 1960s when a new law ended the program and restricted all immigration.

World War II saw eruptions of racial violence against Mexican-Americans with the "zoot suit" riots, but Mexican-Americans were slowly becoming more and more aware of their rights and dissatisfied with their inferior status. By the late 1940s they began to react directly. Cesar Chavez, Reies Lopez Tijerina, and Corky Gonzales are three Chicano leaders who are presently trying to change the plight of the Mexican-American, but in different ways. In addition to these three men, numerous labor, education, and political organizations have brought Mexican-Americans public recognition. La Raza —the race—is being realized. Mexican origins are being studied and interpreted.

1

The Spanish Fantasy Heritage*

The stereotype of the Mexican as a lazy, ignorant peasant usually asleep under the nearest palm tree has been a fairly permanent one. In addition, there are a number of mistaken notions about the Spanish heritage and the Spaniards themselves. While it is true that the Spanish have left a language, religious experience, place names, food, and other aspects of their culture, they also left a legend that Mexican-Americans today have a hard time coping with. Historian Carey McWilliams tells of this fantasy heritage and its relation to modern Mexican-American history.

Questions

1. What is the fantasy heritage?
2. How has it been perpetuated?
3. Did it ever exist?
4. Why is this detrimental to the Mexican-Americans today?

Long, long ago the borderlands were settled by Spanish grandees and caballeros, a gentle people, accustomed to the luxurious softness of fine clothes, to well-trained servants, to all the amenities of civilized European living. Inured to suffering, kindly mission *padres* overcame the hostility of Indians by their saintly example and the force of a spiritual ideal, much in the manner of a gentle spring rain driving the harsh winds of winter from the skies. Life was incomparably easy and indolent in those days. There was none of the rough struggle for existence that beset the Puritans in New England. The climate was so mild, the soil so fertile that Indians merely cast seeds on the ground, letting them fall where chance deposited them, and relaxed in the

*Source: From *North from Mexico: The Spanish Speaking People of the United States* by Carey McWilliams. Copyright © 1948 by Carey McWilliams. Reprinted by permission of the author.

shade of the nearest tree while a provident and kindly nature took over. Occasionally one of the fieldhands would interrupt his siesta long enough to open one eye and lazily watch the corn stalks shooting up in the golden light. . . .

In the evenings one or the other of the patios would witness the gathering of the Spanish dons from the ranchos. Here in the coolness of the evening air they would talk of the day's events, sipping gentle wines that revived memories of castles in Spain. While the men were thus pleasantly engaged, the women would continue their never-ending routine of tasks that kept the large households functioning smoothly. For the young people, it was a life of unrivalled enjoyment; racing their horses over the green-rolling hills and mustard fields of Southern California; dancing the *contradanzas* and *jotas* to the click of castanets. In the evening, the young ranchero strolled beneath the window of his love's boudoir. As the moon rose high over the Sierra Madres, he would sing the old love songs of Spain. . . . All in all, this life of Spain-away-from-Spain in the borderlands was very romantic, idyllic, very beautiful. . . .

Indeed, it's really a shame that it never existed.

Never existed? How can this be said when so much of the public life of Los Angeles is based on the assumption that it did? Why do churches in Los Angeles never hold bazaars? Why are they always called fiestas? Why is a quarter acre and twenty chickens called a rancho? Why does a leading newspaper gossip columnist adopt the nom de plume of "La Duenna"? Why does the largest women's club, composed exclusively of Anglo-American women, hold an annual "gala Spanish fiesta program" in which the ladies appear in "full Spanish costume" to admire Señor Raoul de Ramirez' presentation of *The Bells of San Gabriel?* And, lastly, why do so many restaurants, dance halls, swimming pools, and theaters exclude persons of Mexican descent?

Los Angeles is merely one of many cities in the borderlands which has fed itself on a false mythology for so long that it has become a well-fattened paradox. For example, the city boasts of the Spanish origin of its first settlers. Here are their names: Pablo Rodríguez, José Variegas, José Moreno, Felix Villavicencio, José de Lara, Antonio Mesa, Basilio Rosas, Alejandro Rosas, Antonio Navarro, and Manuel Camero. All "Spanish" names, all good "Spaniards" except—Pablo Rodríguez who was an Indian; José Variegas, first alcalde of the pueblo, also an Indian; José Moreno, a mulatto; Felix Villavicencio, a Spaniard married to an Indian; José de Lara, also married to an Indian; Antonio Mesa, who was a Negro; Basilio Rosas, an Indian married to a mulatto; Alejandro Rosas, an Indian married to an Indian; Antonio Navarro, a mestizo with a mulatto wife; and Manuel Camero, a mulatto. The twelfth settler is merely listed as "a Chino" and was probably of Chinese descent. Thus of the original settlers of Our City the Queen of the Angels, their wives included, two were Spaniards; one mestizo; two were Negroes; eight were mulattoes; and nine were Indians. None of this would really matter except that the churches in Los Angeles hold fiestas rather than bazaars and that Mexicans are still not accepted as a part of the community. When one examines how deeply this fantasy heritage has permeated the social and cultural life of the borderlands, the dichotomy begins to assume the proportions of a schizophrenic mania.

I. The Man on the White Horse

"Three hundred years," writes Tom Cameron in the Los Angeles *Times* of August 29, 1947, "vanished in an instant here in Santa Barbara today as the city and more than 100,000 guests plunged into a three-day round of pageants, parades, street dancing and impromptu entertainment. It is La *Fiesta*. Santa Barbara is a particularly bewitching señorita today. With glowing copa de oro flowers entwined in her raven tresses and with her gayest mantilla swirling above her tight-bodied, ruffled Spanish colonial gown, she is hostess to honored guests from near and far. It is a time when Santa Barbara gazes over her bare shoulders (*sic*) to a romantic, colorful era of leisurely uncomplicated living. . . ."

With one thousand beautiful, "gaily caparisoned" Palomino horses prancing and curveting along State Street—renamed for three days "Calle Estado" —the history of the region is dramatized in costly and elaborate floats. This year, 1947, the Kiwanis Club enters a float in honor of Juan Rodríguez Cabrillo; Rotary honors Sir Francis Drake; the Exchange Club pays homage to Sebastián Viscaíno. "A traditional wedding party of 1818 escorted by caballeros, canters along. It represents the wedding of Anita de la Guerra and Capt. Alfred Robinson." Following the *charros,* riders from San Gabriel and the Spanish grape carts drawn by donkeys with flower girls astride, come the Long Beach mounted police, the Del Rey Palomino Club, *Los Rancheros Visitadores* (headed by J. J. Mitchell of *Juan y Lolita Rancho*), and of course the Los Angeles sheriff's posse headed by Eugene Biscailuz, the sheriff, himself an "early Californian." The celebration comes to a finale with the presentation in the Santa Barbara Bowl of a pageant written by Charles E. Pressley entitled *Romantic California*—and very well titled it is.

"Spanish" food is served; "Spanish" music is played; "Spanish" costumes are worn. For this is the heritage, a fantasy heritage, in which the arbiters of the day are "Spaniards." The Mexicans—those who are proud to be called Mexican—have a name for these "Spaniards." They call them *"Californios"* or *"Californianos"* or, more often, *"renegados."* These are the people after whom streets are named in Los Angeles: Pico, Sepúlveda, Figueroa. It is they who are used by the Anglo-American community to reconcile its fantasy heritage with the contemporary scene. By a definition provided by the *Californios* themselves, one who achieves success in the borderlands is "Spanish"; one who doesn't is "Mexican."

This fantasy heritage makes for the most obvious ironies. Cinco de Mayo is one of the Mexican national holidays which Los Angeles, now a Good Neighbor, has begun to observe. It is celebrated by parades, fiestas, and barbecues; speeches by the mayor and the Mexican consul constitute the principal order of the day. Invariably the parade winds its way through Olvera Street and the Plaza—sections of the old Mexican town now kept in a state of partial repair for the tourist trade—to the City Hall. Leading the parade through the streets, riding majestically on a white horse, is a prominent "Mexican" actor. Strangely enough, this actor, a *Californio* three hundred and sixty-four days of the year, becomes a *"Mexicano"* on Cinco de Mayo. Elegantly attired in a ranchero costume, he sits proudly astride his silver-mounted saddle and jingles his silver spurs as he rides along. The moment he comes into sight, the crowds begin to applaud for he is well known to them through the unvarying stereotypic Mexican roles which he plays in the films. Moreover, they have seen him in exactly this same role, at the head of this or some similar parade, for fifteen years. Of late the applause is pretty thin and it may be that the audience is becoming a little weary of the old routine. A union organizer of Mexican descent once remarked to me: "If I see that white horse once more, I'm going to spit in its eye."

Following the man on the white horse will be other horsemen, few of them with any pretensions of Mexican descent but all similarly attired, mounted on splendid Palominos, horses worth their weight in gold, decorated with their weight in silver trappings. At one time there were men in Mexico who dressed in nearly this fashion. The full irony of the situation dawns when one realizes that the men who lead the parade are dressed like the same class whose downfall is being celebrated. The irony would be no greater if the *Angelenos* put on the brilliant red uniforms of British grenadiers when they paraded on the Fourth of July. For on Cinco de Mayo blood was shed to rid Mexico of grandee landowners who threatened to suck it dry. Here, in Los Angeles, the men who lead the parade symbolically represent the grandees while the Mexicans line the pavements.

These *Californios* are in no small part responsible for the fact that the Mexican population of Los Angeles—the largest minority in the city—is so completely deprived of meaningful civic representation. Since it is impolitic for any Los Angeles official to ignore the Mexican vote completely, care is taken that the roster of civic committees shall always include at least one name which is obviously Spanish or Mexican. If a quick glance is taken of the list of names appearing on the civic committees devoted to housing, juvenile delinquency, racial, and welfare problems, these same names constantly reappear.

It has only been of recent years that the *Californios* have been elevated to this anomalous and largely factitious status. There was a time when they scarcely existed in the eyes of the Anglo-Americans. When the Native Sons of the Golden West were asked, in the early 1900s, to submit a list of "the men who had grown up with Los Angeles," for a civic memorial, they included only Anglo-American names. When the first "pioneer society" was formed in Los Angeles in 1896, not a single Mexican or Spanish name appeared on the membership roster and the by-laws expressly provided that "persons born in this state are not eligible to membership." Ignored throughout this early period, the *Californios* promptly acquired a new and spurious status the moment it became necessary to use them to maintain the subordination of Mexican immigrants in the general scheme of things.

Today the typical *Californio* occupies, in most communities, a social position that might best be compared with that of the widow of a Confederate general in a small southern town. On all ceremonial occasions, the "native Californians" are trotted forth, in their faded finery, and exhibited as "worthy representatives of all that is finest in our Latin-American heritage." In appointing *Californios* to civic committees, most officials realize that they have achieved the dual purpose, first, of having a Mexican name on the roster for the sake of appearances, and, second, that the persons chosen will invariably act in the same manner as Anglo-Americans of equal social status. Thus the dichotomy which exists throughout the borderlands between what is "Spanish" and what is "Mexican" is a functional, not an ornamental, arrangement. Its function is to deprive the Mexicans of their heritage and to keep them in their place.

2

The Zoot Suit Riots*

The United States acquired the Southwest through the Mexican War and the Treaty of Guadalupe Hidalgo in 1848. At the same time an animosity was created between the original inhabitants and

*Source: Robin F. Scott, "The Urban Mexican-American in the Southwest, 1932–55" (Ph.D. dissertation, University of Southern California, History Department, 1969). Reprinted with permission.

the American invaders. From 1850 to 1900 the Americans moved into the Southwest and acquired Mexican land and money, while few Mexicans continued to migrate northwest. The Mexican Revolution caused a wholesale migration of Mexican people toward the north. Railroads and farmers needed unskilled workers, and from 1910 to 1920 more than one million Mexicans came into the United States.

By World War II the Mexican-American community of East Los Angeles was the largest neighborhood of Mexican people outside of Mexico City itself. Second generation Mexican-Americans were feeling more and more frustrated in a white world. Reacting to the dress standards of white society, these pachucos *used their "zoot suit" costumes with suspenders and baggy pants and skin tatoos to differentiate themselves. Growing hostility against the* pachucos *in particular and Mexican-Americans in general burst into open conflict with the zoot suit riots of 1943. Gangs of servicemen waged open war with Mexican-American youths. Here Robin Scott traces the causes and course of the riots.*

Questions

1. What caused the riots?
2. How did the newspapers handle the riots? Was this biased reporting?
3. Who was responsible for the riots?

The stereotype of the zoot-suiter as an undesirable Mexican allowed the people of Los Angeles to feel relieved of any moral obligations to the Mexican-American youth and sanctioned widespread hostile crowd behavior against the zoot-suiters. The general public heard only of the attacks on the "deserving" zoot-suited pachucos while the frequent indiscriminate attacks on innocent Mexican-Americans were ignored.[1] The term "zoot-suiter" was originally used by the newspapers to circumvent the Office of War Information order to the press that the derogatory manner in which the term "Mexican" was used was an insult to the war ally, Mexico.[2] Ralph Turner and Samuel Surace in "Zoot-Suiters and Mexicans: Symbols in Crowd Behavior," discussed the result of the change of terms. "Unlike the symbol 'Mexican,' the 'zoot-suiter' symbol evokes no ambivalent sentiments but appears in exclusively unfavorable contexts."[3] "Zoot-suiter" did not bring to mind the

[1]Ralph H. Turner and Samuel J. Surace, "Zoot-Suiters and Mexicans: Symbols in Crowd Behavior," *The American Journal of Sociology,* 62 (July 1956), p. 20.
[2]Ruth D. Tuck, "Behind the Zoot Suit Riots," *Survey Graphic,* 32 (August 1943), p. 315.
[3]Turner and Surace, "Zoot Suiters and Mexicans," p. 19.

romantic past associated with old California, the Plaza and Olvera Street, the Ramona plays, and Mexican foods. It was far easier for a crowd to become hostile toward the "zoot-suiters" than the "Mexicans."[4]

One can only speculate as to the immediate causes that precipitated the confrontation between Mexican-American youths called zoot-suiters and an Anglo-American group consisting mostly of United States servicemen which occurred in Los Angeles in June, 1943. Edward McDonagh, a sociologist, believed the symbolic status of the uniform versus the zoot suit might have been a factor. The Mexican-American boy wore a long suit coat with trousers pegged at the cuff, draped around the knees and deep pleats at the waist, and a low-hanging watch chain. He kept his hair long and well-greased, presenting a striking contrast to the crew-cut American sailor dressed in his "whites." "In retrospect, it is probably true that many of the Mexican boys desired the patriotic status of the military uniform and many of the sailors wanted the freedom symbolized by the zoot suit."[5]

Another immediate cause of the rioting could be traced to wives and girl friends on both sides. "The most prominent charge from each side was that the other had molested its girls."[6] The Mexican-American girls seemed to cause much of the difficulty. Many of them had also gone in for costumes and were as distinctive as the boys in their short skirts, net stockings, extra-high-heeled shoes, and elaborate hair-do's. The sailors were attracted to these girls and trouble resulted. When the sailors and soldiers dated the Mexican-American girls they invited conflict with the zoot-suited boys. The servicemen were usually badly beaten.[7]

Beatrice Griffith summarized various hostile attacks leading up to the Los Angeles riots. In April, 1943, some United States marines and sailors went to "clean up" two hundred Mexican and Negro zoot-suiters in Oakland, California. The same kind of activity took place in May in Venice, California.[8]

> Rumors, conflict, and incidents between the sailors and the teenage Mexican-Americans continued to increase in Los Angeles . . . Sailors were beaten and robbed in Mexican neighborhoods.[9]

In the latter part of May, 1943, a week before the rioting got under way, taxis carrying individual sailors began to "case" the Mexican-American community in East Los Angeles.[10] Griffith described the feelings of the sailors just

---

[4] *Ibid.*, p. 20.

[5] Edward C. McDonagh, "Status Levels of Mexicans," *Sociology and Social Research*, 33 (July 1949), p. 451.

[6] Turner and Surace, "Zoot Suiters and Mexicans," p. 17.

[7] John A. Ford, *Thirty Explosive Years in Los Angeles County* (San Marino: Huntington Library, 1961), p. 135.

[8] Beatrice Griffith, *American Me* (Boston: Houghton Mifflin Co., 1948), p. 17.

[9] *Ibid.*, p. 19.

[10] *Ibid.*

before going overseas. "It was going to be a good weekend in a war-packed city. The riot fever and community madness had caught on."[11]

The Zoot-Suit Riots began on Thursday, June 3, 1943, in Los Angeles. Sailors left the Chávez Ravine Armory armed with rocks, sticks, clubs, and palm saps. The Georgia Street Emergency Hospital was quickly filled with riot victims.[12] A Mexican-American crime-prevention group was reportedly one of the first victims of the rioting.

> On the evening of Thursday, June 3, the Alpine Club—a group made up of youngsters of Mexican descent—held a meeting in a police substation in Los Angeles. They met in the police station, at the invitation of an officer, because of the circumstance that the nearby public school happened to be closed. With a police officer present, they met to discuss their problems, foremost of which, at this meeting, was the urgent question of how best to preserve the peace in their locality.[13]

When the meeting concluded they were taken in police patrol cars to the street corner which was closest to the neighborhood in which most of the youths lived. "The squad cars were scarcely out of sight, when the boys were assaulted. Thus began the recent weekend race riots in Los Angeles."[14]

On Saturday, June 5, the Los Angeles *Herald-Express* carried the following dispatch:

> "Task Force" Hits Los Angeles Zooters. A Petty Officer says, "We're out to do what the police have failed to do—We're going to clean up this situation to the satisfaction of ourselves and the public. . . ."[15]

In East Los Angeles and Belvedere Gardens, the police arrested nine sailors on charges of disturbing the peace. On June 7, the *Herald-Express* featured photographs which showed two servicemen in the hospital and zoot-suiters in chains being taken to jail after the "Battle of Skid Row," the "Battle of Firestone," and the "Battle of North Broadway."[16]

The *Los Angeles Times* on Tuesday, June 8 featured the riots on its front page:

> Heaviest street rioting in downtown city streets in many years. Thousands of servicemen, joined by thousands of civilians last night surged along Main Street and Broadway hunting zoot-suiters. Chief of Police Horrall declared riot alarm at 10:30 P.M. and ordered every policeman on duty. More than fifty zoot-suiters had

[11]*Ibid.*, p. 22.
[12]*Ibid.*, p. 20.
[13]Carey McWilliams, "The Zoot-Suit Riots," *The New Republic,* 208 (June 21, 1943), p. 818.
[14]*Ibid.*
[15]Los Angeles *Herald-Express* (June 5, 1943), p. A–1.
[16]*Herald-Express* (June 7, 1943), p. A–3.

clothing torn off as servicemen and civilians converged on bars, restaurants, penny arcades, and stores in downtown area searching for zoot-suiters. Streetcars were halted and theatres along Main Street were scrutinized for hiding zoot-suiters . . . [More] clashes broke out later in the evening in various parts of the county with more than 200 servicemen gathering at a theatre at 4th Street and Brooklyn Avenue and rousting zoot-suiters out of their seats. Police were handicapped by the tremendous crowds of civilians who apparently had listened to the police riot calls on the radio and had rushed into downtown. . . . Traffic blocked as groups raced into streets after victims. [They] would disperse only after they "unpan[t]sed" the wearer of the comical clothing.[17]

On June 8, the *Herald-Express* displayed pictures showing "zooters" in "protective custody." They were being held in jail to keep them from being attacked by the angry servicemen. Another picture showed a crowd of typical men and women gathered around servicemen who were man-handling and stripping any zoot-suiters who approached. The crowd cheered the servicemen.[18]

Most of the heavy rioting took place over the week-end but the newspapers did not finish with their stories. On June 9, the *Herald-Express* carried two feature articles with large pictures of the participants.

A Vernon police officer near death from being run down by a carload of zootsuit gangsters who set a trap for him.

A "pachuco woman" held for assertedly being prepared to smuggle aluminum "knucks" to zoot suit hoodlums.[19]

On June 10, the *Herald-Express* headlined the following:

Zoot Girls Stab Woman; State Probes Rioting

Grand Jury to Act in Zoot-Suit War[20]

On June 16, the *Los Angeles Times* headlined the following stories:

Zoot Cyclists Snatch Purses

Mexican Government Expects Damages for Zoot Riot Victims[21]

The editorials of the newspapers left no doubt as to which side the papers were on. The following editorial was entitled "Zoot Suiters Learn."

It was a sad day when zoot suiters began to molest some United States Navy men

---

[17] *Los Angeles Times* (June 8, 1943), p. 1.
[18] Los Angeles *Herald-Express* (June 8, 1943), p. B–1.
[19] *Herald-Express* (June 9, 1943), p. A–1.
[20] *Herald-Express* (June 10, 1943), p. A–1.
[21] *Times* (June 16, 1943), p. 2.

and some members of their families. . . . They promise to rid the community of one of its newest evils—those zoot-suited miscreants who have committed many crimes and have added a very serious side to juvenile delinquency problems.[22]

The Los Angeles County Grand Jury held an investigation of the riots. This body looked into juvenile crime and delinquency. In its final report the Grand Jury acknowledged the seriousness of the situation and the failure of the 1942 Grand Jury investigations and recommendations to stimulate community interest in coping with juvenile gang violence. "When the 1943 Grand Jury came into office the problem seemed no nearer solution than it had six months before. Indeed it seemed to be in an even more aggravated condition."[23] The Grand Jury, however, refused to conclude that this condition had been brought about because of racial prejudice.

The Jury finds that juvenile crimes do not have for their motive or reason class or racial hatred or discrimination. Ill-informed and reckless persons, by unfounded charges of racial discrimination against the Mexican people, have done little to promote harmony between this nation and our sister republic to the south.[24]

Governor Earl Warren also initiated an investigation into the riots. The *Los Angeles Times* reported that this special committee had taken recess after learning "that the zoot suit problem was not a racial one. . . ."[25]

On June 17 and 18, 1943, the *Times* featured the opposing viewpoints of Eleanor Roosevelt and Robert Hotchkis, President of the California State Chamber of Commerce. The First Lady stated that the riots could be traced to what she called long-standing discrimination against Mexicans in that part of the country. " For a long time I've worried about the attitudes toward Mexicans in California and the States along the border."[26] Mrs. Roosevelt added that the riots were not simply youth problems but were provoked by elements which had little to do with youth. Mr. Hotchkis, filled with righteous indignation, answered Mrs. Roosevelt on the next day: "The statement that the citizens of California have discriminated against persons of Mexican-origin is untrue, unjust, and provocative of disunion among people who have lived for years in harmony."[27]

Time magazine devoted some space to zoot-suit riots and added its own opinion. It pointed out that "California's zoot-suit war was a shameful example of what happens to wartime emotions without wartime discipline."[28]

[22] *Herald-Express* (June 8, 1943), p. B–2.
[23] Los Angeles County Grand Jury, *Final Report of the 1943 Los Angeles County Grand Jury: Report of the Special Committee on Racial Problems*, p. 27.
[24] Los Angeles County Grand Jury, *Findings and Recommendations of the Grand Jury of Los Angeles County (1943), Based Upon Its Inquiry into Juvenile Crime and Delinquency in that County*, p. 4.
[25] *Los Angeles Times* (June 16, 1943), p. 2.
[26] *Times* (June 17, 1943), p. 2.
[27] *Times* (June 18, 1943), p. 2.
[28] "California: Zoot-Suit War," *Time* (June 21, 1943), p. 18.

Time criticized local publishers Hearst and Chandler for stirring the violence to higher proportions.[29] *Time* stated that young Mexican-American organized gangs had gotten out of hand. "They had robbed and used their knives on some lone sailors on dark side streets."[30] The magazine added:

"If the pachucos had asked for trouble, they got more than was coming to them last week. The military authorities were notably lax. . . . The Los Angeles Police apparently looked the other way."[31]

The Los Angeles community itself had to share the blame for escalating the riots continued *Time*. "And Los Angeles, apparently unaware that it was spawning the ugliest brand of riot action since the coolie race riots of the 1870s gave its tacit approval."[32]

[29] *Ibid.*
[30] *Ibid.*
[31] *Ibid.*, p. 19.
[32] *Ibid.*

3

Brown Power in the Schools*

It is not completely clear what aroused the Mexican-American community to react forcefully to the prejudice and discrimination they had experienced for years. But with the actions of Cesar Chavez, Tijerina, and others the Mexican-American people began to demand what they had a right to. This militancy was evident in many areas of American society, especially in education where the language barrier had seriously hurt the chances of Mexican-American students for advancement. Here Dial Torgerson explains the militancy behind the Brown Power movement in the Los Angeles schools.

Questions

1. What were the reasons given for the students' militancy?
2. What were the feelings of the students?
3. Did the teachers express the same feelings?
4. What was the significance of the movement?
5. What does the movement expect to accomplish?

"We want to walk out," a group of students at Lincoln High School told teacher Sal Castro last September. "Help us."

The students, like Castro, were Mexican-Americans—at a mostly Mexican-American school deep in the belt of east-of-downtown districts which together comprise the United States' most populous Mexican-American community.

"Don't walk out," Castro told them. "Organize."

And—as has now been seen—they did.

What resulted was a week-and-a-half of walkouts, speeches, sporadic lawbreaking, arrests, demands, picketing, sympathy demonstrations, sit-ins, police tactical alerts and emergency sessions of the school board.

It was, some say, the beginning of a revolution—the Mexican-American revolution of 1968.

In the midst of massive walkouts and police alerts, Dr. Julian Nava, only Mexican-American on the Los Angeles Board of Education, turned to Supt. of Schools Jack Crowther.

"Jack," said Nava, "This is BC and AD. The schools will not be the same hereafter."

"Yes," said Crowther, "I know."

First Mass Militancy

And, in the vast Mexican-American districts of the city and county of Los Angeles—the "barrios" (neighborhoods) where 800,000 people with Spanish names make their homes—leaders of a movement to unite what they call "La Raza" swear the barrios will never be the same, either.

Since World War II the Mexican-American community has had leaders calling for unity, change, better education, civil rights, economic opportunity and an end to what they called second-class citizenship.

But the community never backed them up. Except for a few instances of picketing, nothing happened.

Then came the school walkouts, the first act of mass militancy by Mexican-Americans in Southern California. "Viva la Revolucion," the youngsters' signs read. "Viva la Raza." (Raza translates "race" but is used in a sense of "our people.")

And, surprisingly to some, stunningly to others, the community backed them up.

The men and women of the once-conservative older generation jammed school board and civic meetings, shouting their approval of what their children had done. Parents of students arrested during demonstrations even staged a sit-in in the Hall of Justice.

"The people are with us, now," one young leader says.

Observers within the community say it heralds the entry of a powerful new force on the American scene: a newly united Mexican-American movement drawing a nationalistic, brown-power fervor from 4.5 million people in five Southwestern states.

With underground newspapers, cooperation with Negro groups, plans for political action and economic boycotts, leaders say they will show the country a new type of Mexican-American: one proud of his language, his culture, his raza, ready to take his share of U.S. prosperity.

Some experts, less swept along in the spirit of the movement, say they'll wait a while before they'll believe a few thousand school children can lead the typically divided, splintered Mexican-American millions into becoming a unified power.

But there's no doubt at the grassroots levels, where earlier pleas for unity never reached before—in the minds of the younger men and women on the streets of the barrios, from East Los Angeles to Pico Rivera, from the fringes of Watts north deep into the San Gabriel Valley.

Listen to the voices there of La Raza—and the message observers say these voices bring to the Anglo world:

. . . the scene is a rainy sidewalk outside East Los Angeles Junior College. A white panel truck halts and four young men in brown berets and mixed, cast-off Army fatigues and boots jump out, craning their heads left and right to see if they are pursued, and then file into the campus for a meeting.

They are members of the Brown Berets, the most militant of East Los Angeles Mexican-American groups. They have been accused of inciting high school students to riots, using narcotics, being Communists. There are several hundred of them here and in the Fresno area, their leaders say.

Frankly Admiring Students

"The deputies and the cops have really been harassing us," said David Sanchez, a college student who dropped out to be chairman of the Berets. "Sixty-five Brown Berets have been arrested in the past month. There are warrants out now for five of us because of the school walkouts."

The four sit on a concrete bench and speak in quiet voices to a newsman, glancing at times down the wet, windswept walkway toward the street, nodding in reply to greetings from frankly admiring students with the slightly superior air of young men slightly past 20, slightly revolutionary, and slightly wanted.

"Communism? That's a white thing," said Carlos Montes, mustachioed minister of public relations for the Berets. "It's their trip, not ours," said husky Ralph Ramirez, minister of discipline. Added Montes:

"It's pretty hard to mix Communists and Mexican-Americans. Che (Che Guevara, the late Cuban revolutionary some Berets seem to seek to resemble) doesn't mean a thing to the guy in the street. He's got his own problems."

Despite their vaguely ominous look, the Berets claim wide community support. "A lot of mothers' clubs help us with contributions," said Sanchez. "Men's clubs, too. They're happy to see there is finally a militant effort in the community. And they like what we're doing with the gangs."

In each barrio there are kids' gangs (The Avenues, the Clovers, the White French, Dog Town, Happy Valley) which have long shot up each other, and whole neighborhoods, in senseless warfare.

"Gang fights are going out," said Montes. "We're getting kids from all the different gangs into the Brown Berets. It's going to be one big barrio, one big gang. We try to teach our people not to fight with each other, and not to fight with our blood brothers to the south."

Police say the Berets were among the "outside agitators" who helped cause the student disturbances. "The Chicano students were the main action group," said Sanchez. (Chicano is a term for Mexican-Americans which members of the community use in describing themselves.)

"We were at the walkouts to protect our younger people. When they (law officers) started hitting with sticks, we went in, did our business, and got out." What's "our business"? "We put ourselves between the police and the kids, and took the beating," Sanchez said.

Significance Explored

What significance lies behind the militant movement?

"They've given these people a real revolutionary experience," said Dr. Ralph Guzman, a professor of political science at Cal State Los Angeles. "No Marxist could do better. They're making rebels. When they see police clubbing them, it's the final evidence that society is against them—that existing within the system won't work."

"I don't know what's going to happen. I'm worried. I think there will be violence. I'm not predicting it. But from what I've seen—I saw riots in South America and India when I was with the Peace Corps—I think we all have a potential for violence."

... The scene is Cleland House, a community meeting hall in East Los

Angeles. Two hundred people, most of them adults, jam the hall, facing representatives of police and the sheriff's and district attorney's office invited there by a civic group.

Student Gives Version

"We were at the alley, just breaking out, when the cops charged at us," said Robert Sanchez, 17, student at Roosevelt High. "If I could be allowed to express myself with dignity, I'd do so. But if they're grabbing me, or hitting me, and there's a rock or a brick there, I'd throw it."

"The only reported injury," said Police Inspector Jack Collins, head of the patrol division, calmly, "was a police officer hit in the eye with a bottle . . ."

"Parents got beat up, too!" yelled a man's voice.

"Now try to get out of that one!" shouted Sanchez.

In an office, later, Lincoln High teacher Castro explained the walkouts:

Teacher Tells His Story

"It started with the kids from Lincoln," said Castro, 34, a social studies and government teacher who himself grew up in the East Los Angeles barrios. "They wanted things changed at the school. They wanted to hold what they call a 'blowout'—a walkout.

"I stopped them. I said, 'Blow out now and everyone will think it's because you want short skirts and long hair. Organize. What do you need?'

"They said they needed some help in making signs, printing up demands, things like that. We got them help from college kids—mostly from the United Mexican-American Students at the different colleges. A blowout committee was established at each of the four East L.A. schools. And there was one committee with kids from each school.

Original Plan

"The original plan was to go before the Board of Education and propose a set of changes, without walking out—to hold that back to get what they wanted. Then, at Wilson High Friday (March 1), the principal canceled a play they were going to do ("Barefoot in the Park") as unfit, and the Wilson kids blew out. It was spontaneous.

"Then Roosevelt and Lincoln wanted to blow, too. Garfield, too. Later on (March 8) Belmont, which was never in on the original plan, came in, too.

"These blowouts in the other schools, like Venice and Jefferson, weren't connected with the Chicano blowouts, but they may have been in sympathy. Some of the kids from schools uptown asked us to send representatives to tell them how to organize.

"What do you think of that! The Anglo schools asking the Chicano kids to help them organize. They should've told them 'Ask your dads how they organized to oppress us all these years.' "

Thought Questions

1. Analyze the relevance of the fantasy heritage.
2. How can the "zoot suit" riots be viewed as an example of racial discrimination?
3. Compare and contrast Red Power and Brown Power.

thirteen

ORIENTALS:

The Silent Minority

Today there are over one million people of Oriental descent in the United States, and while they have not been in the United States as long as the Indians, blacks, or Mexican-Americans, they have made substantial contributions to American culture and have frequently borne the worst persecution in the American experience.

The Chinese first came to America during the gold rush days in California. As they grew in numbers, working diligently and successfully at low-paying jobs, economic competition caused hostile feelings among white workers. In the 1860s Chinese also worked successfully on the transcontinental railroad, further antagonizing many white westerners. Obviously, the fact that they looked and sounded differently made them objects of fear and suspicion to an ignorant white populace. By the 1860s and 1870s hostility grew into open violence and "anti-coolie" clubs grew, government passed restrictive legislation, and the Workingman's Party dedicated itself to the exclusion of the Chinese. The growing agitation against the Chinese in California and the West channeled to Congress where some members agitated for an exclusion bill. Eventually, in 1882 Congress solidified growing anti-Chinese sentiment in the Chinese Exclusion Act of 1883. In 1902 Chinese immigration to the United States was banned. But many of the Chinese people remained in the United States, and their children became United States citizens.

The Japanese began to come to America at the time when anti-Chinese feelings were very strong. They did not, however, really arrive in large numbers until the 1890s. From the early 1900s they felt the racial hostility; many Californians talked of having them excluded also. Their children were placed in separate schools, and the California State Legislature tried to legislate them out of existence, particularly through the alien land laws. The climax of anti-Japanese feeling came with World War II and the attack on Pearl Harbor. Some 122,000 Japanese-Americans were moved to relocation camps, even though two-thirds of them were American *citizens*. This action has been justified in many ways, but generally it was seen as a defensive military act. Attorney General Francis Biddle, President Franklin Roosevelt, Secretary of War Stimson all concurred on its necessity. The relocation caused a great deal of suffering and hardship, although the government claimed that "normal living" was maintained in the camps. The general Japanese-American structure was undermined by the evacuation, not to mention the millions of dollars of property that was lost. With the end of the war, the Japanese-Americans reassimilated themselves into American society.

I

Welcome to the Chinese*

The early Chinese who came to America looking for the "Land of the Golden Mountain" were welcomed with open arms by many citizens of California, even Governor Douglas. San Francisco set aside a part of their city for the planting of Little China or Chinatown, and looked upon the people with much civic pride. They proved to be good workers, often better than their American counterparts. Because of white jealousy of their early success as miners and sources of cheap labor, they became subject in California to hostility and even open violence. Mining riots, for example, directed against the Chinese were quite common by the 1860s. Here Reverend William Speer, former missionary to China, writes of the value of the Chinese in America.

Questions

1. What stand does Speer take on the Chinese?
2. Is his picture a positive or a negative one?
3. Were his arguments generally well accepted?

The Chinese are a heathen, and a peculiar people, as yet to us the objects of ignorant wonder and misapprehension. They will soon be better understood and appreciated. Some of their practices have excited great distrust. They are prone to form troublesome guilds, and unite in a species of masonic fraternization. But this is a natural result of their residence under the tyrannical governments, and among the overwhelming masses of population, which they have quitted. The representation, made by ignorant or interested persons here, of their employment in companies as *coolies,* by great capitalists at home,

Source: Rev. William Speer, *China and California* (San Francisco: Marrin and Hitchcock, 1853), pp. 16–17.

is incorrect. This can be sustained by statements from the best authorities in China. But they are wise enough to soon understand their danger and their advantages in this country; and the very opposition to them will assist their fusion into the mass of American civilization and progress. We believe they will keep the promise made in one of the letters published here last year. "If the privileges of your laws are open to us, some of us will doubtless acquire your habits, your language, your ideas, your feelings, your morals, your forms, and become citizens of your country. Many have already adopted your religion in their own, and we will be good citizens. There are very good Chinamen now in the country; and a better class will, if allowed, come hereafter—men of learning and wealth, bringing their families with them." We believe the intellectual countrymen of the famous Ke-ying and Hwang Antung will, in time, be christianized, and add wisdom and dignity even to our halls of legislature.

Let, then, the United States, every considerate man will say, encourage the influx of this people. The wisest of the European colonists in the East, from the days of Miguel de Legazpi, who was despatched from Mexico, in 1564, to conquer the Philippine Islands, and was the first to send vessels across the Great Ocean from Asia to America, until the present time, have everywhere warmly invited and favored a Chinese immigration. Ever since their subjugation to the Tartar yoke, two centuries ago, they have been ready to leave their country in large numbers. Wherever their foot has rested, like the fabulous dragon painted on their imperial standard, they have been the symbol of prosperity. It were unwise to repel or injure those from whose auspices it requires little skill to augur great blessings. They are a proud, a timid, a peace-loving race, and we may scare them away. California, wonderful as has been her advance, may learn a lesson of wisdom from the desolations of once rich and prosperous nations and colonies of the East. "The causes which have eclipsed the prosperity of Borneo, and other former great emporiums of Eastern trade," have been traced justly to "the decay of their commerce," which has chiefly resulted from a barbarous commercial despotism, that put a stop to their direct intercourse with China. This, says an intelligent writer, ended in "first, the destruction of extensive branches of home industry," and to the fatal effect of preventing the annual immigration of large bodies of Chinese, who settled on their shores, and exercised their mechanic arts and productive industry; thus keeping up the prosperity of the country by the tillage of the ground, as well as in the commerce of their ports." For the want of this commerce, many of these lands, once wealthy and prosperous, "have run to jungle," while their cities have sunk down, "like Carthage, to be mere nests of banditti."

But the *scholar,* as well as those who regard only our temporal welfare as a people, has a deep interest in the emigration of the Chinese. The language of the Chinese is to a large degree ideographic—representing ideas independent of speech. Many of its symbolical characters are highly beautiful—as, for instance, that for "leisure, rest," which represents a door, through which the moon is shining. It is, as has been truly said, "a study, which when commenced begets an enthusiasm which is difficult to moderate." It is a mine of boundless riches for our future Pickerings, Websters, and Anthons. In a philological view, the study of this language is important. "The revolution within the last thirty years in the science of philology, is one which for magnitude and rapidity has not been surpassed in the history of the human mind. When the scholars of Europe directed their intellectual vision to that newly-discovered star in the East, the Sanscrit—now so brightly illumining the horizon of philology—they began to anticipate a discovery of no less importance than the means of demonstrating the correctness of those views of the fundamental connection existing between all languages which had long pressed themselves on the attention of critical minds."— . . .

2

The Modern Chinese*

Stereotypes of the Chinese as the Yellow Peril or Charley Chan still exist today, despite the efforts of many Chinese to fit into American society and to make valid contributions. Francis L. K. Hsu describes the relationship between the Chinese today and the American dream. Note how well he feels the Chinese are being allowed into the mainstream of American life.

Questions

1. What is the American dream?
2. Do the Chinese want to become fully Americanized?

Source: From *The Challenge of the American Dream: The Chinese in the United States* by Francis L. K. Hsu. © 1971 by Wadsworth Publishing Co., Inc., Belmont, California 94002. Reprinted by permission of the publisher.

3. How do the Chinese participate in the American dream?
4. Is the American dream still alive and well?

Full Participation in the American Dream

If the Chinese and other immigrant and minority groups fix their sights primarily on self-advancement by pursuing the line of least resistance, they will never be fully American. They and their children may become rich and physically comfortable, and they will have contributed to the American society by their physical labor and skills. But they will not have fully participated in the American Dream, for that dream is not merely the acquisition of material wealth in the form of more skyscrapers, more subdivisions, and a bigger share in the Gross National Product (though that is an important part), but the achievement of a just society which can live in peace with the rest of the world, and in which men are freed from oppression and mutual distrust, and where equal opportunities are open to all. It is toward this part of the American Dream that the Chinese in America have yet to aspire and exert themselves. It is upon the realization of this aspect of the American Dream that the American society will ultimately depend for its future, unless we allow the present unsalutary features of American attitudes and behavior characteristics enumerated before—eternal aggression to enforce American supremacy, internal division due to prejudice and violence, alienation and the decimation of family and kinship—to turn the American Dream into an American Nightmare. What are the Chinese in America doing about the situation?

The Chinese have not, of course, been in America long enough. Since most of them came from humble origins, they simply have not had time to raise their sights to a higher level than limited economic or professional successes.

Then, numerically, Chinese-Americans are insignificant. They constitute the smallest of the minority groups in the United States. Under the circumstances, they are even more likely to be threatened by what Alexis de Tocqueville described as the tyranny of the majority. He spoke of this tyranny in terms of a majority which controls the public force, the judiciary decisions, and legislative processes, and leaves no choice for the minority except abject submission. This tyranny can be especially crippling to some member of the minority whose attempt to make some positive contribution is scornfully spurned by the majority, as the following episode would indicate.

Fong Chow was a Cantonese who came to northern California in the latter part of the nineteenth century during the Gold Rush days. In spite of white prejudice and disabling discrimination, he made a small fortune in his limited way. In appreciation of what his children's school and its teacher had done, Fong spent the colossal sum (for him) of $100 to purchase an elaborately embroidered Chinese silk hanging for a school wall. A storm of protest was raised by the white parents of the mining town, who did not want their children subjected to any aspect of the inferior Chinese cultural influence. Fong's face was temporarily saved when the teacher threatened resignation in mid year if the silk hanging were removed. However, the tapestry and the teacher left the town together at the end of the school year.

The American social and psychological climate in which the minorities find themselves in the 1970's is vastly different from that of Fong Chow in northern California during the Gold Rush days. Unless we are satisfied with things as they are, white Americans as well as minority Americans must proceed on the assumption that the American society is perfectable. In that context, the Chinese in the United States need not feel that they are in any less advantageous position than other groups.

Contribution to the American Dream can be made in large or small packages. For example, the semi-fictional Hakka woman, Char Nyuk Tsin, wife of a leper in the late nineteenth century, whose saga occupied a place in James A. Michener's *Hawaii,* devoted herself for several years not only to serving her dying husband in the leper colony in Molokai, but after his death also worked to transform the leper society from one of total chaos into a sort of organized community. Hers was a selfless dedication of the highest order to a cause which is also exemplified by Western greats from Florence Nightingale to St. Francis Xavier. But, characteristically Chinese, Char Nyuk Tsin devoted the rest of her life to the rearing and betterment of her five sons once she left the abnormal environment of the leper colony. She was not any less admirable for it, but the fact is that the scope of her dedication was defined by kinship and pseudo-kinship.

Another Chinese of humble origin was responsible for the establishment of the Department of Chinese and the Chinese library at Columbia University. In the Gold Rush days, Dean Lung was a domestic in the employ of a naturalized American who was a retired French army general. He was extremely devoted to his employer and his devotion was not shaken by the latter's bad temper and abuse. Instead, he would quote his own half-baked version of Confucian sayings to his erratic employer to explain why he did not leave. One day when Lung's employer asked him what he would like as an expression of his employer's gratitude, Lung replied:

> You pay me for my service. I desire for myself nothing more. But United States people know little about Chinese culture and philosophy. Could you do something about that?

Lung's employer made a very large contribution to Columbia University for the establishment of the Chinese department and library. Into that contribution Lung added the sum of $12,000 representing his entire savings from many years' work as a servant. Therefore, Columbia University also inaugurated the Dean Lung Professorship of Chinese.

We need more Chinese–Americans who will excel not merely in their own crafts and specialties and the amassing of wealth. We need more Chinese who, whatever their occupational endeavors, will apply themselves in earnest and with zeal to the human side of the American Dream. They will not just search for rewards and accolades within the boundaries of the established scheme of things. Instead, they will address themselves to ways and means for realizing the progressive idealism embodied in the American Dream.

It was the vision of our forefathers in the New World that began the American Dream. Throughout American history not all who called themselves Americans were in tune with that dream. In fact, many of them tried their best to destroy it. But it was men and women such as Lincoln, Jefferson, Jackson, John Brown, Harriet Beecher Stowe, Henry David Thoreau, Martin Luther King, Robert Kennedy, Charles Evers, James Earle Fraser, Orestes Brownson, and many others, whose dedication moved the American reality closer to that dream, at least in some respects. These men and women were not all in high places or equally famous. They and others like them are men and women who dared to stand up and be counted on important issues, to dissent and champion unpopular causes at the risk of loss of income, ostracism, or even persecution and jail. Their successors today are speaking up against the Vietnam War and against racial and other injustices at home.

It is easy, in the face of mounting internal and external violence and other problems, to be cynical and say that today we are farther from that Dream than before. Yet, those who care to look will surely realize it is not accident that, as we saw in the previous chapter, the egalitarian patterns of our legal, educational, and social institutions are in sharp contrast to those which prevail in the racist Union of South Africa. Those who are disgusted with American military ventures abroad must at least concede that the change from the pursuit of a purely military victory to a policy of negotiated settlement in Vietnam and the restraints on the use of our enormous powers are directly related to the opposition at home. Did Napoleonic France and Imperial Japan exercise such restraints? Did any European powers in their heyday of colonialism and world-wide expansion exercise restraints with reference to any of the Asian or African peoples they conquered?

The Chinese in America must actively participate in the American Dream by seeking its further realization. In this their Chinese cultural heritage is an advantage and not a liability. In contrast to Whites, they can more easily draw on that heritage for ideas and for behavior patterns which may be instrumental in remedying the defects of the American reality and adding to its progressive idealism. They can more easily take advantage of their ancestral cultural heritage for two reasons. Because they will always be linked with some or all aspects of Chinese culture in the eyes of non-Chinese (whether or not they care for such a linkage), they can speak about the Chinese ways to the non-Chinese public with greater authority. More importantly, since most of them were and will be raised wholly or partly by Chinese parents and grandparents, the Chinese in America cannot help but carry with them some of the content of the Chinese orientation towards men, gods, and things. They can, therefore, more readily attain insight into the Chinese ways and exhibit them behavior-wise. Since they live or were born in America, are raised in American schools, work in the American environment, and read and speak English, they have the opportunity to communicate and enjoy a unique cross-cultural facility for this task.

The problem is not merely to recognize this unique opportunity; having recognized it, will the Chinese in America seize it—to their own advantage and to the advantage of the United States of America with whose future they have, by their American citizenship, identified themselves?

3

The Relocation Camps*

In 1924 the Immigration Act, which set up a quota system, did not give a quota to Japan. It appeared that the Japanese problem was being handled in essentially the same way as the Chinese problem had been. Anti-Japanese feelings did not disappear with the passage of the Immigration Act, for the Japanese remained evident and hostile feelings surfaced again with the attack on Pearl Harbor. After a series of military decisions, the West Coast Japanese were moved from the "military zones" to temporary then permanent relocation camps until the end of the war. When some Japanese-Americans attempted to take their case to the Supreme Court, the Court went along with the reasoning of government officials and decided that relocation was legal because of military necessity. Carey McWilliams describes the relocation centers where Japanese-Americans lived during most of the war.

*Source: From *Prejudice* by Carey McWilliams. Copyright © 1955 by Carey McWilliams. Reprinted by permission of the author.

Questions

1. What were the conditions in the centers?
2. How was housing arranged?
3. What was the government structure?
4. What were the general advantages and disadvantages of the camps?

The WRA centers are, in essence, ten government-sponsored Little Tokyos located in isolated regions of the inter-mountain West. The projects, as such, were designed by the army engineers. Only in the imagination of an investigator for the Dies Committee could they be described as "adequate housing." The barracks themselves are merely temporary shelters, hastily constructed, inadequately planned. In the original plan, one room was provided for each family; but this standard has been more honored in the breach than in the observance. Given the monotonous character of the construction itself and the desolate character of the environment, it is not surprising that the centers are such dreary establishments. They are surrounded by barbed-wire fences, with watchtowers and armed guards, and searchlights play upon the area at night. Community washrooms and toilets are established for each block within the area. In huge mess halls within each block the evacuees are fed at a cost to the government between 34 and 42 cents per day. No one has starved in these centers and no one has frozen to death; everyone has shelter and sustenance. But this is about as much as can be said in defense of the centers as housing projects.

During the first weeks and months after its establishment, WRA was primarily concerned with getting the centers ready for occupancy, recruiting personnel, and establishing certain administrative policies. Recruiting a staff for such a unique agency as WRA was a difficult assignment. There were few persons in the field of government service who had had any experience in dealing with the Japanese or who had any knowledge of Japanese culture or language. The distant location of the centers and their isolation were major obstacles in securing personnel. Fortunately, the Indian Service could be tapped, as it was, for a nucleus of experienced administrators around whom a staff was built. By and large, the staff has been, in the words of Dr. Robert Redfield, more than "ordinarily high," including "men and women with devotion to liberal and humanitarian principles." It is to the lasting credit of the administration that men such as Milton Eisenhower and Dillon Myer were selected to head the authority. It is also to the credit of the administration that political considerations have played virtually no part in the selection of the staff. With the exception of a few clerical employees in the Washington office and in the various relocation employment offices, the entire staff is Caucasian. No Japanese or Japanese-Americans occupy posts in the administrative staff as such.

"Nothing quite like these relocation centers," observes Dr. Redfield, "has ever appeared before in the history of America." They resemble army camps; they are like Indian reservations; they resemble the FSA resettlement projects, and they are somewhat like the internment camps for dangerous enemy aliens. To call them "concentration camps" after the pattern of Dachau and Oranienburg would be a gross exaggeration. A degree of self-government is permitted in the camps, and, so far as possible, the constitutional rights of the evacuees have been respected. Complete freedom of religious worship has been safeguarded; every variety of church service may be found. There is no censorship of mail. Open meetings may be held with the approval of the project director as to time and place, and both English and Japanese may be spoken. Newspapers are published in most of the centers and are certainly outspoken, as an examination of the files will readily show. Obviously, it would be an exaggeration to say that the rights of free speech and of a free press are exercised in the centers with the same freedom from restraint that exists outside. But the point is that these rights have not been wholly suppressed nor altogether restrained.

Through their co-operative organizations, evacuees carry on many important community enterprises in the centers, including such personal services as shoe-repair shops, mending and pressing shops, beauty parlors and barbershops, and the sale of such goods as clothing, confections, toilet goods, stationery, and books and magazines. These enterprises pay WRA a minimum rental for the space they occupy. They have been financed by the evacuees; they are operated by the evacuees; and they are all co-operative nonprofit enterprises. Certain of these co-operatives have accumulated substantial assets.

Evacuees in the relocation centers are governed by three categories of law and regulations: (1) the general law of the United States and the state in which the center is situated; (2) the regulations of the WRA and the project director; and (3) regulations made by the community council under the authority of the project director and with his approval. The maintenance of internal security is a function of WRA; external security is an army function discharged by small detachments of military police. To assist in maintaining law and order within the centers, WRA has established a special detention center in Leupp, Arizona, to which "incorrigibles"—chronic violators of center regulations—are sent on the authority of the project directors (there are about seventy evacuees in the Leupp center).

Approximately 90 per cent of the employable residents of the centers are employed by WRA—in all manner of administrative and work projects, in the offices of mess halls, hospitals, farms, work projects, and so on. These evacuees receive cash allowances of twelve, sixteen, or nineteen dollars a month, according to the nature of their duties. No one seems to know how these rates were determined, except that they were supposed to bear some relation to basic army pay which, at the time the centers were opened, was twenty-one dollars a month. Medical care and hospitalization are furnished without charge; and, to date, health conditions in the centers have been remarkably good. No charge is made for room and board.

Initially, WRA toyed with the idea of creating genuine resettlement projects; but this policy was virtually abandoned by the autumn of 1942. In fact, the idea was abandoned before even the basic policies for the proposed projects could be formulated. Three factors were responsible for this basic shift in policy: (*a*) the surprising success of the seasonal leave program; (*b*) strenuous public opposition to competing commercial projects in the centers; and (*c*) the ever-increasing manpower shortage outside the centers. At the present time, only a restricted works program is carried on in the centers. There are a few small-scale industrial projects, such as the manufacture of camouflage nets for the Army, silk screen posters for the Navy, ship models for the Navy's construction program, and similar projects.

The farming operations are conducted solely for the purpose of supplying the center residents with a portion of the food they consume. Vegetable production, in all the centers, for the year 1943, was valued at $2,750,000. "We are not planning to produce crops for the market at these centers," to quote from Mr. Myer's testimony before the Dies Committee. Since most of the land was raw, undeveloped land, requiring drainage, irrigation, and the construction of extensive canals and laterals, it would have taken an estimated five years to bring 20,000 acres under cultivation. In its current efforts to avoid the "institutionalization" of the evacuees, WRA has deliberately sought to minimize its agricultural and industrial projects.

There are nearly 30,000 Japanese-American youngsters of school age in the centers. Due to the abnormal population pyramid, there is a higher percentage of school-age children among the evacuees than among the total population, and a striking concentration in the number of students of high-school age. Establishing complete school systems in each of the ten centers has been, in itself, a major undertaking. Local school authorities have not been uniformly co-operative. Proposals that evacuee students be admitted to the state colleges and universities in Arkansas (where two of the centers are located) met with emphatic opposition. Requests from the WRA to the University of Arizona for extension courses, library books, and faculty lectures for the evacuees in that state have been consistently denied. In the words of President Alfred Atkinson: "We are at war and *these people* are our enemies." Even the request of WRA to have twelve or fifteen Japanese children admitted to the Oregon School for the Deaf was curtly denied by the local authorities. "This is no time," to quote from their refusal, "to admit Japanese children to the Oregon deaf school, particularly in view of the war."

Despite all of these handicaps, including a serious shortage of teachers, WRA has improvised a makeshift school system. Some centers have much better schools than others. The schools at the Granada (Colorado) Relocation Center are the best that I have seen. In some of the centers, evacuee personnel has been drafted to meet the demand for teachers; thereby creating a serious rift in the teaching staff between the regularly paid Caucasian personnel and the evacuee personnel paid nineteen dollars a month for precisely the same service. The whole atmosphere of the centers is so abnormal that it is debatable whether, given the best in personnel and equipment, much could be done in creating an adequate educational program. Fortunately it has been possible to relocate a good many college and university students in Eastern and Middle Western institutions (largely through the assistance of private organizations).

In some of the centers, excellent adult educational programs have been conducted. At Topaz, for example, 3250 adults are enrolled in 165 different classes: democracy in action, auto mechanics, cabinetmaking, carpentry, cooperatives, radio repairing, American history, American foreign affairs, current events, psychology, English, German, shorthand, public administration, practical electricity, first aid, and so on. Both Issei and Nisei are enrolled in these courses; and, from my own observation, I should say that the Issei evince a greater interest than the Nisei. For the centers as a whole, over 25 per cent of the adult population is currently enrolled in such courses and the two most popular subjects are English and American history. It is unquestionably true that, for some of the Issei, relocation has afforded an opportunity for study and self-improvement previously denied them. Even in the assembly centers, where the circumstances were most unfavorable, a real and active interest was shown in these courses.

By and large, there has been only a slight impairment of the rights of the Nisei as American citizens. On January 28, 1943, they were declared eligible for enlistment in the combat team; still more recently they have been removed from the 4-F classification, for selective service, into which they had been put after Pearl Harbor. Today they are at liberty to leave the centers whenever they wish (subject only to the liberal clearance rules of WRA) and to go wherever they wish, with the exception of those portions of the Western Defense Command (the coastal areas) from which they were excluded. While citizens in the relocation centers cannot qualify as voters in the areas to which they have been removed, since they lack technical "residence" within the meaning of state statutes, nevertheless they may continue to vote by absentee ballot in the communities in which they formerly resided and in which they still retain residence.

Thought Questions

1. Compare and contrast the general treatment of Japanese and Chinese people in America.
2. Compare and contrast the reasons for Japanese-American relocation.
3. Analyze the position of the modern Japanese and Chinese in America.

fourteen

GENERAL CULTURE:
The Intellectual Tradition
Revisited

American culture as mirror of the American mind reflects, and at the same time sets the trend for, what Americans think and how they act. Modern American culture is still rooted in the colonial period. During the colonial period, European trends in literature and science influenced American thinkers greatly. Early education and literature frequently reflected the influence of religion, but with the American Revolution state and church were separated and growth in science was noticeable.

The period of national growth from the American Revolution to the Civil War was also a period of growing cultural maturity. More writers were dealing with more varied themes. Scientists were becoming more prominent and science sophisticated. And education was moving from a one-room schoolhouse to a modern classroom. The upheaval that came with the growth of the industrial city was reflected in the American consciousness of thinkers and writers who pondered the present and future of America.

The frustration of twentieth century culture is seen in the frustrations of modern America. Wars, birth control, Women's Liberation, the Civil Rights Movement, passivism, and other themes have caused American thinkers to branch out and become more intense in their search for truth. Computers seem to be beginning to almost think for themselves. Writers are discussing themes involving blacks, whites, and Indians. Best-sellers today range from sex manuals to automechanics for women to historical novels. But society may not be keeping up with these changes. The educated are not being completely employed, and many writers see a future with little air and too many people. Yet writers and thinkers, paradoxically, both formulate and clarify culture, as they are molded by it themselves.

Thoreau*

Henry David Thoreau wrote not only in ecological terms of the beauty of nature and solitude in the wilderness, but also of an idea that the best government is that which governs least. His ideas have appealed to many who believe in passive resistance, such as Martin Luther King, Jr. Writer Van Wyck Brooks talks of Thoreau—the man and writer.

Questions

1. How does Brooks describe Thoreau?
2. Does he seem to be described as a loner?
3. What type of person would you say that Thoreau was from this reading?

In Emerson's white house on the Boston turnpike, Henry Thoreau had taken up his quarters. He occupied the room at the head of the stairs, a little room, but he was a little man: his nose and his thoughts were the biggest things about him. Emerson, and especially Emerson's children, had formed a warm affection for their difficult Henry, difficult, that is, for the rest of Concord but a treasure for the household of a sage. He was short, lean, frail, although nobody guessed it, he was so tough and muscular, with a meagre chest, long arms falling from the collar-bone, a workman's hands and feet, a huge Emersonian beak, rather like Julius Caesar's, bright blue eyes and flaxen hair. He walked with the swinging stride of an old campaigner. His manners were of the homespun sort, different indeed from Emerson's. But, after the first encounter, one perceived that, if Henry Thoreau was a thorn-bush, he was the kind that bears the fragrant flowers.

*Source: From the book *The Flowering of New England* by Van Wyck Brooks. Copyright 1936, 1952 by Van Wyck Brooks. Renewal © 1964 by Gladys Brooks. Published by E. P. Dutton & Co., Inc. and used with their permission.

He was the son of the pencil-maker, who had his little house and shop on Main Street: "J. Thoreau and Sons." The Thoreaus were a mercantile family of small pretensions who had seen better days. They were well-connected in the Channel Islands, where the French Thoreaus were prosperous wine-merchants. Their other forbears in Maine, the Scottish Dunbars, had taken the royalist side in the Revolution. As a barefoot village boy, Henry had driven the turkeys and the cow to pasture, and Emerson had vaguely heard of him as a poor student at Harvard. He had written to President Quincy, suggesting Henry's name for a scholarship. Later, Henry walked in to Boston, eighteen miles from Concord, to hear Emerson speak, and walked home again after the lecture. Emerson, touched by this, was still more touched when, after one of his Concord lectures, his sister-in-law, who was boarding with Mrs. Thoreau, said to him, "Henry Thoreau has a thought very like that in his journal." A friendship had soon sprung up between them, and when, one day, the Emersons went on a picnic, to the Cliffs on the Concord river, they asked Henry to join them and bring his flute. The village people looked askance at him because he was so pugnacious. He had queer ideas about teaching school, refusing to use the ferule; for with children and simple folk he was always gentle. With others, he was obstinate and harsh. He liked to administer doses of moral quinine, and he never thought of sugaring his pills. He had with-drawn from Dr. Ripley's church with a thesis more defiant than Martin Luther's. He liked to speak of a cold spot as "sultry," and he had a way of calling the woods "domestic." But at boating and camping he was a master-woodsman, skilled as Ulysses, shrewd as any fox. The redskins had forgotten the arts he knew. Arrowheads and Indian fireplaces sprang from the ground when he touched it. He charmed the snakes and fishes. Wild birds perched on his shoulder. His fingers seemed to have more wisdom in them than many a scholar's head.

This young Briareus of the hundred hands was something more than Emerson's factotum. There was nothing he could not do in the matter of painting and papering, building walls, repairing chicken-houses, pruning and grafting fruit-trees, surveying, tinkering, gardening. But these were trifles in his bag of tricks, useful to pay his way in the world and justify his creed of self-reliance. He was a master of other arts that Emerson also knew, and a scholar of unusual distinction; and he wished to be a philosopher, not a mere thinker of subtle thoughts but one who, loving wisdom, lived a life that was simple, magnanimous, free. In fact, he recalled those ancient sages who, when an enemy took the town, walked out of the gate empty-handed, without a care for the morrow. Why should one be burdened with impedimenta? Henry liked the soldier's life, always on the stretch and always ready for a battle. Each of his mornings brought its strenuous sortie. He lived "for to admire and for to see." He had spoken his mind in his college themes about the "blind and unmanly love of wealth" that actuated most of his fellow-beings. The order of things, he said, should be reversed. The seventh should be man's day of toil, wherein to earn his living by the sweat of his brow; he should keep the rest of the week for his joy and wonder.

These views delighted Emerson. In fact, the two agreed on so many subjects, always with an edge of difference, that one might well have supposed the relation between them was that of master and pupil. Emerson was fourteen years the elder; and it was true that Henry had acquired some of his traits and mannerisms: his handwriting, his voice, even his nose seemed to have gone to school to Emerson. There was something contagious in Emerson's aura; everyone was affected by it, nobody seemed able to resist it. Alcott was more than a little Emersonized; and as for Ellery Channing, what did the lady say who heard him lecture?—that his gait, his inflections, the very turn of his eyebrow were Emerson to the life. Henry Thoreau had felt this influence, as he had felt the influence of Carlyle. He had his own form, none the less. Emerson and he had grown in Concord, as two flowers grow in a common bed, one of them larger and more luxuriant, the other with a much more pungent odour; but they stood in different corners of the bed, with an ample space between them, so that the breeze could blow upon each of them freely. They were different enough in temperament, as in their personalities; and Henry phrased their common points of view with a sort of acidulous accent that was never heard on Emerson's lips.

They were of one mind in a dozen matters, not least in regard to the reformers. "As for these communities," said Henry, expressing their joint opinion, "I had rather keep bachelor's hall in hell than go to board in heaven." Much as he liked Alcott, the "best-natured man" he had ever met,—"the rats and mice make their nests in him,"—he turned up his nose at Fruitlands as well as at Brook Farm. He meant to bake his own bread in heaven, and wash his own clothes there. And suppose, he said, these grievances do exist? So do you and I. And the universal soul prefers the man who sets his own house in order first. A foul thing, this "doing good," observed the contemptuous Henry, instead of looking after one's own life, which ought to be one's business, taking care to flourish, and taste and smell sweet, refreshing all mankind. He had had encounters with reformers that filled him with abhorrence. They would not keep their distance. They tried to cover him with a slimy kindness that fairly took the starch out of his clothes. These "lovers" of their kind were almost more injurious to their kind than the feeble souls that met in drawing-rooms, fabulating and paddling in the social slush, and going to their beds unashamed, to take on a new layer of sloth.

2

Literature in the Late 1800s*

Nineteenth century literature reflected both the positive and negative aspects of American society. The local color writers told of the beauty of their own regions, while naturalists saw human life in terms of uncontrollable cosmic forces. There was often little tangible difference between the realistic and naturalistic writers of the time, for if they wrote truthfully there were many problems in the growing cities, as yet not dealt with or solved. One of the more sarcastic critics of American life was Ambrose Bierce. In this selection from his book Ashes of the Beacon, *he looks back at America from a perspective in 1930.*

Questions

1. What was Bierce's description of life in America?
2. What was his critique of American government?
3. Why did he think it failed?

Politics, which may have had something of the character of a context of principles, becomes a struggle of interests, and its methods are frankly serviceable to personal and class advantage. Patriotism and respect for law pass like a tale that is told. Anarchy, no longer disguised as "government by consent," reveals his hidden hand, and in the words of our greatest living poet,

> lets the curtain fall,
> And universal darkness buries all!

*Source: Ambrose Bierce, *Works* (New York: The Neale Publishing Co., 1909), Vol. I, pp. 17–22.

The ancient Americans were a composite people; their blood was a blend of all the strains known in their time. Their government, while they had one, being merely a loose and mutable expression of the desires and caprices of the majority—that is to say, of the ignorant, restless and reckless—gave the freest rein and play to all the primal instincts and elemental passions of the race. In so far and for so long as it had any restraining force, it was only the restraint of the present over the power of the past—that of a new habit over an old and insistent tendency ever seeking expression in large liberties and indulgences impatient of control. In the history of that unhappy people, therefore, we see unveiled the workings of the human will in its most lawless state, without fear of authority or care of consequence. Nothing could be more instructive.

Of the American form of government, although itself the greatest of evils afflicting the victims of those that it entailed, but little needs to be said here; it has perished from the earth, a system discredited by an unbroken record of failure in all parts of the world, from the earliest historic times to its final extinction. Of living students of political history not one professes to see in it anything but a mischievous creation of theorists and visionaries—persons whom our gracious sovereign has deigned to brand for the world's contempt as "dupes of hope purveying to sons of greed." The political philosopher of to-day is spared the trouble of pointing out the fallacies of republican government, as the mathematician is spared that of demonstrating the absurdity of the convergence of parallel lines; yet the ancient Americans not only clung to their error with a blind, unquestioning faith, even when groaning under its most insupportable burdens, but seem to have believed it of divine origin. It was thought by them to have been established by the god Washington, whose worship, with that of such *dii minores* as Gufferson, Jaxon and Lincon (identical probably with the Hebru Abrem) runs like a shining thread through all the warp and woof of the stuff that garmented their moral nakedness. Some stones, very curiously inscribed in many tongues, were found by the explorer Droyhors in the wilderness bordering the river Bhitt (supposed by him to be the ancient Potomac) as lately as the reign of Barukam IV. These stones appear to be fragments of a monument or temple erected to the glory of Washington in his divine character of Founder and Preserver of republican institutions. If this tutelary deity of the ancient Americans really invented representative government they were not the first by many to whom he imparted the malign secret of its inauguration and denied that of its maintenance.

Although many of the causes which finally, in combination, brought about the downfall of the great American republic were in operation from the beginning—being, as has been said, inherent in the system—it was not until the year 1995 (as the ancients for some reason not now known reckoned time) that the collapse of that vast, formless fabric was complete. In that year the defeat and massacre of the last army of law and order in the lava beds of California extinguished the final fires of enlightened patriotism and quenched in blood the monarchical revival. Thenceforth armed opposition to anarchy was confined to desultory and insignificant warfare waged by small gangs of mercenaries in the service of wealthy individuals and equally feeble bands of proscripts fighting for their lives. In that year, too, "the Three Presidents" were driven from their capitals, Cincinnati, New Orleans and Duluth, their armies dissolving by desertion and themselves meeting death at the hands of the populace.

The turbulent period between 1920 and 1995, with its incalculable waste of blood and treasure, its dreadful conflicts of armies and more dreadful massacres by passionate mobs, its kaleidoscopic changes of government and incessant effacement and redrawing of boundaries of states, its interminable tale of political assassinations and proscriptions—all the horrors incident to intestinal wars of a naturally lawless race—had so exhausted and dispirited the surviving protagonists of legitimate government that they could make no further head against the inevitable, and were glad indeed and most fortunate to accept life on any terms that they could obtain.

But the purpose of this sketch is not bald narration of historic facts but examination of antecedent germinal conditions; not to recount calamitous events familiar to students of that faulty civilization, but to trace, as well as the meager record will permit, the genesis and development of the causes that brought them about. . . .

3

Greenwich Village Declines[*]

The jazz age of the 1920s was a time of literary disillusionment. Many writers and artists abandoned America for Europe at this time, becoming what is called the Lost Generation. Still, there grew in America places such as Greenwich Village, a colony of intellectu-

---

*Source: *The Improper Bohemians* by Allen Churchill. Copyright © 1958 by Allen Churchill. Published by E. P. Dutton & Co., Inc. and used with their permission.

*als who remained in America, but felt aloof from the mass of
Americans. Allen Churchill in his book* The Improper Bohemians *describes the end of the free spirit of Greenwich Village.*

Questions

1. What happened to Greenwich Village?
2. What exactly caused the changes?
3. What were the results on the Village culture?

Greenwich Village, in the minds of many had been ruined by Prohibition.
But late in 1929 the Prohibition Village was in turn wiped out by the depression. The Provincetown Players were not the only Village institution to suffer
from the collapse of the nation's finances. The entire Village reeled from the
shock. What one writer has called "an element of joy" fled Bohemia with the
coming of the depression. The old, clear, carefree Bohemian spirit seemed to
depart forever. One reason was that many young Villagers—girls, especially
—had subsisted on money from home, for as George Bernard Shaw once
pointed out, nothing creates a Bohemian faster than a steady check from
bourgeois parents. Checks from home ceased, Villagers lost jobs. But such
things constituted the surface of Bohemia's plight. Far deeper was the fact
that, in the midst of depression, the Village could no longer be the weightless
spot in a weightless world. Everywhere, now, life was real, life was earnest.
Once Greenwich Village seemed to have led the country in its plunge to
national lightheadedness. Now it turned to follow as the nation moved into
bleak depression years.

All of which brought upheaval. "As I look back on the year 1930," Malcolm
Cowley has written, "it seems to me that there never were so many shifts in
personal relations of people one knew well or faintly or by reputation."
Bohemians, no less than the rest of the country, thought the world truly lost
and sought desperately for new footholds. For a time the wild parties continued as of yore, but in these the element of joy was particularly lacking.
Continues Cowley: "People no longer drank to have a good time or as an
excuse for doing silly things and amusing things they could talk about afterwards. . . . There was as much horseplay and laughter as before, but it seemed
strained and even hysterical."

It could be that Greenwich Village was growing up. Where once its
Bohemians had insisted on acting like privileged children, they now found
that no one rated privilege in a world laid low by financial disaster. It was
a process of change highlighted by the fortunes of Robert Clairmont. On the
Blue Monday of October 29, 1929, the millionaire playboy lost some three
hundred thousand dollars. The rest of his paper fortune also shot down the
Wall Street drain. Since he had been the most conspicuous playboy of his
time, Clairmont was also the most conspicuous loser. Newspaper stories

about him were headlined POET RHYMES HIMSELF OUT OF A MILLION. But Clairmont continued debonair through the awful days of his money debacle. "Have you sold out?" a reporter shouted as he left his broker's office. "Hell, no, I'm wiped out," Clairmont called back. Touched by his plight, newspaper readers sent him candy and cigarettes. For a month he waited, hoping like everyone else that a crazy world would right itself. Then he gave up. With his last thousand, he financed a final revel of the Greta Garbo Social Club. Attired in white robes with gold-paper crowns, Clairmont, Boggs, Gildea, Bodenheim, and Siegel rampaged New York as of old. Fittingly they wound up at a ball in Webster Hall. But when he woke up the morning after this final, tumultuous fling Clairmont was broke.

But in a sense, perhaps, the Depression was good to Bohemia. As hard times continued, rents in the Village dropped. Further, the hordes of sight-seers, spenders and tourists both, dwindled. The more blatant speakeasies folded, leaving the field to spots like Julius', Goody's and Nick's (for jazz), which were more typical of the real Village. For a short time Greenwich Village seemed almost as quiet as the Village of 1912–1918—and with almost the same capacity for drawing intellectual lightning. Early in the depression a Villager named Howard Scott rose to propound the science of Technocracy. In a desperate world, this was seized on as a flaming hope, and for a while the country looked to Greenwich Village for salvation.

With the election of Franklin D. Roosevelt, the WPA with its projects for writers, artists, actors and musicians proved still another boon. The WPA gave many Villagers the steady, though minimum, salary lacked by most others in the United States. In charge of these WPA projects were some old Villagers—Orrick Johns, for instance, was important in the Writer's Project —and no true Bohemian ever forgets an old friend.

Yet in the midst of this comparative good fortune, Villagers remained discontented. In a world of dire reality, there seemed to be no place for Bohemia, and Bohemians did not like this. "The Depression did it," states Joseph Freeman, saluting the demise of his once Happy Island. Bohemians, unhappy or otherwise, have always been Utopian dreamers, and now the Village showed its difference from the rest of the country by the blind, visionary ardor with which it embraced a cause. "The year 1930 marked the end of the Age of Innocence," Freeman goes on, "and with it went the age of innocent Bohemianism. That year opened the Age of the Assassins and with it came the age of violent Bohemianism." Painting, prose, and poetry seemed to have failed. Politics remained and, Bohemia being what it was, only extremes of politics would do.

While the nation went Democratic, the Village—or a large segment of it— went Communist. A few voices were raised in protest. One was that of Max Eastman who had returned from a trip to Russia disillusioned, though he had married the sister of the Russian prosecutor Krylenko. Few bothered to listen. Except for those too artistic to care, most Villagers at one time or another flirted with Communism, to bring the locality to a pitch where, in the words of Heywood Broun, "If it comes from Moscow, there is nothing to do except swallow it whole." Boring from within, the Communists got control of the magazine *New Masses*. The most active Party group in the area loudly proclaimed itself a John Reed Club.

"Idealogy became more important than experiences," a Villager has said of this period of Village history. Yet in a short time the rigidities of Communist doctrine antagonized most Villagers. Experience once again became interesting. Opportunities for richer experience arrived with the repeal of Prohibition, which brought new contours to Village life. Again MacDougal Street and its environs—notably Third Street—sprang violently to life, though this time the life was not primarily intellectual. On the block below the Provincetown Playhouse, between Third and Houston Streets, the Minetta Tavern and the San Remo became the places where lusty Bohemians could now drink openly. Opposite the Provincetown itself a new kind of district began evolving. Here male and female homosexuals became dominant. Ever the home of the free, the old Greenwich Village had always included homosexuals in its groupings. Members of the third sex had mingled with everyone else and had been tolerated if not encouraged, as an example of Bohemian broadmindedness. But now the homosexual influx reached such a point that its members formed a society of their own. As headquarters, this new group chose the block of night clubs in the now-ratty buildings immediately opposite the Provincetown Playhouse. This area was callously named the Auction Block, and an interesting new note was introduced in this Village netherworld by a mannish-looking girl singer beating out a song called *Youse a Viper*. *Viper* was contemporary slang for marijuana smoker.

In uptown areas the term "café society" was fast coming into use, but the Village remained a cafeteria society. Hubert's on Sheridan Square was torn down to make way for a bank, and the nearby Life Cafeteria became the haunt for those who had enjoyed Hubert's. Next, the cafeteria group switched headquarters to the Waldorf, on Sixth Avenue just below Eighth Street. Locally this was called the Waxworks, in part because of the eerie glow cast by the lights in an establishment which has been compared to "an enormous bathroom bathed in sickly yellow-green light."

But the Waxworks also derived its name from the increasing sallowness (and sadness) of the group that frequented it. Prominent among them was Bodenheim, who on good nights did his drinking at the San Remo or Minetta Tavern. In the former, he was especially honored. Sometimes he was allowed to sit on a Thonet chair in the middle of the floor imbibing gin out of a water glass while expounding his philosophy of hopeless gloom in still-brilliant phrases. On bad nights—or after the San Remo closed at 4 A.M.—here again his person seemed to reflect what many considered the decline of Greenwich Village.

Like other writers, Bodenheim went on the WPA, but his personal demons kept pushing him ever downward. At the San Remo he began writing poems on scraps of paper and selling them for drinks, asking first one dollar, then fifty cents, and finally a ten-cent beer. He would drink anything bought for him, then go raging through the streets of the Village "shouting imprecations at a society that returned his hate by ignoring him." Those who bought his scribbled poetry found it more doggerel than verse, clever rhymes with pretentious thoughts, as empty, really, as his oft-repeated epigram, "Greenwich Village is the Coney Island of the soul."

Bodenheim was not unaware of his decline. Often his battle cry, "I have a malady of the soul," would ring over the bardin at the San Remo or Minetta. To anyone who bought him a drink, he might confess, "I am a scarecrow body and a dead soul." To Ben Hecht, who on a visit to New York sought out his old friend, Bodenheim said, "I know of no sensible reason why I should not commit suicide and put an end to the whole stupid nonsense."

He never did. Instead, he continued to act the bizarre Village character. So did Joe Gould, who haunted the Minetta Tavern, a figure (to use Bodenheim's words) "with his tonsured head, piebald ecclesiastical beard, and bent, shrunken frame . . . like a fugitive from a medieval monastery." As the Village regained some of its former gaiety, it became customary for girls to kiss the tiny author of *An Oral History of the World* on the top of his bald pate, so that by almost any midnight his head was covered by the imprint of bright, scarlet lips. Once a girl had kissed Joe Gould's head, her escort was supposed to buy the little man a drink. The mild, soft-spoken Gould possessed one of the gentlest dispositions in the world. If the drink were not forthcoming, he displayed no resentment.

When sufficiently plied with drink, Gould—an elfish 5–4, less-than-100 lbs.—would imitate a sea gull by skipping, cawing, and flapping his arms. His startling proficiency at this gained him the bar-named Professor Seagull, and when the *New Yorker* magazine meticulously profiled him, this title was used on the article. At other exhilarated moments, the odd, gnomelike figure would perform what he called the Joseph Ferdinand Gould Stomp, a dance which also involved violent physical gyrations. Joe Gould's meal-of-the-day was often the crusts nature-lovers tossed out to birds. He liked to douse all food with an ocean of tomato ketchup. He often slept in flophouses or on subway trains, but every night—legend has it—he added a few thousand words to his ambitious *Oral History of the World.* He wrote in longhand in notebooks which he carried lovingly under his arm. When finished with one set of notebooks, he stored them away. It is said that he inscribed some ten million words in this fashion.

As the nation pulled itself out of depression, the Village achieved a new type of color. One of its brightest spots became the Village Vanguard, born of the depression at 1 Charles Street and presided over by a man named Max Gordon who, like Barney Gallant, had roots in Middle Europe. For a long time the Vanguard held no liquor license, yet Gordon had a liking for, and tolerance of, Bohemians that won the Village to him. At various times Harry

Kemp, Bodenheim, John Rose Gildea, and other poets declaimed their verse at the Vanguard in return for food. (Gildea simplified this by being satisfied to eat mustard.) In time the Vanguard prospered to such an extent that it moved to its current location at 178 Seventh Avenue, where it occupies downstairs premises "shaped like a crazy piece of pie." Here the Village conspicuously acted as a generator of talent. Judy Holliday made an early appearance at the Vanguard as a member of the Revuers, with Betty Comden and Adolph Green. Leonard Bernstein, Burl Ives, Pearl Bailey, Josephine Premice, and others used the Vanguard as a step to fame. "It was a nice, charming, simple, innocent place—no nonsense," Gordon says of his early Vanguard.

By 1940, when the Village Vanguard had prospered to the point where it could afford a liquor license, further changes were in store for the Village. No one could call these improvements. With the coming of war, a great anonymous wave seemed to surge over the area. With most young Villagers away fighting, soldiers and sailors on leave took possession of the district. Most GI's visiting New York went to Times Square for thrills, but enough had heard of Greenwich Village to make the district seem like a boomtown for servicemen. On Saturday nights, Sheridan Square and upper MacDougal Street were like any honkytonk district the country over. Resident Villagers staggered back, and even today thought of the wartime Village renders some numb. "What happened in the Village during the forties?" one was recently asked. A glazed expression spread over his features. "Oh, I don't know," he said. "The war, I guess."

4

Modern Culture*

It is difficult to be objective about the effects of mass education, scientific advances, and modern art from our present perspective. Someday critics will be able to look back and make a more valid

*U.S. Department of Health, Education and Welfare, *Toward a Social Report* (Washington, D.C.: Government Printing Office, 1968), pp. 65–78.

evaluation, but in the 1960s the Department of Health, Education and Welfare attempted a study of modern learning, science, arts, and other aspects of modern culture. Here is Chapter 7 of that report.

Questions

1. How much learning is taking place in America today?
2. What are the problems encountered in education?
3. What advances in science have occurred? What is the value of the scientific changes?
4. What is the appeal of the arts?
5. What are the weaknesses of performing arts?
6. What conclusions about modern culture can be derived from this study?

Learning

EXPOSURE TO LEARNING

The average American has spent far more time in school than his parents did. Today, three-fourths of the Americans just old enough to have done so have finished high school—roughly the same proportion that finished the eighth grade in 1929. Today, about 15 percent of Americans in their late twenties have graduated from college—about the same proportion that had graduated from high school at the time of World War I.

In addition there has been an increase in the proportion of each year that the student spends in school. Since 1900, 34 days have been added to the average academic year. Pupils are also absent much less often, so the actual number of days of school attendance per year by the average pupil has increased by more than half.

The difference in years of schooling received by different groups of Americans has at the same time decreased. Among Americans born in 1901 or shortly before, those in the 90th percentile had 13.5 years of schooling, and those in the 10th percentile 2.6 years of schooling, for a difference of almost 11 years. Among those born between 1932 and 1936, those in the 90th percentile had 16.4 years of schooling, and those in the 10th percentile, 8.4 years, for a difference of 8 years. This difference is projected to decline to about 5.5 years for those born between 1956 and 1960. The gap in median years of schooling between whites and Negroes has fallen from an average of 3.4 years for those born in 1901 or before to one-half year for those born between 1942 and 1946, and appears to be narrowing still further.

The amount of resources used to educate each pupil is also increasing. In 1956, there were 27 pupils for each teacher; now there are 24. Teachers have also had more formal training; 93 percent of the teachers now have college degrees, as compared with 78 percent only 13 years ago. The one-room school, commonplace in rural areas as late as World War II, has largely disappeared. Total expenditures per pupil in elementary and secondary public schools increased from $2.25 to $3.43 per day (in constant dollars) between 1954 and 1964. There have also been improvements in curricula, especially in science and mathematics.

It is generally assumed that these increases in the length of schooling and expenditures on education have brought about an increase in the amount children have learned. There is, however, almost no direct evidence on this point—unless it be the evidence that parents often have difficulty with their children's homework. The *Digest of Educational Statistics,* for example, contains over a hundred pages of educational statistics in each annual issue, yet has virtually no information on how much children have learned. The Department of Health, Education, and Welfare has recently encouraged an attempt at a "national assessment" of educational achievement in the United States. This assessment would involve administering tests measuring standard academic skills to a representative sample of Americans of various ages. Such an assessment, if repeated periodically, would yield for the first time a series of estimates of the change taking place in the intellectual skills and knowledge of the population. . . .

THE POLICY CHALLENGE

The greatest challenge to American education today is to find effective ways of helping low income children learn the basic intellectual skills so that they can be more successful in school and compete more successfully for jobs and rewarding positions in the community when they become adults.

How much a child learns depends upon his mother's diet before he was born, his own nutrition and health, his access to books, and the psychological and intellectual influences in the home. Most psychologists seem to agree that the preschool years are a period of particularly rapid development, and that attitudes acquired in these years can have enduring effects. Even after he reaches school age, a child typically spends only one-third of his working hours in school. Television programs and conversations with parents and playmates take up much of a child's time. The motivation to learn is obviously important, and there is every reason to believe it is decisively influenced by the home environment.

Some of the findings in the *Survey of Educational Opportunity* suggest the importance of the educational impact of factors outside of school. The *Survey* found that the socioeconomic status of a child's parents, and of his classmates, were major determinants of a student's academic performance. Once the impact of the socioeconomic status of parents and peers had been accounted for, such differences in quality of schooling as were observed and measured explained very little of the remaining variation in student performance.[1] The only observed school characteristic that had a significant effect was the verbal ability of its teachers, and this effect was much smaller than that of socioeconomic status of parents and classmates.

Despite the limitations of the *Survey* the conclusion that a child's socioeconomic environment is an important determinant of how much he learns is almost certainly right. This conclusion, in turn, suggests that we cannot take full advantage of the potential for learning simply by spending more on schools. Higher incomes and better jobs for parents may have more influence on their children's learning than any "compensation" which can be given to the children themselves. Better television programing and help for parents in how to talk with and stimulate their own children may also be important. Improved housing arrangements which give children from poor families the opportunity to attend schools and live in neighborhoods with children of different social and economic status may also be of crucial importance.

Nevertheless, it is clear that schools could do far more to stimulate and foster the curiosity and creativity of children—not just poor children, but all children. We must somehow find a way to do two things. First, we need to channel more resources into education especially in areas where the needs are very high in relation to the tax base and present spending. It takes money to attract sensitive, intelligent, and highly trained people into teaching and education administration, and to replace rat-infested old schools, especially in the center cities, with attractive convenient structures.

But resources alone will not solve the problems of American education. A new spirit of acceptance of change and desire for improvement is needed. Progressive industries often spend 5 to 10 percent of their funds on research and development. But expenditures on education research and development are now miniscule, perhaps a half of 1 percent of the total education budget.

Furthermore, much "research and development" in education consists of small projects having little impact on actual learning in the schools. There is a need for major departures, for developing whole new curricula and approaches to education, for trying the new approaches with real children and real schools. This kind of effort is expensive, by the present standards of

[1]The *Survey* did not measure the quality of schools well and its conclusions are subject to varying interpretations. The conclusion that the socioeconomic status of the families of a student's classmates is an important determinant of a student's performance could be interpreted as evidence that differences in the quality of schooling are important, because high status parents usually want and can afford to live in neighborhoods with good schools. Since variations in the quality of schooling were measured only partially and crudely in the *Survey*, it is possible that the average socioeconomic status of the families of the students in a school measures the quality of that school better than the explicit measures of school quality used in the *Survey*.

education research, although not by the standards of military and industrial research and development.

But even a major effort to find more effective methods in education through research and development will not be sufficient unless the schools as a whole adopt a new attitude toward change. School systems must learn to see themselves as continuous laboratories trying new things, evaluating results, and making changes.

Science

The advance of science has an effect on the Nation's capacity to produce more goods and services, better health, and a stronger defense. Our society also values scientific truth for its own sake. And because it is clear that the state of a nation's science is related to its productivity, the health of its people, and even to national security, Americans are concerned whenever any other nation excels us in an important area of scientific capability.

RESOURCES DEVOTED TO SCIENCE

What is the state of American science and how much are we adding to the stock of systematic knowledge? Unfortunately, useful measures of scientific productivity do not exist.

A frequent measure of our scientific capital is the number of scientists and the amount of resources devoted to scientific pursuits. Between 1950 and 1965 the number of scientists and engineers nearly doubled, reaching about a million and a half in the latter year. About a million were engineers, a half a million scientists. This increase in the number of scientists and engineers was 4.5 times the rate of growth of the total labor force. The number of scientists and engineers getting doctorates has doubled in the last 10 years.

Between 1953 and 1965 the Nation's research and development expenditures increased fourfold, from 5.2 billion to 20.5 billion. This means that these expenditures increased at a compound annual rate of 12 percent per year, and that the percent of the Gross National Product used for these purposes rose from 1.4 to 3.0 percent. No other nation comes close to devoting a similar proportion of its resources to scientific research and development.

THE DIVERSITY OF SCIENCE

Three hundred years ago all experimental sciences were grouped together in one specialty called "natural philosophy." An individual could attempt to master almost all important scientific knowledge. In 1958, the National Science Foundation counted 120 subfield groupings and 142 groupings in 1968. The number of particular specialties increased even faster: 695 specialties were listed in 1958, 1,235 in 1968.

This increase of specialization does not measure the pace of scientific advance. Classifications and new specialties are sometimes created for reasons unrelated to the growth of knowledge. Nonetheless, the statistics on the increasing diversity and division of labor in science reflect the rapid growth of scientific exploration and knowledge.

THE ADVANCE OF TECHNOLOGY

The remarkable advances of industrial technology in recent years are too obvious to need documentation. Television, supersonic jets, computers, nuclear power and many other advances have revolutionized our lives and made possible feats, like trips around the moon, that earlier generations thought sheer fantasy. Whereas the *Mayflower* took 2 months to cross the Atlantic, in the 1890's it took 1 week, in the 1930's a day, and now about 7 hours. But advancing technology has also created problems for society—noise, congestion, pollution, and the like.

Some insight into the level of technological achievement in the United States can be obtained from what is called the "technological balance of payments." This is an accounting of payments foreigners have made to us for the use of patented techniques or technical expertise, minus our payments for their patents and technical expertise.[2] The United States enjoys a huge surplus in the technological balance of payments, and this surplus appears to be growing. Our surplus was $311 million in 1956 and $1,097 million in 1965. The ratio of our payments to our receipts was one to seven in 1956 and one to nine in 1965. If the transfers within multinational firms are left out, our surplus is still growing; it rose from $110 million in 1956 to $235 million in 1965.

These striking figures on our technological lead can easily mislead us. Science is international, and any major scientific achievement is likely to be of mixed ancestry. Moreover, many scientists have come to this country from other lands. Although the "brain drain" increases the inequality of income among nations, it is nonetheless an encouraging indicator about the state of American science.

THE POLICY CHALLENGE

The main challenge presented by the state of American science is the need to lay the foundations for a science policy. We are confronted with

---

[2]This is not an ideal measure because of problems of definition and the bias against basic science.

burgeoning advance that offers great promise. Can we formulate policies that will nurture our invaluable scientific resources and ensure the fulfillment of prospects that lie ahead?

The competition for public resources will amost certainly be more intense, either between science and other programs, or between different scientific endeavors. The Nation will also continue to find itself at the center of controversies concerning the condition and needs of world science.

If there is almost sure to be more heat generated by issues of science policy in the future, ways must be found to generate more light. Priorities in science could be laid out more systematically, and farther in advance. Issues involving such priorities could be exposed to wider public debate. The very unpredictability of scientific breakthroughs could be made the basis for more rational development of scientific manpower, institutions, and communications with an emphasis on keeping these resources flexible.

The international character of the scientific enterprise poses a special challenge. The United States, as we have seen, spends a larger *percentage* of its income on scientific research and development than do other countries. One possible explanation for this is that some of the benefits of scientific advance are readily available to any nation in the world. For example, people of any country can take advantage of such medical advances as heart transplants. Because of its size and affluence, the United States gets a larger share of the benefit of a basic scientific advance than other countries, and therefore had an incentive to spend more of its national income on basic research. Even the biggest countries do not, however, reap all of the benefits of the basic research they finance. Thus the world as a whole probably tends to spend too little on basic science.

The benefits of basic research are international, and worldwide cooperation in science is essential. A cooperative recognition of the universality of basic science could benefit all mankind.

Art

Artistic creativity and its appreciation are an important part of our national life. There is art not only in museums, theaters, opera houses, and books but in every aspect of life—in cooking, dress and industrial design. Although this section concentrates on the conventionally most professional and "highbrow" forms of art, we must not forget that this is only a small part of the total and may not be the most important.

ACCESS TO ART

Access to many forms of art is easier today than it has ever been before. Modern technologies of communication and transportation have given the entire population an access to a variety of art forms that could in an earlier age have been open only to a privileged few. Even the most fortunate in earlier periods could not possibly have heard as wide a variety of symphonies, or seen such a diversity of drama, as the connoisseur of records and motion pictures can enjoy today.

This improvement in the accessibility of art has continued even in recent years. Twenty-five years ago almost no one owned a television set; by 1952, 30 percent of the households owned at least one set, and this percentage rose to 67 percent in 1955, 88 percent in 1960, and 94 percent in 1967.

Notwithstanding the obvious shortcomings in television programing, the growth in the number of television sets has given more Americans an access to at least some serious attempts at artistic expression. National Educational Television's 148 stations now reach almost all metropolitan areas, and surveys have shown that the NET audience about doubled between 1961 and 1966, by which time it reached over 6 million homes and an estimated 14 million viewers weekly, apart from school programs. Of 160 hours of programing supplied last year to NET's affiliates, about half or more were in the field of art and culture.

Television is, to be sure, only one of the technologies that has made art more accessible. Even such an old technology as that involved in making books has changed with the "paperback revolution," which has made books more accessible to millions of Americans. This development, along with expanding incomes, increased education, and other factors, has brought about a 90-percent increase in the number of new books and editions between 1960 and 1967, and a 65-percent increase in books classified in the arts or humanities. These increases considerably exceed the rates of growth of population and income.

Improved methods of transportation and increased incomes have also widened the range of possible artistic experience for many Americans by facilitating foreign travel. In 1929 about half a million Americans traveled abroad, but in 1967 almost three and a half million did so.

New technologies have not only widened the access to art, but also permitted new forms of artistic expression, from films to new kinds of sculpture and music.

THE PERFORMING ARTS

At the same time that technology and economic advance have improved the accessibility of many types of art, they have also created problems for other art forms, especially for those involving live performances. There is evidence that live performances of certain kinds are not increasing in proportion to the growth of population and the economy, and in some cases are perhaps even in an absolute decline.

The Broadway theaters are the largest single part of the American theater, and they have been keeping records in a consistent way longer than other theaters. These records reveal that Broadway attendance has not expanded in proportion to our population or economic growth. The Broadway theater reached its peak quite some time ago, probably about 1925. No new Broadway theater has been built since 1928.[3] There has been no clear trend in attendance since World War II, and there clearly has not been enough of an increase to offset rapidly rising costs. Since 1950, ticket prices have risen only half as much as costs. Though a few "hits" make great profits, the Broadway theater as a whole is in serious financial difficulty.

The off-Broadway theater grew rapidly from the late 1940's until the mid-sixties, but it has an attendance of about one million, compared with seven million for Broadway. More recently, the off-Broadway theater has suffered, too; the number of productions is now smaller than it was in 1961–62.

There has been little or no growth in the number of professional symphony orchestras since 1950. In 1967 there were 28 entirely professional symphony orchestras playing for seasons ranging from 22 to 52 weeks. There are about twice as many "metropolitan" orchestras, mainly professional but having smaller budgets, and a large number of partially amateur community orchestras.

Chamber music groups are generally less well organized than symphony orchestras. Receipts from ticket sales to the small halls appropriate for chamber groups are generally low, and the cost of the individual performer relatively high. Some orchestras are organizing chamber groups to achieve the advantages of a longer season for some of their members.

Opera is perhaps the most vulnerable of the arts because it is easily the most expensive, requiring large casts, an orchestra, a chorus, and a ballet company as well as expensive scenery and costumes. The only major opera companies are the Metropolitan, the New York City Opera, the Chicago Lyric Opera, and the San Francisco Opera. There are about 40 other professional and semiprofessional organizations, but they usually give no more than 25 performances in a year. Estimating total attendance at these performances requires a good deal of guesswork, but the figure has been placed at less than 2 million in 1963–64.

Ballet as a separate artistic undertaking is characterized by high costs in many of the same areas as opera. Annual attendance for dance performances is estimated at less than 1 million, with dance tours showing a marked relative growth in popularity since 1952. At the present time, however, there is little chance to see a professional dance company perform any place except in one of the largest cities or in a college town.

Notwithstanding the paucity of information in this area, it does seem very

[3]Unless Lincoln Center is counted.

likely that there is no "cultural boom" where direct attendance at live perfor- mances is involved. The rate of growth in such performances is probably slower than that of the economy as a whole, and expenditures on these art forms have certainly not risen at anything like the rate at which expenditures on science and education have increased.

VULNERABILITY OF THE PERFORMING ARTS

To some extent, the relative decline in live artistic performances is probably a natural result of the development of modern communications technology. The new technologies offer a less expensive substitute for live performance.

But there is another factor at work. One explanation of the slow growth of audience participation in the performing arts is the tendency for this participation to become even relatively more expensive as the economy ad- vances. There is little increase in productivity per worker in the performing arts: a string quartet continues to require four performers. In the economy in general productivity increases regularly, and so then do wage levels. Since this does not happen in the performing arts, someone must make sacrifices. If it is not the public or the patrons, it will be the artists themselves, who will have to choose other careers or forego higher incomes.

This systematic tendency for the relative cost of live performance to rise is made somewhat less serious by the technological improvements in ways of disseminating culture, such as by phonograph records, motion pictures, and television, providing substitutes for the audiences and additional earn- ings for some performers. But if there is presumably also a need to enjoy culture at first hand, these technological developments do not altogether fill the gap from the audiences' point of view. From the performers' point of view, the fact that only a relatively small number can expect careers in the media may be discouraging.

There is another cultural sector, where the problem of productivity can be considered not to exist at all. This is what we might call amateur or subsis- tence culture: artistic work carried on by the artist primarily for his own enjoyment. Increased incomes may allow more of this, as growth of amateur community symphonies, for example, seems to show. Sometimes amateur efforts can create or enlarge a commercial audience, as with rock music.

The probable long run tendency for a relative decline in certain types of live performance does not automatically indicate a "social" or "public" prob- lem. Nevertheless, live performances are needed to give the typical performer (or composer or playright) a chance to develop. The quality of records, motion pictures and television could decline if live performances fell off beyond some point, since the lack of this large testing and training opportunity could become critical.

The performing arts indirectly benefit others besides members of live audiences in other ways as well. Their quality is tied up with the capacity to educate, and probably also the capacity to communicate. The cultural inheritance of a nation is also a source of important values in a civilized society—understanding, appreciation, and respect for other people. Finally, the taste for art is in part an acquired taste: those who have a broader cultural experience tend to have the greatest concern for art. The demand for art might be greater if the opportunities to enjoy it were more numerous. These arguments suggest that the prospect of a relative decline in live performances is a matter of general public concern, and something to keep in mind in any assessment of the condition of American society.

Thought Questions

1. Describe the changes in culture as seen in Thoreau and Bierce.
2. Does modern culture reflect past culture?
3. Trace the specific evolution of literature from the colonial period to the twentieth century.
4. In what general directions is modern culture going?

fifteen

POPULAR CULTURE:
The Rise
of Mass Amusements

The growth of popular culture has been a very dominant and noticeable trend in American history. Today there are so many activities that no American has enough time to completely participate in every phase of popular culture.

In colonial America, culture was limited by a strict religious outlook, and idleness was often considered devil's work. In the early 1800s industrial life still occupied most of the working hours of many Americans, but promoters such as P. T. Barnum tried to provide entertainment with his freak show and circus. And the theater was becoming more important too. Spectator sports did not come into being until the late 1800s with increasing leisure time and more money to spend on it. Popular music continued to change and reflect the black experience in jazz, while the movies and radio were in their beginning stages.

From the 1920s to the present popular culture has literally exploded with movies, spectator sports, music, radio, and that greatest spectator sport of all —television. Television became popular in America during the 1950s and today is almost universal. Yet spectator sports have grabbed the popular mind too, and pro football appears to rank first among them. Americans spend more money on sports and leisure time activities than ever before in history. The need for mass amusements seems insatiable.

1

Sports in Colonial America*

Many of the sports that existed in colonial America were regional in nature. In the southern colonies, for example, cock fighting, boxing, and hunting were quite popular, while in New England drinking and gambling were common pastimes. Historian Louis B. Wright describes some of the early colonial amusements.

Questions

1. What popular colonial sports were described here?
2. In what areas were they most popular?
3. Do these same activities exist today? To what extent?

Although horse racing was a particular addiction of the southern colonies, it was not confined to this region. New Englanders in the eighteenth century raced horses, with the excuse that it was a useful way of improving the breed. Rhode Island, which had plantations somewhat like those in the South, raised horses for export to the West Indies, and enjoyed racing them. Cockfighting was another sport that anyone with the inclination to breed gamecocks could enjoy, and cockfighting took place on all levels of society.

An Anglican parson in New York, the Reverend John Sharpe, kept a journal between the years 1710 and 1713 in which, among other things, he wrote down the times that he attended cockfights. Sometimes he went from his church service directly to the cockpits. Planters bred gamecocks and bet on their favorites as they did on their horses. Backwoods chick-raisers also bred gamecocks and fought them for the entertainment of themselves and their neighbors. This sport has never completely died out and is still carried on

*Source: Reprinted by permission of G. P. Putnam's Sons from *Everyday Life in Colonial America* by Louis B. Wright. Copyright © 1965 by Louis B. Wright.

surreptitiously in many rural areas even though in most jurisdictions it is now illegal.

Hunting and fishing were universal sports throughout the colonies, though the type of hunting varied with the nature of the game and the customs of the region. Foxes were at first regarded as vermin and were killed as were other pests. Not until late in the eighteenth century did fox hunting in the English manner become a fashionable sport in Virginia and in Maryland. Since deer were prized for food and for their skins, deer hunting everywhere from the earliest times was a sport that every boy and man enjoyed. Boys learned to shoot at an early age, and the highest ambition of almost every boy was to own a gun of his own.

In seventeenth-century New England wolves were a menace and a bounty was offered for wolf heads. Men and boys in the time that they could spare from routine tasks hunted wolves and brought in their heads to the magistrates of the townships. It was the custom in many districts to hang wolf heads against the outside walls of the meetinghouse.

Fishing, like deer hunting, was a useful sport, for fish were a valuable food in all areas. Furthermore it was the most democratic of all sports, for fancy and expensive fishing tackle had not yet been invented, and anybody with a cane pole, a line, and a hook could enjoy an hour or two on the bank of some stream.

Besides fishing with hook and line, seining with nets was an activity that provided not only profit from the huge catches of fish but a great deal of fun for the boys and young men who took part. During the runs of herring in the New England rivers, however, the great loads of fish scooped from the streams must have been more labor than sport. In the South, seining was a sport that even gentlemen-planters enjoyed. John Harrower, an indentured white servant of Colonel William Daingerfield's of Fredericksburg, Virginia, tells in his *Journal* for April 22, 1775, of such fishing:

> At three p.m. went to New Post where the Colonel and several gentlemen had been all day hauling a seine net and had catched a good deal [of] herrings and white fish; but at noon their net got foul of some driven tree at bottom and continued so until I went off in a canoe and got it cleared.

Harrower, who had been brought over as a schoolmaster, was invited from time to time to go fishing with Colonel Daingerfield. An entry in his *Journal* for June 11, 1774, reads:

> At nine a.m. left school and went afishing on the river with the Colonel, his eldest [son], and another gentleman in two canoes. Mrs. Daingerfield, another lady, and the other two boys met us at Snow Creek in the chair [two-wheeled buggy] at two p.m. when we all dined on fish under a tree.

Such fishing picnics were frequent with all classes.

Since fish and game abounded in all the colonies and the woods and streams were free of any restrictions, these outdoor sports were available to everyone. Even a boy unable to own a gun could trap and snare animals, or track them to their dens in the snow. Rabbit hunting, when the rabbits could not run fast enough in soft snow to escape, was regarded as great fun. Hunting and fishing, so important in the economic life of early America, became traditional sports that have endured in popularity to the present time. Only the destruction of forests and the closing of open land has diminished hunting as a universal sport. Even though many streams have been ruined by pollution, fishing continues to be one of our favorite outdoor activities.

2

Football at the Turn of the Century*

Spectator sports came into their own in the late 1800s. Horse racing and boxing had always been very popular, but now football and baseball began to attract considerable public attention. In the 1800s the colleges and universities fielded competitive teams and the popularity of the game expanded. In baseball the American and national leagues were founded, and although conditions were much different than today, the game was undergoing a real change. Historian Foster Rhea Dulles here writes of the popularity of football in the early 1900s.

Questions

1. What accounted for the popularity of football in the early 1900s?
2. What changes were taking place in the game?
3. What accounted for the rise of pro football?

A History of Recreation: America Learns to Play, 2nd ed., by Foster Rhea Dulles, pp. 347–50. Copyright © 1940, D. Appleton-Century Company, Inc., and Copyright © 1965, Meredith Publishing Company. Reprinted by permission of Appleton-Century-Crofts.

After the turn of the century, intercollegiate football continued to forge ahead as one of the country's outstanding spectator sports. But it had first to survive a crisis even more serious than that of the 1890's for the reforms which had then been adopted to combat both professionalism and roughness did not entirely resolve football's problems. Injuries and even fatalities continued to mount (the death-roll reached forty-four in 1903) and the press so universally condemned the game as it was being played that many colleges and universities contemplated abolishing it altogether. With football thus becoming a national issue, President Theodore Roosevelt stepped resolutely into the fray and summoned its leaders to a White House conference to work out reforms that might save the game. The forward pass, the on-side kick, and separation of the rush lines were thereupon devised to make football less dangerous, and these innovations gradually led to a more open—and also far more interesting—game.

By the 1920's football was consequently more popular than ever before and the several hundred thousand spectators crowding the college stadia every Saturday afternoon were supplemented by the many millions of fans who hovered over their radios in comfortable, heated living-rooms to follow the games play-by-play, and then spent Sunday mornings devouring long accounts in the newspapers' sports sections of how it had all happened. Football reigned supreme from the opening of early practice to the Tournament of Roses. "It is at present a religion," a contributor to *Harper's* stated in 1928— "sometimes it seems to be almost our national religion."

It was not only Harvard, Yale and Princeton which now attracted the great crowds. Universities and colleges throughout the country had built great new concrete stadia (the Yale and California bowls seated eighty thousand each; Illinois, Michigan, Ohio State and several other universities could handle seventy thousand) which altogether boasted a total capacity of two million. Empty almost every day of the year except for those fabulous Saturday afternoons in the autumn, the quickened interest of the public then taxed them to the utmost. It was estimated that during the season as many as twenty million spectators (attendance generally doubled between 1921 and 1930) watched a game which had been largely taken away from college undergraduate or graduate and given over to a sports-hungry public which supported football as a grandiose commercial amusement.

It was a colorful, exciting show. Every year saw a new sensation: the "praying colonels" of Centre College blazing through the sky like a meteor, and as quickly fading out; Princeton's "Team of Destiny" briefly lighting up the dimmed prestige of the one-time Big Three; and Red Grange, an Illinois team by himself, flashing past all other heroes. Even in this glamorous period the line between intercollegiate football and the newly set up professional game was sometimes hardly distinguishable. Red Grange was one of the first of college players who deftly stepped over it after his last college season. While student admirers framed his football jersey at Illinois (also circulating a petition to nominate him for Congress), he joined the Chicago Bears at a salary of $30,000, signed a $300,000 movie contract, and was presented to President Coolidge. Here was fame—and also fortune.

Educators continued to be something less than enthusiastic over an emphasis on football that seemed to make the academic standing of their institutions a negligible factor in the public mind in comparison with a football championship. But the general public—and also the greater part of the nation's college alumni—only asked for more victories. An editorial in the magazine *Liberty* found the protesting faculty members jealous. "The problem is not the elimination or restriction of football," it declared, "but how long it will be before red-blooded colleges demand the elimination or restriction of those afflicted with this inferiority complex." In 1929 a report of the Carnegie Foundation heavily scored the mounting overemphasis and professionalism in the sport, but the colleges now had too great a vested interest in football for it to fan the old fires of controversy into a very fierce flame.

Football suffered something of a setback during the depression. The sale of big-game tickets declined just as severely as that of any other market commodity. But it withstood these slings of outrageous fortune; it kept its strong hold on the public. And then after the interruption of war it zoomed forward to still greater heights of popularity. Television even more than radio made college football the country's most popular Saturday afternoon indoor attraction, but ever greater crowds also crammed the stadia whose capacity was enlarged, whenever possible, in some individual cases now accommodating as many as 100,000 persons.

The game had its usual vicissitudes. There were repeated outcries against excessive commercialization, an unsavory game-fixing scandal in 1947, and continued controversy over football scholarships. University faculties periodically renewed their old struggle against the exaggerated role of football in college life and the concentration on winning championships at whatever cost. But far from submitting to any such move to deemphasize football, its sponsors extended the season by setting up more regional championships— the Rose Bowl, the Sugar Bowl, the Cotton Bowl, the Orange Bowl.

There were various changes in the game—the T-formation, the two-platoon system, constantly shifting regulations on substitutions—but it remained essentially the same. Every season had its quota of "upsets, surprises, thrills, records" and a new set of popular heroes. The Saturday afternoon ritual was ever more deeply fixed in American life. Even though in some ways it did not quite recapture the glamor of the 1920's or seem to provide such exciting players as the legendary stars of that earlier decade, college football in postwar years more than held its own. It was reported in 1961 that something like twenty-five million persons had attended the countrywide games and no one could measure how many more watched them over television.

In the meantime, new developments had given a tremendous impetus to the professional sport. Its beginnings could be traced back to the opening of

the century and the American Professional Football Association was organized in 1920. But while the game attained a measure of popularity in the
days of Jim Thorpe, the great Indian athlete, and was further boosted when
Illinois' Galloping Ghost joined the ranks, professional football did not come
of age until after 1945. With the veteran National League supplemented by
the American League, it then became the fastest growing of all spectator
sports both in actual game attendance and its nationwide television audience.

The teams adopted wonderfully expressive names—the Green Bay Packers,
the Houston Oilers, the Boston Patriots, the Buffalo Bills, the Denver Broncos
—and they had their own galaxy of stars. With a more open game and such
special features as the sudden-death extra period, professional football thereupon built up a popular following that rivalled if it did not surpass that of
the somewhat ambiguously amateur sport. While yearly attendance (in spite
of packed stadia) could never attain the total drawn to the hundreds of college
games, it had risen to three million in 1960, and then in another three years
added over two million more.

3

Baseball—The All-American Game *

*Since the 1920s spectator sports have attained greater importance
than ever before. Dynasties have been built upon million and mul-
timillion dollar investments. Today the professional athlete has high
social acceptance and is extremely well paid. Here Henry Aaron
describes the feelings of a baseball player in the World Series.*

Questions

1. How does Aaron feel about the World Series?

*Source: Reprinted by permission of the World Publishing Company from *The Henry Aaron
Story* as told to Furman Bisher. Copyright © 1968 by Henry Aaron and Furman Bisher.

2. How does Aaron feel about baseball in general?
3. How has baseball fared in modern America?

I wish I could write about what it's like to play in a World Series and make you understand the feeling. You put on your uniform the same way, the personal equipment, the undershirt, the sanitary stockings and the outer stockings with the rubber bands that hold them up, the spikes and the shirt with "Braves" across the front. You do that for 162 games a year (in 1957 the season was 154 games), but there's nothing special about it then. That's your day's work. You're merely on the job like any other salaried employee.

But the World Series! Man, that's something different in every way. You do everything the same way, I said, and yet it's not the same way. You give every little act an extra touch, like a ritual. After all, you're going out on the field to play for the world's championship of baseball. Every eye that can see will see you a little better in a World Series. People who never go to a baseball game during the season will be watching the World Series. Celebrities who never read a box score and couldn't tell you what Cooperstown is famous for show up for the World Series. If you're playing in a World Series and your spine doesn't tingle some that first day you walk out of the clubhouse onto the field, you're dead and don't know it.

Our World Series with the New York Yankees in 1957 opened in Yankee Stadium and closed there. It was a long one and a busy one, running seven games from October 2 to October 10, and in between some real hell broke loose.

The Yankees took us in the first game with Whitey Ford pitching, and it looked like we were goners. He'd beaten Warren Spahn, our best pitcher, and I'd read somewhere that teams that lost the first game of a World Series don't usually win it.

Lew Burdette beat Bobby Shantz in the second game, then we flew to Milwaukee for the third. It was like a state fair when we got back there. Downtown Milwaukee was dressed up like the Fourth of July. Store windows were decorated, and businesses had banners hanging out saying, "Welcome Home Braves," "Home of the Next World's Champions," and all kinds of hoopla.

The Yankees flew into Chicago and came by train from Chicago to Milwaukee. A few miles out of Milwaukee some newspapermen got aboard, buttonholed Manager Casey Stengel and squeezed some quotes out of him. He made the mistake of saying something about Milwaukee being a "bush town," and they never let the old man forget it.

We played like a bush-town team in the third game. The Yankees bombed our pitchers, and our pitchers threw nothing but base hits or balls. Bob Buhl never finished the first inning. The score was 12–3, and it may have been for the best. It sobered the Milwaukee fans some. If we had come in from New

York and swept the three games there, those wild people might have burned the town to the ground.

Everything you read about in sports seems to have a turning point, and I don't think there's any doubt about what was the turning point in the 1957 World Series. If it wasn't, it will have to do for a turning point in this book, because that's the way I saw it.

Back in June when we lost Joe Adcock—he'd fractured an ankle sliding into a base, you'll recall—our bench had been left short. We had Frank Torre to take Adcock's place at first base. There was no sweat there. Torre had always been a clever fielder. One year in Atlanta, when he played on the Braves' old farm club there, he had a string of more than one thousand chances without making an error, and everybody knows the first baseman gets more traffic than anybody on the field. By this time, his second season in the big leagues, he was becoming a pretty good hitter, too.

Just for insurance and pinch-hitting, the Braves bought an old-timer named Nippy Jones from the Sacramento club in the Pacific Coast League. Jones had been in the major leagues before. One year he batted .300 for the Cardinals, and he had played for them in the 1946 World Series, but he had had some kind of back trouble, and since the 1952 season with the Phillies he had been back in the minors.

I never did get to know him, except to say "hello" and ride elevators with him. He didn't say much, and I didn't know enough about him at that time to ask him any questions about his exciting career. He had a sort of bony face and dark, sad eyes that were set deep under his brows.

He hadn't had much of a hand in our pennant-winning. He didn't get much of a chance, because as I said, Torre was taking care of first base in a great way. Jones played a few games and hit a couple of home runs, but he went to bat only about seventy-five times. He was the kind of a guy that a sports writer would identify as a "most forgettable" member of the Braves.

So we go into this fourth game of the World Series. We are now down to the Yankees, one game to two. Worst thing about it is, we're in our own ball park, but the Yankees have taken us apart, humiliated us before our own people in the only game we've played there.

We get to the ninth inning with a 4–1 lead, Spahn pitching. You've got to feel as safe as if you're in a bomb shelter, Spahn pitching with a 4–1 lead. We got the four runs in the fourth inning, all on home runs. Logan had walked. Mathews had followed him with a double, and I hit a home run over the left-field fence off Tom Sturdivant. Torre followed me with a home run over the right-field fence.

There wasn't any more scoring until the ninth inning, and it came like a bomb. I could see people filing out of the ball park as the Yankees came to bat. They were heading for their cars, pretty sure that the Braves had won and tied the series at two games apiece. But the Yankees got two men on base, and with two men out, Elston Howard hit a home run over the left-field fence and the score was tied 4–4.

We could have folded then. I really believe that. You never saw a quieter dugout in your life when we came in from the field. We all looked as if we'd been watching a murder. I don't remember anybody saying anything, unless it was the usual routine, meaningless stuff about going out there and gettin' 'em.

The Yankees shut us out in the bottom of the ninth inning, then they took the lead in their half of the tenth. Hank Bauer hit a triple that scored Tony Kubek, and so we went into our half of the tenth on the short side, 4–5, and it began to look as if we were dead for the whole series, as well as the fourth game.

Spahn was due to be the lead-off batter in the tenth inning. He was always a good hitter, and I think any of us on the Braves would just about as soon see him at bat in a clutch as a lot of our regulars. Surely, we'd as soon have seen him up as Nippy Jones. But Haney called for Jones to bat for him. In any other situation—what I mean is, if Spahn hadn't been tired—it wouldn't have been that way. Haney was taking him out as a pitcher now, not as a batter. Besides, Spahnie was a left-handed batter and the Yankees had Tommy Byrne, a left-handed pitcher, in the game. Jones batted right-handed.

He stepped in and Byrne pitched. It was low and looked like it was in the dirt, and the ball got through Howard. The next thing I know, Jones is jawing with the plate umpire, Augie Donatelli, and as I said before, Jones wasn't a very talkative sort. But he was talking now, and he was having it out with Donatelli chin to chin. I didn't know what it was all about until I heard Red Schoendienst holler from the on-deck circle.

"Hey, Augie, it hit his foot! It hit his foot!"

While Donatelli and Jones were arguing, the ball came rolling between their feet and just died there. It had hit the retaining wall and bounced back. Jones suddenly reached down and picked up the ball and showed it to Donatelli. Nobody in the crowd knew what was going on, but there was some flutter of anticipation going around, and when the fans saw Donatelli wave Jones to first base, a roar went up.

What happened was this. When Jones looked down and saw the ball at his feet, he also saw a black spot on it left by the polish on his spikes. He picked up the ball, showed it to Donatelli, and, as I heard him telling sports writers in the clubhouse later, he said, "Here, see the shoe polish! Doesn't that prove it?"

He was on his way to first base before Haney could even get out of the dugout. The Yankees argued back. Stengel came out and grumbled some, but Jones had his base. He held it about ten seconds. Haney sent Mantilla in to run for him, and Jones faded away into the obscurity of the dugout. He'd left us something to go on, though, and we took it and ran, though I didn't have a hand in it. My turn at bat never came up.

After Stengel finished arguing—and I guess he dragged it out some to get a relief pitcher heated up—he sent to the bull pen for Bob Grim, who was a right-hander. Grim pitched to Schoendienst, and Red sacrificed Mantilla to second. Logan was up next, and he really clothes-lined a drive to the left-field corner. Mantilla scored, and we were tied now 5–5.

That brought up Mathews, and this was the reason I never got to bat. I was kneeling in the on-deck circle with a box-seat view watching it all. Grim tried to slip a fast ball by Mathews, but Ed caught it on the nose and hit a home run over the right-field fence. Ball game, 7–5, from death to life again. The series was tied 2–2. We knew we could win then, but not if it hadn't been for Nippy Jones. I believe that.

Thought Questions

1. Compare and contrast twentieth century football and baseball.
2. How has culture changed since colonial days?
3. Compare and contrast sports in colonial America with modern sports.
4. How has TV changed mass amusements?

sixteen

THE CITY:
From Jamestown to
Megalopolis

Modern America is urban America. Today better than eight out of every ten Americans live in urban centers. The country is no longer the symbol of America. But in early America the situation was reversed; the vast majority of Americans lived on farms and few Americans lived in cities. Urban planners today talk of urban renewal, green areas, and rapid transit and feel that since the city has become the American way of life, it must be improved. And the city, with its stores, shops, and night life, is also the key to modern culture.

In colonial times the early cities were small seacoast towns. They relied upon trading and fishing, and they faced the same problems of police, fire protection, and garbage disposal—sometimes dealing with them in rather backward ways. With the early 1800s urban conditions in established towns improved, while new towns grew in the wilderness. The Civil War brought rapid changes to American cities, for it marked the transformation from agricultural America to industrial-urban America. People came into the city to work and live. The increased immigration from Eastern Europe also compounded the growth of the cities.

By 1920 more Americans lived in cities than on farms. And by then many of the problems in the industrial city, such as slums and health conditions, were being improved. The automobile was helping to make suburban America possible, as successful city dwellers left for more pleasant environs. From the 1920s to the present the city has undergone renovation and internal revolutions. The "central city" is now controlled primarily by minorities. Crime is still a major problem; garbage collection has become one. But the age of the super city is here. And Americans have no choice but to live with it —or in it.

The Colonial City*

*The early inhabitants of America brought knowledge of the Eu-
ropean cities, and the growth of colonial towns reflected their experience. Many of the colonial cities such as Boston, Philadelphia, and
New York were carefully planned communities located on good
harbors. Boston was the largest city and the early urban leader, but
by the American Revolution, Philadelphia had grown larger. Traveler Andrew Burnaby in the years 1759–1760 wrote his impressions of colonial Philadelphia and Boston. Here are his thoughts.*

Questions

1. How does he describe Philadelphia?
2. What stands out in Boston?
3. Compare and contrast his description of Philadelphia and Boston.
4. Does he make any comments upon city life in general?

Philadelphia

Philadelphia, if we consider that not eighty years ago the place where
it now stands was a wild and uncultivated desert, inhabited by nothing but
ravenous beasts, and a savage people, must certainly be the object of every
one's wonder and admiration. It is situated upon a tongue of land, a few miles
above the confluence of the Delaware and Schuylkill; and contains about
3,000 houses, and 18 or 20,000 inhabitants. It is built north and south upon
the banks of the Delaware; and it is nearly two miles in length, and three
quarters of one in breadth. The streets are laid out with great regularity in
parallel lines, intersected by others at right angles, and are handsomely built:

*Source: Rufus R. Wilson, ed., *Burnaby's Travels through North America* (New York, 1904), pp.
88–90, 132–33.

on each side there is a pavement of broad stones for foot passengers; and in most of them a causeway in the middle for carriages. Upon dark nights it is well lighted, and watched by a patrol: there are many fair houses, and public edifices in it. The stadt-house is a large, handsome though heavy building; in this are held the councils, the assemblies, and supreme courts; there are apartments in it also for the accommodation of Indian chiefs or sachems; likewise two libraries, one belonging to the province, the other to a society, which was incorporated about ten years ago, and consists of sixty members. Each member upon admission, subscribed forty shillings; and afterward annually ten. They can alienate their shares, by will or deed, to any person approved by the society. They have a small collection of medals and medallions, and a few other curiosities, such as the skin of a rattlesnake killed at Surinam twelve feet long; and several Northern Indian habits made of furs and skins. At a small distance from the stadt-house there is another fine library, consisting of a very valuable and chosen collection of books, left by a Mr. Logan; they are chiefly in the learned languages. Near this there is also a noble hospital for lunatics, and other sick persons. Besides these buildings, there are spacious barracks for 17 or 1800 men; a good assembly-room belonging to the society of Free Masons; and eight or ten places of religious worship; viz. two churches, three Quaker meeting-houses, two Presbyterian ditto, one Swedish ditto, one Romish chapel, one Anabaptist meeting-house, one Moravian ditto: there is also an academy or college, originally built for a tabernacle for Mr. Whitfield. At the south end of the town, upon the river, there is a battery mounting thirty guns, but it is in a state of decay. It was designed to be a check upon privateers. These, with a few alms-houses, and a school-house belonging to the Quakers, are the chief public buildings in Philadelphia. The city is in a very flourishing state, and inhabited by merchants, artists, tradesmen, and persons of all occupations. There is a public market held twice a week, upon Wednesday and Saturday, almost equal to that of Leadenhall, and a tolerable one every day besides. The streets are crowded with people, and the river with vessels. Houses are so dear, that they will let for 100 £. currency per annum; and lots, not above thirty feet in breadth, and a hundred in length, in advantageous situations, will sell for 1,000 £. sterling. There are several docks upon the river, and about twenty-five vessels are built there annually. I counted upon the stocks at one time no less than seventeen, many of them three-masted vessels.

Can the mind have a greater pleasure than in contemplating the rise and progress of cities and kingdoms? Than in perceiving a rich and opulent state arising out of small settlement or colony?

Boston

Boston, the metropolis of Massachusetts Bay, in New England, is one of the largest and most flourishing towns in North America. It is situated upon a penninsula, or rather an island joined to the continent by an isthmus or narrow neck of land half a mile in length, at the bottom of a spacious and noble harbour, defended from the sea by a number of small islands. The length of it is nearly two miles, and the breadth of it a half a one; and it is supposed to contain 3,000 houses, and 18 or 20,000 inhabitants. . . .

The buildings in Boston are in general good; the streets are open and spacious, and well paved; and the whole has much the air of some of our best country towns in England. The country round about it is exceedingly delightful; and from a hill, which stands close to the town, where there is a beacon to alarm the neighborhood in case of any surprise, is one of the finest prospects, the most beautifully variegated, and richly grouped, of any without exception that I have ever seen.

The chief public buildings are, three churches; thirteen or fourteen meeting-houses; the governor's palace; the court-house, or exchange; Faneuil Hall; a linen manufacturing-house; a work-house; a bridewell; a public granary; and a very fine wharf, at least half a mile long, undertaken at the expense of a number of private gentlemen, for the advantage of unloading and loading vessels. Most of these buildings are handsome: the church, called King's Chapel, is exceedingly elegant; and fitted up in the Corinthian taste. There is also an elegant private concert-room highly finished in the Ionic manner. I had reason to think the situation of Boston unhealthy, at least in this season of the year, as there were frequent funerals every night during my stay there.

2

Problems of the Industrial City*

The technological revolution of the late 1800s caused rapid changes in the cities. The trend to the suburbs had started, certain cities developed specialized industries, the ghetto of immigrants from East-

---

*Source: Josiah Strong, *Our County: Its Possible Future and Its Present Crisis* (New York, 1885), pp. 128–31; Jacob A. Riis, *How the Other Half Lives* (New York: Charles Scribner's Sons, 1890), pp. 5–8.

ern Europe was growing, political bossism was at its height, and tenements and slums abounded. There were few health regulations and building codes. Overcrowding, disease, poverty were characteristics of the industrial cities of the late 1800s. There was a definite need for reform. These two writers, Josiah Strong and Jacob Riis, not only commented upon the conditions of the cities, but tried to reform them. Reforms, however, were slow to come to the city, and it was not until the general impetus of the Progressive Era that the cities began to be fit places for people to live.

Questions

STRONG

1. What were the basic problems of the city?
2. Were there any possible solutions?
3. Why would people live there?

RIIS

1. What is a tenement?
2. What was the origin of the tenement?
3. What were the evils of tenements?
4. Do tenements exist today? Are they necessary to modern cities?
5. Compare and contrast the ideas of Strong and Riis on the city.

Strong

The city is the nerve center of our civilization. It is also the storm center. The fact, therefore, that it is growing much more rapidly than the whole population is full of significance. In 1790 one-thirtieth of the population of the United States lived in cities of 8,000 inhabitants and over; in 1800, one twenty-fifth; in 1810, and also in 1820, one-twentieth; in 1830, one-sixteenth; in 1840, one-twelfth; in 1850, one-eighth; in 1860, one-sixth; in 1870, a little over one-fifth; and in 1880, 22.5 per cent., or nearly one-fourth. From 1790 to 1880 the whole population increased a little less than four fold, the urban population thirteen fold. From 1870 to 1880 the whole population increased thirty per cent., the urban population forty per cent. During the half century preceding 1880, population in the city increased more than four times as rapidly as that of the village and country. In 1800 there were only six cities in the United States which had a population of 8,000 or more. In 1880 there were 286.

The city has become a serious menace to our civilization. . . . It has a peculiar attraction for the immigrant. Our fifty principal cities contain 39.3 per cent. of our entire German population, and 45.8 per cent. of the Irish. Our ten larger cities only nine per cent. of the entire population, but 23 per cent. of the foreign. While a little less than one-third of the population of the United States is foreign by birth or parentage, sixty-two per cent. of the population of Cincinnati are foreign, eighty-three per cent. of Cleveland, sixty-three per cent. of Boston, eighty-eight per cent. of New York, and ninety-one per cent. of Chicago.

Because our cities are so largely foreign, Romanism finds in them its chief strength.

For the same reason the saloon, together with the intemperance and the liquor power which it represents, is multiplied in the city. East of the Mississippi there was, in 1880, one saloon to every 438 of the population; in Boston, one to every 329; in Cleveland, one to every 192; in Chicago, one to every 179; in New York, one to every 171; in Cincinnati, one to every 124. Of course the demoralizing and pauperizing power of the saloons and their debauching influence in politics increase with their numerical strength.

It is the city where wealth is massed; and here are the tangible evidences of it piled many stories high. Here the sway of Mammon is widest, and his worship the most constant and eager. Here are luxuries gathered—everything that dazzles the eye, or tempts the appetite; here is the most extravagant expenditure. Here, also, is the *congestion* of wealth severest. Dives and Lazarus are brought face to face; here, in sharp contrast, are the *ennui* of surfeit and the desperation of starvation. The rich are richer, and the poor are poorer, in the city than elsewhere; and, as a rule, the greater the city, the greater are the riches of the rich and the poverty of the poor. Not only does the proportion of the poor increase with the growth of the city, but their condition becomes more wretched. The poor of a city of 8,000 inhabitants are well off compared with many in New York; and there are no such depths of woe, such utter and heart-wringing wretchedness in New York as in London. Read in "The Bitter Cry of Outcast London," a prophecy of what will some day be seen in American cities, providing existing tendencies continue. . . .

Socialism not only centers in the city, but is almost confined to it; and the materials of its growth are multiplied with the growth of the city. Here is heaped the social dynamite; here roughs, gamblers, thieves, robbers, lawless and desperate men of all sorts, congregate; men who are ready on any pretext to raise riots for the purpose of destruction and plunder; here gather foreigners and wage-workers; here skepticism and irreligion abound; here inequality is the greatest and most obvious, and the contrast between opulence and penury the most striking; here is suffering the sorest. As the greatest wickedness in the world is to be found not among the cannibals of some far off coast, but in Christian lands where the light of truth is diffused and rejected, so the utmost depth of wretchedness exists not among savages, who have few wants, but in great cities, where, in the presence of plenty and of every luxury men starve. Let a man become the owner of a home, and he is much less susceptible to socialistic propagandism. But real estate is so high in the city that it is almost impossible for a wage-worker to become a householder. The law in New York requires a juror to be owner of real or personal property valued at not less than two hundred and fifty dollars; and this, the Commissioner says, relieves seventy thousand of the registered voters of New York City from jury duty. Let us remember that those seventy thousand voters represent a population of two hundred and eighty thousand, or fifty-six thousand families, not one of which has property to the value of two hundred and fifty dollars. "During the past three years, 220,976 persons in New York have asked for outside aid in one form or another." Said a New York Supreme Judge, not long since: "There is a large class—I was about to say a majority —of the population of New York and Brooklyn, who just live, and to whom the rearing of two or more children means inevitably a boy for the penitentiary, and a girl for the brothel." Under such conditions smolder the volcanic fires of a deep discontent.

Riis

The first tenement New York knew bore the mark of Cain from its birth, though a generation passed before the writing was deciphered. It was the "rear house," infamous ever after in our city's history. There had been tenant-houses before, but they were not built for the purpose. Nothing would probably have shocked their original owners more than the idea of their harboring a promiscuous crowd; for they were the decorous homes of the old Knickerbockers, the proud aristocracy of Manhattan in the early days.

It was the stir and bustle of trade, together with the tremendous immigration that followed upon the war of 1812 that dislodged them. In thirty-five years the city of less than a hundred thousand came to harbor half a million souls, for whom homes had to be found. Within the memory of men not yet in their prime, Washington had moved from his house on Cherry Hill as too far out of town to be easily reached. Now the old residents followed his example; but they moved in a different direction and for a different reason. Their comfortable dwellings in the once fashionable streets along the East River front fell into the hands of real estate agents and boarding-house keepers; and here, says the report to the Legislature of 1857, when the evils engendered had excited just alarm, "in its beginning, the tenant-house became a real blessing to that class of industrious poor whose small earnings limited their expenses, and whose employment in workshops, stores, or about the warehouses and thoroughfares, render a near residence of much importance." Not for long, however. As business increased, and the city grew with rapid strides, the necessities of the poor became the opportunity of their wealthier neighbors, and the stamp was set upon the old houses, suddenly become valuable, which the best thought and effort of a later age has vainly struggled to efface. Their "*large* rooms were partitioned into *several smaller ones,* without regard to light or ventilation, the rate of rent being lower in proportion to space or height from the street; and they soon became filled from cellar to garret with a class of tenantry living from hand to mouth, loose in morals, improvident in habits, degraded, and squalid as beggary itself." It was thus the dark bedroom, prolific of untold depravities, came into the world. It was destined to survive the old houses. In their new rôle, says the old report, eloquent in its indignant denunciation of "evils more destructive than wars," "they were not intended to last. Rents were fixed high enough to cover damage and abuse from this class, from whom nothing was expected, and the most was made of them while they lasted. Neatness, order, cleanliness, were never dreamed of in connection with the tenant-house system, as it spread its localities from year to year; while reckless slovenliness, discontent, privation, and ignorance were left to work out their invariable results, until the entire premises reached the level of tenant-house dilapidation, containing, but sheltering not, the miserable hordes that crowded beneath smouldering, water-rotted roofs or burrowed among the rats of clammy cellars." Yet so illogical is human greed that, at a later day, when called to account, "the proprietors frequently urged the filthy habits of the tenants as an excuse for the condition of their property, utterly losing sight of the fact that it was the tolerance of those habits which was the real evil, and that for this they themselves were alone responsible."

Still the pressure of the crowds did not abate, and in the old garden where the stolid Dutch burgher grew his tulips or early cabbages a rear house was built, generally of wood, two stories high at first. Presently it was carried up another story, and another. Where two families had lived ten moved in. The front house followed suit, if the brick walls were strong enough. The question was not always asked, judging from complaints made by a contemporary witness, that the old buildings were "often carried up to a great height without regard to the strength of the foundation walls." It was rent the owner was after; nothing was said in the contract about either the safety or the comfort of the tenants. The garden gate no longer swung on its rusty hinges. The shell-paved walk had become an alley; what the rear house had left on the garden, a "court." Plenty such are yet to be found in the Fourth Ward, with here and there one of the original rear tenements.

Worse was to follow. It was "soon perceived by estate owners and agents of property that a greater percentage of profits could be realized by the conversion of houses and blocks into barracks, and dividing their space into smaller proportions capable of containing human life within four walls. . . . Blocks were rented of real estate owners, or 'purchased on time,' or taken in charge at a percentage, and held for under-letting." With the appearance of the middle-man, wholly irresponsible, and utterly reckless and unrestrained, began the era of tenement building which turned out such blocks as Gotham Court, where, in one cholera epidemic that scarcely touched the clean wards, the tenants died at the rate of one hundred and ninety-five to the thousand of population; which forced the general mortality of the city up from 1 in 41.83 in 1815, to 1 in 27.33 in 1855, a year of unusual freedom from epidemic disease, and which wrung from the early organizers of the Health Department this wail: "There are numerous examples of tenement-houses in which are lodged several hundred people that have a *pro rata* allotment of ground area scarcely equal to two square yards upon the city lot, court-yards and all included." The tenement-house population had swelled to half a million souls by that time, and on the East Side, in what is still the most densely populated district in all the world, China not excluded, it was packed at the rate of 290,000 to the square mile, a state of affairs wholly unexampled. The utmost cupidity of other lands and other days had never contrived to herd much more than half that number within the same space. The greatest crowding of Old London was at the rate of 175,816. Swine roamed the streets and gutters as their principal scavengers.[1] The death of a child in a tenement was registered at the Bureau of Vital Statistics as "plainly due to suffocation in the foul air of an unventilated apartment," and the Senators, who had come down from Albany to find out what was the matter with New York, reported that "there are annually cut off from the population by disease and death enough human beings to people a city, and enough human labor to sustain it." And yet experts had testified that, as compared with uptown, rents were from twenty-five to thirty per cent. higher in the worst slums of the lower wards, with such accommodations as were enjoyed, for instance, by a "family with boarders" in Cedar Street, who fed hogs in the cellar that contained eight or ten loads of manure; or "one room 12 X 12 with five families living in it, comprising twenty persons of both sexes and all ages, with only two beds, without partition, screen, chair, or table." The rate of rent has been successfully maintained to the present day, though the hog at least has been eliminated.

---

[1] It was not until the winter of 1867 that owners of swine were prohibited by ordinance from letting them run at large in the built-up portions of the city.

A Big City Mayor Reflects*

The Progressive Era brought needed physical and political changes to urban America. By 1920 America had become more urban than rural. The introduction of automobiles and electric power changed the habits of Americans and brought the city to life. But many writers had begun to contemplate what the future of cities would be and what forces were shaping the future.

Los Angeles is often considered the epitome of the city of the future with its urban sprawl, air pollution, crime, and lumbering hugeness. Sam Yorty was mayor of Los Angeles for several years. In 1966, before a Senate subcommittee, he reflected on the problems of his city.

Questions

1. What were his general impressions of the city?
2. Analyze the governmental structure.
3. What did he feel were the major problems?
4. How can race relations be improved?
5. Can a mayor really run a big city any more?
6. What are your impressions of Mayor Yorty?

Mayor Yorty. Thank you, Senator. First of all, I want to thank you for inviting me here and inviting the mayors to express our opinions directly to this committee about some of the Federal programs, and what we foresee as being needed in the future.

I would like to start by saying I think it is very important that it be

*Hearings before the Subcommittee on Executive Reorganization of the Committee on Government Operations, *Federal Role in Urban Affairs, Part 3,* 45 Senate, 89th Cong., 2d sess., August 22–23, 1966, pp. 671ff.

recognized here at the Federal level that the cities, while maybe from the vantage point of Washington they all look about the same, with population figures differing, the structure of the cities are very different, and therefore the programs need to be tailored, I think, more to the individual cities than they have sometimes in the past. I might say, for instance, that in Los Angeles, of the larger cities of the Nation, it is the only really large city that has a nonpartisan city government.

Governmental Structure of Los Angeles

Also, we have a different structure from the other cities. The mayor of Los Angeles has nothing to do, for instance, with the school system. We have an independently elected school board, with their own taxing power and they make up their own budget.

Also, the mayor of Los Angeles has nothing to do with the welfare program. This is handled by the county for the State. So I am not involved as mayor in any of those programs either. We don't have a department of employment in the city. This is another State function, the State department of employment which is entirely separate and I have no jurisdiction over that.

The health department is part of the county structure. Our effort to build a rapid transit system is through State agency, with the members originally appointed by the Governor, but now with some local appointments, but still the transit district is much larger than the city.

Our housing authority, while it is called a city housing authority, is nevertheless a State agency, and it is presently at our request being operated by the Federal Government.

Also, another difference that we have from some other cities is that we have not only what we call a weak mayor–strong council type of government, but we have a commission form of government. The major departments of the city of Los Angeles are actually headed by commissioners who are dollar-a-year type people, receive no real compensation for the work that they do, coming in usually once a week and heading a department.

Minority Group Representation in City Government

When I became mayor in 1961 I completely integrated these commissions for the first time in the history of the city. Before that, there was sort of a token representation for minorities on these commissions, and my first exhibit there is a talk that I made to a U.S. conference of mayors shortly after I became mayor, suggesting that in all cities that minorities should be given more of a voice in the government, and it was my intention at that time to try and make Los Angeles a model city as far as race relations were concerned, and this was the first step within my jurisdiction to do something about these commissions.

Major Problem in Los Angeles Is Unemployment

What would you say is the major problem that you have to face now, Mr. Mayor, in connection with the city of Los Angeles?

Mayor Yorty. It depends on what field you mean, but I would say primarily in the field of where we have human relations. It still gets back to taking the people who are unskilled and unemployed, and if they had skills they would have jobs because there are jobs available, as you know, but only for skilled people.

I think, No. 1, these people must be provided with the opportunity to work, and as I said before, I think Dr. King must have been wrestling with this problem a lot, because he said the other day that our problem is primarily economic, and I think we should have a guaranteed annual income for everyone. So I can see what he is thinking is that if you cannot get them a job, he thinks they should at least have an income, but basically I think we must realize that they cannot compete in a capitalistic competitive system, and so we modify it as to them and supply them with some kind of work and try and make it meaningful work. But if it cannot be so meaningful, at least it should be some kind of work that they can do and draw income. I think if they did this, this would solve a lot of other problems.

Senator Kennedy. How would you go about doing that?

Mayor Yorty. Well, I think it can only be done by some kind of an effort under OEO probably. The kind of work that we supply them with I do not know. I would hope that maybe we could work in cooperation with the private sector, so that what benefit they could get for their services they would pay for, and there is some of this being done.

Senator Kennedy. Have you worked out yourself the kind of a program you would like to see?

Mayor Yorty. We have worked it out with this opportunities industrialization center, which we hope, of course, will not just hire them after they get out of a job, but we hope are going to fit them for jobs that are available.

We feel that a good job was done in Philadelphia by Reverend Sullivan, and I hope that it is going to work in our community.

The Ford Foundation did make a grant, a great cross section of the people are involved in the program.

What Should Be Done to Improve Race Relations in United States?

Mr. Mayor, what is your feeling about how you would work toward improving the relationship that exists between the races, not only in Los Angeles but across the country?

What are your ideas about that? Would you say that is a problem?

Mayor Yorty. It is one of the great problems of course, and as I pointed out before, one of the problems I have with the city and that all the mayors have is that we are the head of law enforcement, and when the politicians run around and make a lot of promises that are not kept and some that cannot be kept, and get people agitated, expecting more than is going to be made available to them, and then they reach out illegally to get it, it is the policeman who has to stop them, and it has created an intolerable situation for the police departments. And of course I think Los Angeles, as proven by the record, has basically good race relations. Certainly the Negroes have proved by the Urban League and others to be better off in Los Angeles than any large city in the Nation. We are pretty proud of that record and we hope to improve it.

Senator Kennedy. Would you say with the unemployment rate in Watts of 35 per cent that the Negro is better off?

Mayor Yorty. No, I did not say that. I said that based on a study of all the cities, that the Negroes in Los Angeles have a higher average income, better housing and are better off than in New York or say Chicago or Detroit or some of the rest. They have better standards. But that as Sam Rayburn used to say, all of this does not mean anything to the guy that is out of a job, because if everybody else is working, as Mr. Sam used to say, that man is in a depression.

Senator Kennedy. That is right.

Mayor Yorty. And so we want to take care of all those people just as much as anybody else does certainly, and I would like to get jobs for all of them. We will do everything we can to stimulate projects at our level to make jobs, but we have to do it within our means and within our jurisdiction. We have to rely on other jurisdictions, and Federal jurisdiction too, for some of the funds and for some of the help with the projects.

Thought Questions

1. Compare and contrast life and problems in the colonial cities and twentieth century cities.
2. Compare life in the cities of the late 1800s and today.
3. What trends are evident in all periods of urban development? What are the major differences?

seventeen

THE FUTURE:
The Past Revisited?

Americans have talked of the future since their earliest beginnings. If Americans are, as the Greek philosopher Aristotle said, basically searching for happiness, it is a past theme as well as a future theme. And American history has shown that the future is frequently the past revisited. War, racism, ecology have all joined with the American heritage; and we will continue to add other things to that heritage in the future. Many fear the unknown that is the future, but we all must live with it and watch it become, rather, the past.

Reich on the Future*

Writers display an avid interest in social changes and the future. One writer, Charles Reich, in the book The Greening of America, *feels that the future is taking place today and that this movement (called consciousness III) is the movement of the future. Here he gives some of the characteristics of consciousness III.*

Questions

1. What are the characteristics of consciousness III?
2. How is society changing?
3. Is this really happening?

If this is true, then it is also true that a new way of life does not have to wait for a new world, it can be built out of the elements now available. Pop art illustrates this process. The artifacts of modern life, such as neon signs, juke boxes, Campbell's Soup cans, present dominating images of sterility, forming man's life in a sterile pattern. But the pop artist regains power over his environment by using these elements in his own creations, thereby taking responsibility for their ultimate form. He has selected and chosen what he wants, and thereby transcended the artifacts. Likewise the new music chooses from many elements of earlier music, and from many forms of technology, to produce the form it wants.

Tom Wolfe recognized this process in his preface to *The Kandy-Kolored Tangerine-Flake Streamline Baby* (1965). He was writing about subcultures such as stock-car racing or surfing. He came to see that affluence had made it possible for various groups to "build monuments" to their own life-styles. By implication, this meant that various groups were getting to a position where they could choose a way of life. The lifestyles they chose, which Wolfe described, were not very meaningful, and they were still closely tied to the machine. But the element of creativity, of artistry, was unmistakably there. Using such artifacts of the Corporate State as the 1955 Chevrolet, the hamburger drive-in, the technology of neon, groups were able to create something of their own. To do this with a job, to do it with an institution, to do it under all the pressure and burdens of the present society will take much more. It will require imagination, strategy, cunning. But it will be the cunning of art, for it is art when we make something of our own out of the elements of the existing world. It only requires that we not lose sight of what we are doing: creating a way of life that is better for human beings.

The first major theme of this new way of life must be education—education not in the limited sense of training in school, but in its largest and most humanistic meaning. The central American problem might be defined as a failure of education. We have vastly underestimated the amount of education and consciousness that is required to meet the demands of organization and technology. Most of our "education" has taught us how to *operate* the technology; how to function as a human component of an organization. What we need is education that will enable us to make use of technology, control it and give it direction, cause it to serve values which we have chosen.

We have already shown, in discussing the industrialization of America and the New Deal, that Americans never faced the question of how much education and understanding would be necessary if mass democracy were really to be effective in a technological society. Even before technology, de Tocqueville and others expressed well justified skepticism about self-government by poorly educated masses. The New Deal tried to rely on experts and specialists, but quite aside from their own failings, they could not govern an electorate that did not understand. Our failure in democracy has now been surpassed by our failure in control of the things we have made, and our even greater failure to realize the affirmative possibilities of technology. We know how to drive a car, but we do not know how to keep cars from destroying our environment, or how to use a car to make cities and countryside more beautiful and more of a community, and to make man's life more creative and liberated. Henry James was acutely aware of this incapacity; he believed that time, tradition, and sensibility were needed to "civilize" manufactured innovation. We can give his ideas a contemporary meaning by saying that today education and consciousness are needed to humanize all the new forms of work, things, and experiences that are thrust upon us.

We are prone to think of the capacity to make affirmative use of innovations as a moral quality, an aspect of "character." A man who drives to the country for a picnic, drowns out the sounds of nature with a transistor radio, and leaves beer cans strewn around when he departs is said to lack "character." This is the same fallacy of the human heart that has made us see so many issues of government and technology as moral questions. Capacity to appreciate nature, to benefit from it, and to be enhanced by it is a matter of education. The beauty and fascination of nature is not available to the uneducated eye, any more than the beauty of painting or poetry. But it is not just a question of specific education, it is a question of a more general consciousness, a readiness to receive new experiences in a certain way.

2

Life in 2001*

What will American society and life be like in thirty or forty years? The way that America has changed since the 1920s makes one wonder about the future. Al Martinez imagines life in California in the year 2001.

Questions

1. What is Joaquin–1?
2. Describe regulated growth.
3. What is rapid transit?
4. How have education and population control changed?
5. What will life be like in the future?
6. Do we see any of these changes taking place today?

Not so long ago, when Ray Bradbury and Arthur Clarke first spun their futuristic visions into novels, the future seemed impossibly far away.

And now, already, we have walked upon the moon and seen the face of Mars. An exploding technology thrust the world into the future ahead of the novelists' timetable.

*Source: Al Martinez, "California 2001—Better Life Follows Environmental Wars," Los Angeles *Times*, September 17, 1972. Copyright, 1972, Los Angeles Times. Reprinted by permission.

The future continues to arrive at a faster and faster pace, often creating the future shock of a world arriving too soon, to a people unprepared. And Clarke's "2001" is only 29 years away.

The novelists' visions proved remarkably close to reality, but the technologists are developing ever surer methods of prediction and control of realities still to come.

For three months, The Times has consulted with more than a score of planners who look to the future as a renewed world of surprise.

It may be—in fact CAN be—very much like this . . .

Morning comes to California, gleaming off the amber dome of a transpoliner that streaks south out of San Francisco on a cushion of air.

The linear induction motors accelerate smoothly, pressing the multiunit commuter to its cruising speed of 300 m.p.h. just clear of the sprawling San Jose megalopolis.

The six-forty-fiver is nonstop to Los Angeles. The trip will take an hour and 20 mintues.

The day is Tuesday, Sept. 25, 2001.

Overhead, on its regular 18-day orbit, the manned station Skylab glides through space, its sensitive scanning equipment geared now to monitor the life of the Golden State in the golden autumn: the rush of rivers and traffic, the purity of air and ocean, the sum of resources and population, the health of crops and forests, the subtle movement of mountains and the barely perceptible erosion of granite.

All of this, translated in a flicker to analog-video-digital telemetry, is flashed to Sacramento as Skylab, its passover done, moves out of range, and as the transpoliner slips by Joaquin-1 on the western edge of the great Central Valley near Polonia Pass.

Joaquin-1 is the first of the cities conceived by a coalition of planners from government and the private sector to relieve the pressure of urbanization from California's overpopulated metropolitan centers, and it is aborning now at the confluence of a network of water and power and transportation, where need and nature destined it should be.

Here business and industry will flourish in a population complex designed to overcome the enigma of wasted space and congestion that still threaten the survival of the big cities. Here new knowledge utilizes land for capacity and privacy and creates an architecture at peace with nature.

The transpoliner, its computerized acceleration system ignorant of the dream coming true, is past Joaquin-1 in a twinkling and flies through the morning toward its final destination—by towns that appear with disturbing unplanned frequency in the distance, near low hills that mask the nuclear power plants of an energy-hungry state, through the far-flung outskirts of the L.A. suburbs that sprawl into Ventura County.

Finally, Los Angeles.

Its brakes hissing softly as the speed drops, the transpoliner dips through an underground opening to the mammoth subsurface downtown DOT (Department of Transportation) terminal and glides to a stop, settling gently through the cushion of air to its base.

The doors slide open automatically and the passengers leave their cars. They board electrically operated feeder pods, the so-called people movers, that transport them to key points throughout the big city.

The pods glide with a soft whir on fixed guideways 20 feet aboveground, over the elevated pedestrian walkways and the protected malls and the small clean cars that dart through a shimmery day in a world that has discovered the value of clear air after a choking haze.

The city comes to life. The business of the day is beginning.

Thirteen miles northwest of the downtown section, in a multi-use highrise building near the intersection of Mulholland Drive and the San Diego Freeway, morning has come with the clicking awake of an automated household.

A medium-impact Homemaster, the miniaturized and simplified version of a business computer, has been pre-programmed to bring the essentials of a new day to the six-room apartment.

Indirect lighting spreads automatically through each room, a microwave oven heats up, music plays, a coffee maker turns on and a video screen flashes a reminder of the day's commitments.

A family of three yawns and stretches into the routine of the morning in a scene that is repeated again and again in other high-activity centers and in the suburbs, the New Towns and the desert developments.

Now the works of men stand sharply defined against the iridescent sky, and nowhere—not piled against the mountainsides nor stagnant in the land basins—is there even a hint of smog.

Water pollution is also only a distant battle—won in the war to preserve the environment.

The victory is evident as the sun at noon shimmers off the revitalized streams and the once dying lakes of California, the level of their purity monitored by instruments 1,000 times more sensitive than they once were.

Pollution is measured in parts per trillion, where yesterday such minutiae was not even detectable.

Natural Coastline

But environment involves some abstracts too, and one of them is beauty. Toward esthetic considerations, mansions along with shanties have been removed by law as shoreline barriers to the blue Pacific.

And private vehicular traffic has been permanently barred from the mountain recreation areas in favor of public monorails to help preserve California's forest lands in perpetuity.

All these are triumphs of the environment wars, a conglomerate name for the crusade to survive that finally unlocked the ecologists and the economists from what had become a private struggle and got them working together for the good of the future.

Their union spawned creation in the early 1980s of the California Committee, an independent, privately financed, quasi-official forum with Sacramento representation and approval.

Advisory Board

Initially a coalescence of environmental organizations, the California Committee assumed special status as an advisory body to the Legislature upon successful submission of a master plan for California.

The plan, until then only a long-standing dream, lays out state responsibility for orderly growth and assumes the function of an outline for the more substantive progress of today.

Today.

It begins to fade now as afternoon comes sliding down the western slope of the Cascade Range and flattens out over Mountain Country, the state's newest tourist mecca.

The mecca rises from the brushland southeast of Redding in the shadow of Mt. Lassen, a Disneylandish recreation center half-history and half-carnival.

To Draw Population

Essentially concerned with re-creating and animating early California, Mountain Country embodies at least one element of a philosophy of population dispersion.

A private undertaking encouraged by tax incentives and a state transportation system, it will hopefully be the nucleus of a whole new population center in a wide-open region.

Until it becomes that nucleus, Mountain Country at least serves to shift a portion of the yearly tourist trade away from those areas barely able to handle the influx of visitors.

Masses of people have long been a critical consideration in California's concept of the future.

Threat of Megalopolis

Demographers were warning three decades ago that unchecked growth could result in one giant megalopolis covering 50,000 square miles from San Fransciso to San Diego and jammed with 40 million people.

Those who feared its inevitability were already calling it San-San and were saying that a total state population as high as 50 million-plus by the year 2000 was not unrealistic.

The population of California today is 33 million.

Even at that, power needs have quadrupled over the last 30 years, urban water waste needs have doubled, solid waste has increased at five times the population growth, demands on the state park system have doubled.

The needs have so far been met, even to the closed-loop recycling of solid waste into new uses.

But they didn't know then, in the edgy days of the fading 20th century, that they would, or even could, be met.

They called for strict migration control into California, for laws to remove all legal barriers to abortion, for tough marriage requirements among minors, for mandatory birth control classes.

But as the population boom ended (the birthrate dropped, in-migration eased), the emphasis shifted from control to guidance.

Today, to assure that growth remains at a moderate level, revised income tax deductions discourage large families, a national employment policy has opened new job opportunities in other states and the creation of a uniform welfare system throughout the nation has ended California's reign as one of the places to go for public assistance.

Efforts at Dispersion

New energy is being concentrated now in dispersing the population within the state.

One of the results is Joaquin-1 along the route of the San Francisco–Los Angeles transpoliner and in close proximity to Interstate 5, the San Luis Reservoir, the California Aqueduct and a major power tie-in.

Joaquin-1 remains largely experimental to determine whether a so-called New Town, a prepackaged community of homes, services and industries, can survive—and to test how successful it might be in redirecting the state's population away from the cities.

Another effort at population redistribution is also being made in the Mojave east of Barstow where the Desert Campus of the University of California is in fall session.

College in Desert

Desert Campus contributes to the birth of a new university town, its creation enhanced by piped-in water, a direct major highway connection out of Barstow, a new jet field for STOL aircraft and the promise of air-cushion feeder service out of the Pasadena substation.

Here, around the 10th campus of the 150,000-student statewide UC system, tax incentives are again being offered to induce controlled residential and industrial development.

The state hopes that the new campus will have impact beyond education, and that simply by existing it will encourage the establishment of other desert cities—their outdoor activities domed, their transportation underground, their life geared to a blazing sun that hangs low even now over the Calico Mountains this Tuesday in September.

The day is fading over a California in transition.

Much has been done at this moment in time to make the Golden State a better place to live. Much remains to be done throughout the 21st century.

The sins of the past are the problems of the present. Economic ghettos exist even though low-cost housing in any residential development is a fact of law.

Inequities Persist

Some forms of animal life continue to face extinction even though hunting has been all but regulated out of existence and game reserves are widespread in the strenuous effort to preserve our wildlife.

There are inequities based on the historic divisions of race and religion and political commitment. Crime plagues the New Towns as well as the old cities. Taxes are high. Prices continue to rise. There is never enough money.

But there is hope. The California Committee will convene tomorrow in Sacramento to consider once more quality of life and to materialize that abstract into manageable substance.

There is talk that the committee itself has become unmanageable, that perhaps there ought to be a North Committee and a South Committee, and the irony of these internal problems is not lost on the members.

But there will be time enough for that tomorrow and the day after tomorrow and all the days after that.

For now the evening has come and the families have gathered and the business of the day has ended.

The night is Tuesday, Sept. 25, 2001.

California sleeps.

Thought Questions

1. Compare life in the future as described by Reich and Martinez.
2. Is Charles Reich accurate in his ideas on future societal movement?